Berlitz

Russian

phrase book & dictionary

ФАЛИН Н.С
СЕРЖАНТ МОРОЗОВ И.А.
ДОВОЙ ШАЙКИН Я.П
ДОВАЯ Виноградова КЛАВА
ЛЕЙТЕНАНТ БРЕЧКО И.Д
ЙТЕНАНТ РАЗНИК
СЕРЖАНТ КУДРЯВЦЕВ С.П
СТ.ЛЕЙТ. ШЕЛУДЯКОВ О.Л.
ЛЕЙТ НЕМОВ П.А.
РМЕЙ ДОЛГАНОВ В.С.

Berlitz Publishing
New York London Singapore

No part of this book may be reproduced, stored in a retrieval system, or transmitted in any form or means electronic, mechanical, photocopying, recording, or otherwise, without prior written permission from APA Publications.

Contacting the Editors
Every effort has been made to provide accurate information in this publication, but changes are inevitable. The publisher cannot be responsible for any resulting loss, inconvenience or injury. We would appreciate it if readers would call our attention to any errors or outdated information. We also welcome your suggestions; if you come across a relevant expression not in our phrase book, please contact us at: **comments@berlitzpublishing.com**

All Rights Reserved
© 2019 Apa Digital (CH) AG and Apa Publications (UK) Ltd.
Berlitz Trademark Reg. U.S. Patent Office and other countries. Marca Registrada. Used under license from Berlitz Investment Corporation.

Printed in China

Editor: Helen Fanthorpe
Translation: updated by Wordbank
Cover Design: Rebeka Davies
Interior Design: Beverley Speight
Picture Researcher: Steven Lawrence

Cover Photos: iStock
Interior Photos: APA Richard Schofield 12, 39, 40, 58, 61, 65, 77, 91, 104, 118, 124, 130, 150, APA Abe Nowitz 45, 57, 81, 101,133, 141, APA Lucy Johnston 165, Istockphoto 70, 83, APA Greg Gladman 112, APA Britta Jaschinski 47

Distribution

UK, Ireland and Europe
Apa Publications (UK) Ltd
sales@insightguides.com
United States and Canada
Ingram Publisher Services
ips@ingramcontent.com
Australia and New Zealand
Woodslane
info@woodslane.com.au
Southeast Asia
Apa Publications (SN) Pte
singaporeoffice@insightguides.com

Worldwide
Apa Publications (UK) Ltd
sales@insightguides.com

Special Sales, Content Licensing, and CoPublishing
Discounts available for bulk quantities. We can create special editions, personalized jackets, and corporate imprints. sales@insightguides.com; www.insightguides.biz

Contents

Survival

Food & Drink

People

Leisure Time

Special Requirements

In an Emergency

Dictionary

Pronunciation

This section is designed to make you familiar with the sounds of Russian using our simplified phonetic transcription. You'll find the pronunciation of the Cyrillic (Russian) letters explained below, together with their 'imitated' equivalents. To use this system, found throughout the phrase book, simply read the pronunciation as if it were English, noting any special rules below. Keep in mind that stress in Russian is irregular. In this phrase book, the stress is indicated with an underline.

Consonants

Letter	Approximate Pronunciation	Symbol	Example	Pronunciation
б*	like b in bit	b	был	_bihl_
в	like v in vivid	v	ваш	_vahsh_
г	like g in go	g	город	_goh•raht_
д	like d in do	d	да	_dah_
ж	like s in pleasure	zh	жаркий	_zhahr•keey_
з	like z in zoo	z	завтра	_zahf•trah_
к	like k in kitten	k	карта	_kahr•tah_
л	like l in lily	l	лампа	_lahm•pah_
м	likew m in my	m	масло	_mahs•lah_
н	like n in not	n	нет	_nyet_
п	like p in pot	p	парк	_pahrk_
р	trilled r	r	русский	_roos•keey_
с	like s in see	s	слово	_sloh•vah_
т	like t in tip	t	там	_tahm_
ф	like f in face	f	ферма	_fyer•mah_
х	like ch in Scottish loch	kh	хлеб	_khlyep_
ц	like ts in sits	ts	цена	_tsih•nah_

ч	like ch in chip	ch	час	_chahs_
ш	like sh in shut	sh	ваша	_vah•shah_
щ	like sh followed by ch	shch	щи	_shchee_

Capital **б** in writing appears as **Б**.

The pronunciation of Russian consonants can be either hard or soft. Consonants are soft when followed by the vowels **я, е, и, ё, ю** and the soft sign, **ь**. In the Russian phonetic transcription system, when a letter is soft it is generally followed by y + a vowel (as in **нет** _nyet_), or by an apostrophe (for example, **сколько** _skol'•kah_). The apostrophe, included in the phonetics, is commonly used to represent the soft sign when Russian is written in the Latin alphabet. When the letter **ъ**, known as the hard sign, is used, it precedes a vowel and is pronounced like the y in yet. It indicates that the preceding consonant is hard.

Vowels

Letter	Approximate Pronunciation	Symbol	Example	Pronunciation
а	between a in cat and u in cut	**ah**	**как**	_kahk_
е	like ye in yet	**ye/yeh**	**где**	_gdyeh_
ё*	like yo in yonder	**yo/yoh**	**мёд**	_myot_
и	like ee in see	**ee**	**синий**	_see•neey_
й	like y in boy	**y**	**бой**	_boy_
о	like o in hot	**o/oh**	**стол**	_stol_
у	like oo in boot	**oo**	**улица**	_oo•lee•tsah_
ы	like i in ill	**ih**	**вы**	_vih_
э	like e in met	**e/eh**	**эта**	_eh•tah_

| ю | like you in youth | **yoo** | **юг** | *yook* |
| я | like ya in yard | yah | **мясо** | *myah·sah* |

Capital **ё** in writing appears as **Ё**.

The vowels **o**, **e**, **a** and **я** are pronounced differently depending on whether or not they are stressed. This explains why a given vowel is not always represented the same way in phonetic transcription.

Vowel Combinations

Letter	Approximate Pronunciation	Symbol	Example	Pronunciation
ай	like y in my	**ie**	**май**	*mie*
яй	like y in my, preceded by y in yes	**yie**	**негодяй**	*nee·gah·dyie*
ой	like oy in boy	**oy**	**вой**	*voy*
ей	like ey in obey, preceded by y in yes	**yey**	**соловей**	*sah·lah·vyehy*
ий	like ee in see, followed by y in yes	**eey**	**ранний**	*rahn·neey*
ый	like i in ill, followed by y in yes	**iy**	**красивый**	*krah·see·viy*
уй	like oo in good, followed by y in yes	**ooy**	**дуй**	*dooy*
юй	as уй above, preceded by y in yes	**yooy**	**плюй**	*plyooy*

Like most of the languages of Eastern Europe, Russian is a Slavic language. It uses the Cyrillic alphabet.

How to use this Book

Sometimes you see two alternatives separated by a slash. Choose the one that's right for your situation.

ESSENTIAL

I'm here on vacation [holiday]/business.

Я здесь в отпуске/по делу. *yah zdyes' v ot·poos·kee/pah dyeh·loo*

I'm going to...

Я еду в... *yah yeh·doo v...*

I'm staying at the...Hotel.

Я живу в гостинице... *yah zhih·voo v gahs·tee·nee·tseh...*

Words you may see are shown in YOU MAY SEE boxes.

YOU MAY SEE...

ПРИБЫТИЕ *pree·bih·tee·yeh* — arrivals
ОТПРАВЛЕНИЕ *aht·prahv·lyeh·nee·yeh* — departures
ВЫДАЧА БАГАЖА *vih·dah·chah bah·gah·zhah* — baggage claim

Any of the words or phrases listed can be plugged into the sentence below.

Train

Where is/are...?	**Где...?** *gdyeh...*
the ticket office	**билетные кассы** *bee·lyet·nih·ee kah·sih*
the information desk	**справочное бюро** *sprah·vahch·nah·yeh byoo·roh*
the luggage lockers	**камеры хранения** *kah·mee·rih khrah·nyeh·nee·yah*

Russian phrases appear in purple.

Read the simplified pronunciation as if it were English. For more on pronunciation, see page 7.

Telephone Etiquette

Hello. This is…   **Алло. Это…** *ah·loh eh·tah…*
I'd like to speak   **Я хотел m /хотела f бы поговорить с…** *yah*
to…   *khah·tyel/khah·tyeh·lah bih pah·gah·vah·reet' s…*
Extension…   **Добавочный номер…** *dah·bah·vahch·niy*
                             noh·meer…

For Numbers, see page 157.

Related phrases can be found by going to the page number indicated.

When different gender forms apply, the masculine form is followed by *m*; feminine by *f.*

Parking is usually unrestricted, except in central areas of Moscow and St. Petersburg, where parking meters and no-parking zones can be found. Illegally parked cars are subject to clamping and towing.

Information boxes contain relevant country, culture and language tips.

Expressions you may hear are shown in You May Hear boxes.

YOU MAY HEAR…
Ваш паспорт, пожалуйста.   Your passport,
vahsh pahs·pahrt pah·zhahl·stah   please.

Color-coded side bars identify each section of the book.

Survival

Arrival & Departure

ESSENTIAL

I'm here on vacation
[holiday]/business.

Я здесь в отпуске/по делам. *yah zdyehs'
v ot-poos-kee/pah dee-lahm*

I'm going to...

Я еду в... *yah yeh-doo v...*

I'm staying at
the...Hotel

Я живу в гостинице... *yah zhih-voo
v gahs-tee-nee-tseh...*

YOU MAY HEAR...

Ваш билет/паспорт, пожалуйста. *vahsh
bee-lyet/pahs-pahrt pah-zhahl-stah*

Your ticket/
passport, please.

Цель Вашего визита? *tsel' vah-shee-vah
vee-zee-tah*

What's the purpose
of your visit?

Где вы остановились? *gdyeh vih
ahs-tah-nah-vee-lees'*

Where are you
staying?

Сколько вы пробудете здесь? *skol'-ka vih
prah-boo-dee-tee zdyes'*

How long are you
staying?

С кем вы приехали? *s kyem vih
pree-yeh-khah-lee*

Who are you with?

Border Control

I'm just passing
through.

Я проездом. *yah prah-yez-dahm*

I would like to
declare...

Я хочу предъявить...таможне. *yah
khah-choo pree-dyah-veet'...tah-mozh-nyeh*

I have nothing to
declare.

Мне нечего декларировать. *mneh
nyeh-chee-vah dee-klah-ree-rah-vaht'*

YOU MAY HEAR...

Есть ли у Вас вещи, подлежащие декларированию? *yest' lee oo vahs vyeh•shchee pahd•lee•zhah•shchee•yeh dee•klah•ree•rah•vah•nee•yoo*

Do you have anything to declare?

Вам надо оплатить пошлину. *vahm nah•dah ah•plah•teet' posh•lee•noo*

You must pay duty on this.

Откройте эту сумку. *aht•kroy•tee eh•too soom•koo*

Please open this bag.

YOU MAY SEE...

ТАМОЖНЯ *tah•mozh•nyah*	customs
ТОВАРЫ БЕЗ ПОШЛИНЫ *tah•vah•rih byez posh•lee•nih*	duty-free goods
ТАМОЖЕННЫЙ ДОСМОТР *tah•moh•zhih•niy dah•smotr*	goods to declare
СВОБОДНЫЙ КОРИДОР *svah•bod•niy kah•ree•dor*	nothing to declare
ПАСПОРТНЫЙ КОНТРОЛЬ *pahs•pahrt•niy kahnt•rol'*	passport control
МИЛИЦИЯ *mee•lee•tsih•yah*	police

Money

ESSENTIAL

Where's…?	**Где…?** gdyeh…
the ATM	**банкомат** bahn-kah-_maht_
the bank	**банк** bahnk
the currency exchange office	**обмен валюты** ahb-_myen_ vah-_lyoo_-tih
What time does the bank open/close?	**Во сколько открывается/закрывается банк?** va _skol'_-kah aht-krih-_vah_-ee-tsah/ zah-krih-_vah_-ee-tsah bahnk
I'd like to change dollars/pounds into rubles.	**Я хотел m /хотела f бы обменять доллары/фунты на рубли.** yah khah-_tyel_/ khah-_tyeh_-lah bih ahb-mee-_nyaht'_ _dol_-lah-rih/ _foon_-tih nah roob-_lee_
I want to cash some traveler's checks.	**Я хочу обменять дорожные чеки.** yah khah-_choo_ ahb-mee-_nyaht'_ dah-_rozh_-nih-ee _cheh_-kee

At the Bank

Can I exchange foreign currency here?	**Можно обменять валюту здесь?** _mozh_-nah ahb-mee-_nyaht'_ vah-_lyoo_-too zdyes'
What's the exchange rate?	**Какой курс?** kah-_koy_ koors
How much is the fee?	**Сколько процентов комиссионный сбор?** _skol'_-kah prah-_tsen_-tahf kah-mees-see-_on_-niy zbor
I think there's a mistake.	**Я думаю, здесь ошибка.** yah du-ma-yoo zdes' ash-_eeb_-kah

15

I've lost my traveler's checks [cheques].	**Я потерял *m* /потеряла *f* дорожные чеки.**
	yah pah•tee•ryahl/pah•tee•ryah•lah
	dah•rozh•nih•ee cheh•kee
My card was lost.	**Я потерял *m* /потеряла *f* свою карточку.**
	yah pah•tee•ryahl/pah•tee•ryah•lah
	svah•yoo kahr•tahch•koo
My credit cards have been stolen.	**У меня украли кредитные карточки.**
	oo mee•nyah ook•rah•lee kree•deet•nih•ee
	kahr•tahch•kee
My card doesn't work.	**Моя карточка не работает.** *mah•yah*
	kahr•tahch•kah nee rah•boh•tah•eet
The ATM ate my card.	**Банкомат забрал мою карту.**
	bahn•kah•maht zahb•rahl moh•yoo kahr•too

For Numbers, see page 157.

Contact your travel agent or the Russian embassy before your trip to determine the latest regulations regarding how much foreign currency you can bring into the country. In major towns and cities, currency exchange offices can be found in banks, hotels, stores and even street kiosks. Some operate 24 hours a day.

Others are open from early morning to late evening, with a break for lunch. All currency exchange offices accept U.S. dollars and euro, and some pounds sterling; however, notes that are not clean and crisp are often rejected and you may be required to show your passport. You may have difficulty changing notes issued before 1993. For other currencies and traveler's checks, it's best to use banks and large hotels.

Warning: You may be approached by someone on the street offering attractive exchange rates. It is highly inadvisable to take up such offers.

YOU MAY SEE...

ВСТАВЬТЕ КАРТУ *fstahf'·tyeh kahr·too*	insert card
ОТМЕНИТЬ *aht·mee·neet'*	cancel
ОЧИСТИТЬ *ah·chees·teet'*	clear
ВВОД *vvot*	enter
ПИН-КОД *peen·kot*	PIN
СНИМАТЬ *snee·maht'*	withdraw funds
С ТЕКУЩЕГО СЧЕТА *s tee·koo·shchee·vah shchoh·tah*	from checking [current] account
СО СБЕРЕГАТЕЛЬНОГО СЧЕТА *sah zbee·ree·gah·teel'·nah·vah shchoh·tah*	from savings account
ЧЕК *chehk*	receipt

YOU MAY SEE...

The monetary unit is the ruble (**рубль** *roobl'*), which is divided into 100 kopecks (**копеек** *kah·pyeh·yek*).
Coins: 1, 5, 10, 50 **kopecks**; 1, 2, 5 **rubles**
Notes: 10, 50, 100, 500, 1000 **rubles**

Getting Around

ESSENTIAL

How do I get to town?	**Как мне добраться до города?** *kahk mnyeh dah·brah·tsah dah goh·rah·dah*
Where's...?	**Где...?** *gdyeh...*
the airport	**аэропорт** *ah·eh·rah·port*
the train [railway] station	**вокзал** *vahg·zahl*

the bus station	**автовокзал** ahf·tah·vahg·<u>zahl</u>
the metro [underground] station	**станция метро** <u>stahn</u>·tsih·yah mee·<u>troh</u>
How far is it?	**Как далеко это отсюда?** kahk dah·lee·<u>koh</u> eh·tah aht·<u>syoo</u>·dah
Where can I buy tickets?	**Где можно купить билеты?** gdyeh <u>mozh</u>·nah koo·<u>peet'</u> bee·<u>lyeh</u>·tih
A one-way [single]/ return-trip ticket.	**Билет в один конец/туда и обратно.** bee·<u>lyet</u> v ah·<u>deen</u> kah·<u>nyets</u>/too·<u>dah</u> ee ahb·<u>raht</u>·nah
How much?	**Сколько?** <u>skol'</u>·kah
Are there any discounts?	**Есть какая-нибудь скидка?** yehst' kah·<u>kah</u>·yah·nee·<u>boot'</u> skeet·kah
Which gate/line?	**Какой выход/путь?** kah·<u>koy</u> vih·khaht/poot'
Which platform?	**Какая платформа?** kah·<u>kah</u>·yah plaht·<u>for</u>·mah
Where can I get a taxi?	**Где можно взять такси?** gdyeh <u>mozh</u>·nah vzyaht' tahk·<u>see</u>
Please take me to this address.	**Пожалуйста, отвезите меня по этому адресу.** pah·<u>zhahl</u>·stah aht·vee·<u>zee</u>·tee mee·<u>nyah</u> pah eh·tah·moo <u>ahd</u>·ree·soo
Where can I rent a car?	**Где можно взять машину напрокат?** gdyeh <u>mozh</u>·nah vzyaht' mah·<u>shih</u>·noo nah·prah·<u>kaht</u>
Could I have a map?	**Можно мне карту?** <u>mozh</u>·nah mnyeh <u>kahr</u>·too

Tickets

When's…to Moscow?	**Когда…в Москву?** kahg·<u>dah</u>…v mahs·<u>kvoo</u>
the (first) bus	**(первый) автобус** (<u>pyer</u>·viy) ahf·<u>toh</u>·boos
the (next) flight	**(следующий) рейс** (<u>slyeh</u>·doo·yoo·shcheey) reys

the (last) train	**(последний) поезд** (pahs-*lyed*-neey) *poh*-eest
Where can I buy tickets?	**Где можно купить билеты?** gdyeh *mozh*-nah koo-*peet'* bee-*lyeh*-tih
One ticket/Two tickets, please.	**Один билет/Два билета, пожалуйста.** ah-*deen* bee-*lyet*/dvah bee-*lyeh*-tah pah-*zhahl*-stah
For today/tomorrow.	**На сегодня/завтра.** nah see-*vod*-nyah/ *zahf*-trah
A first/economy class ticket.	**Билет на первый/туристический класс.** bee-*lyet* nah *pyer*-viy/too-rees-*tee*-chees-keey klahss
A...ticket.	**Билет...** bee-*lyeht*
one-way	**в один конец** v ah-*deen* kah-*nyets*
return trip	**туда и обратно** too-*dah* ee ahb-*raht*-noh
business class	**бизнес-класс** biz-nes klahss
How much?	**Сколько?** *skol'*-kah
Is there a discount for...?	**Есть скидка...?** yest' *skeet*-kah...
children	**на детей** nah dee-*tyey*
students	**студентам** stoo-*dyen*-tahm
senior citizens	**пенсионерам** peen-see-ah-*nyeh*-rahm
tourists	**туристам** too-*rees*-tahm
I have an e-ticket.	**У меня электронный билет.** oo mee-*nyah* ee-leek-*tron*-niy bee-*lyet*
Can I buy a ticket on the bus/train?	**Я могу купить билет в автобусе/поезде?** yah mah-*goo* koo-*peet'* bee-*lyet* v ahf-*toh*-boo-see/*poh*-eez-dee
Do I have to stamp the ticket before boarding?	**Нужно ли перед посадкой компостировать билет?** *noozh*-nah lee peret pah-*saht*-koy kam-pas-*tee*-ro-vat' bee-*lyet*

How long is this ticket valid?	**Как долго действителен билет?** *kahk* <u>dol</u>·go dey·<u>stvee</u>·tee·lyen bee·<u>lyet</u>
Can I return on the same ticket?	**Могу я вернуться по этому билету?** *mah·<u>goo</u> yah vyer·<u>noo</u>·tsah poh <u>yeh</u>·tah·moo bee·<u>lye</u>·too*
I'd like to…my reservation.	**Я хотел *m* /хотела *f* бы…свой предварительный заказ.** *yah khah·<u>tyel</u>/ khah·<u>tyeh</u>·lah bih…svoy preed·vah·<u>ree</u>·teel'·niy zah·<u>kahz</u>*
cancel	**отменить** *aht·mee·<u>neet'</u>*
change	**изменить** *eez·mee·<u>neet'</u>*
confirm	**подтвердить** *paht·tveer·<u>deet'</u>*

For Days, see page 160.
For Time, see page 159.

Plane

Airport Transfer

How much is a taxi to the airport?	**Сколько стоит такси в аэропорт?** *<u>skol</u>'·kah stoh·eet tahk·<u>see</u> v ah·eh·rah·<u>port</u>*
To…Airport, please.	**В аэропорт…, пожалуйста.** *v ah·eh·rah·<u>port</u>… pah·<u>zhahl</u>·stah*
My airline is…	**Я лечу самолётом авиакомпании…** *yah lee·<u>choo</u> sah·mah·<u>lyoh</u>·tahm ah·vee·ah·kahm·<u>pah</u>·nee·ee…*
My flight leaves at…	**Мой рейс отправляется в…** *moy reys aht·prahv·<u>lyah</u>·ee·tsah v…*
I'm in a rush.	**Я спешу.** *yah spee·<u>shoo</u>*
Can you take an alternate route?	**Вы можете поехать другим путём?** *vih <u>moh</u>·zhih·tee pah·<u>yeh</u>·khaht' droo·<u>geem</u> poo·<u>tyom</u>*
Can you drive faster/slower?	**Не могли бы вы ехать быстрее/медленнее?** *nee mahg·<u>lee</u> bih vih <u>yeh</u>·khat' bihs·<u>tryeh</u>·yeh/<u>myed</u>·leen·nee·yeh*

YOU MAY HEAR...

Рейсом какой авиакомпании вы летите? What airline are you
rey•sahm kah•koy ah•vee•ah•kahm•pah•nee•ee flying?
vih lee•tee•tyeh

Внутренний или международный? Domestic or
vnoot•reen•neey ee•lee meezh•doo•nah•rod•niy International?

Какой терминал? *kah•koy teer•mee•nahl* What terminal?

YOU MAY SEE...

ПРИБЫТИЕ *pree•bih•tee•yeh*	arrivals
ОТПРАВЛЕНИЕ *aht•prahv•lyeh•nee•yeh*	departures
ВЫДАЧА БАГАЖА *vih•dah•chah bah•gah•zhah*	baggage claim
ВНУТРЕННИЕ РЕЙСЫ *vnoo•treen•nee•yeh rey•sih*	domestic flights
МЕЖДУНАРОДНЫЕ РЕЙСЫ *meezh•doo•nah•rod•nih•yeh rey•sih*	international flights
РЕГИСТРАЦИОННАЯ СТОЙКА *ree•gee•strah•tsih•on•nah•yah stoy•kah*	check-in desk
РЕГИСТРАЦИЯ ЭЛЕКТРОННЫХ БИЛЕТОВ *ree•gee•strah•tsih•yah ee•leek•tron•nihkh bee•lyeh•tahf*	e-ticket check-in
ВЫХОД НА ПОСАДКУ *vih•khaht nah pah•saht•koo*	departure gates

Checking In

Where is check-in?	**Где регистрация?** *gdyeh ree•gees•<u>trah</u>•tsih•yah*
My name is…	**Меня зовут…** *mee•<u>nyah</u> zah•<u>voot</u>…*
I'm going to…	**Я лечу в…** *yah lyee•<u>choo</u> v…*
I have…	**У меня есть…** *oo mye•<u>nyah</u> yest'*
one suitcase	**один чемодан** *ah•<u>deen</u> chee•mah•<u>dahn</u>*
two suitcases	**два чемодана** *dvah chee•mah•<u>dah</u>•nah*
one piece of hand luggage	**одна единица ручной клади** *od•<u>nah</u> yeh•dee•<u>nee</u>•tsa rooch•<u>noy</u> <u>klah</u>•dee*
How much luggage is allowed?	**Сколько багажа разрешается провозить?** *<u>skol'</u>•kah bah•gah•<u>zhah</u> rahz•ree•<u>shah</u>•ee•tsah prah•vah•<u>zeet'</u>*
Is that pounds or kilos?	**Это в фунтах или килограммах?** *<u>eh</u>•tah v <u>foon</u>•tah ee•lee kee•lo <u>gram</u> mahkh*
Which gate does flight…leave from?	**У какого выхода посадка на рейс…?** *oo kah•<u>koh</u>•vah <u>vih</u>•khah•dah pah•<u>saht</u>•kah nah reys…*
Which terminal?	**Какой терминал?** *kah•<u>koy</u> tyer•meeh•<u>nal</u>*
I'd like a window/ an aisle seat.	**Я бы хотел m /хотела f место у окна/ прохода.** *yah bih khah•<u>tyel</u>/khah•<u>tyeh</u>•lah <u>myes</u>•tah oo ahk•<u>nah</u>/prah•<u>khoh</u>•dah*
When do we leave/ arrive?	**Во сколько мы вылетаем/прилетаем?** *vah <u>skol'</u>•kah mih vih•lee•<u>tah</u>•eem/ pree•lee•<u>tah</u>•eem*
Is there any delay on flight…?	**Рейс в…задерживается?** *reys v… zah•<u>dyer</u>•zhih•vah•ee•tsah*
How late will it be?	**На сколько задерживается?** *nah <u>skol'</u>•kah zah•<u>dyer</u>•zhih•vah•ee•tsah*

For Numbers, see page 157.

YOU MAY HEAR...

Следующий! *slyeh·doo·yoo·shcheey* Next!

Ваш билет/паспорт, пожалуйста. *vahsh* Your ticket/
bee·lyet/pahs·pahrt pah·zhahl·stah passport, please.

Сколько у Вас мест багажа? *skol'·kah oo* How much luggage
vahs myest bah·gah·zhah do you have?

У Вас перевес багажа. *oo vahs pee·ree·vyes* You have excess
bah·gah·zhah luggage.

Этот слишком тяжёлый/большой That's too heavy/
для ручной клади. *eh·taht sleesh·kahm* large for a carry-on
tee·zhoh·liy/bahl'·shoy dlyah rooch·noy klah·dee [to carry on board]

Вы сами упаковывали багаж? *vih sah·mee* Did you pack these
oo·pah·koh·vih·vah·lee bah·gahsh bags yourself?

Вас просили что-нибудь перевезти? *vahs* Did anyone give you
prah·see·lee shtoh·nee·boot' pee·ree·vees·tee anything to carry?

Выньте всё из карманов. *vihn'·tee fsyoh ees* Empty your
kahr·mah·nahf pockets.

Снимите обувь. *snee·mee·tee oh·boof'* Take off your shoes.

Производится посадка на рейс... Now boarding
prah·eez·voh·dee·tsah pah·saht·kah nah reys... flight...

Luggage

Where is/are...?	**Где...?** *gdyeh...*
the luggage trolleys	**багажные тележки** *bah·gahzh·nih·ee tee·lyesh·kee*
the luggage lockers	**камеры хранения** *kah·mee·rih khrah·nyeh·nee·yah*
the baggage claim	**выдача багажа** *vih·dah·chah bah·gah·zhah*

| My luggage has been lost/stolen. | **У меня пропал/украли багаж.** *oo mee·nyah prah·pahl/oo·krah·lee bah·gahsh* |
| My suitcase was damaged. | **Мне повредили чемодан.** *mnyeh pah·vree·dee·lee chee·mah·dahn* |

Finding your Way

Where is…?	**Где…?** *gdyeh…*
the currency exchange office	**обмен валюты** *ahb·myen vah·lyoo·tih*
the car hire	**прокат автомобилей** *prah·kaht ahf·tah·mah·bee·ley*
the exit	**выход** *vih·khaht*
the taxis	**такси** *tahk·see*
Is there…into town?	**Есть…в город?** *yest'…v goh·raht*
a bus	**автобус** *ahf·toh·boos*
a train	**поезд** *poh·eest*
a metro [subway]	**метро** *mee·troh*

For Asking Directions, see page 34.

Train

How do I get to the train station?	**Как мне добраться до вокзала?** *kahk mnyeh dah·brah·tsah dah vahg·zah·lah*
Is it far?	**Это далеко?** *eh·tah dah·lee·koh*
Where is/are…?	**Где…?** *gdyeh…*
the ticket office	**билетные кассы** *bee·lyet·nih·ee kah·sih*
the information desk	**бюро информации** *byoo·roh een·fahr·mah·tsee·ee*
the luggage lockers	**камеры хранения** *kah·mee·rih khrah·nyeh·nee·yah*
the platforms	**платформы** *plaht·for·mih*
Could I have a schedule [timetable]?	**Можно расписание?** *mozh·nah rahs·pee·sah·nee·yeh*

How long is the trip?	**Сколько длится поездка?** _skol'_•kah _dlee_•tsah pah•_yest_•kah
Is it a direct train?	**Это прямой поезд?** _eh_•tah pryah•_moy_ _poh_•yest
Do I have to change trains?	**Мне надо делать пересадку?** mnyeh _nah_•dah _dyeh_•laht' pee•ree•_saht_•koo
Is the train on time?	**Поезд приедет вовремя?** _poh_•yest pree•_ye_•dit _voh_•vre•myah

For Asking Directions, see page 34.

For Tickets, see page 18.

YOU MAY SEE...

К ПЛАТФОРМАМ k plaht•_for_•mahm	platforms
ИНФОРМАЦИЯ een•fahr•_mah_•tsih•yah	information
ЗАКАЗ БИЛЕТОВ zah•_kahz_ bee•_lyeh_•tahf	reservations
ЗАЛ ОЖИДАНИЯ zahl oh•zhee•_dah_•nee•yah	waiting room
ПРИБЫТИЕ pree•_bih_•tee•yeh	arrivals
ОТПРАВЛЕНИЕ aht•prahv•_lyeh_•nee•yeh	departures

An often-quoted line by the great Russian writer Nikolai Gogol (1809-1852) states that Russia's roads are one of its greatest misfortunes. While the state of Russian roads is still a source of national frustration, the excellent rail system built during the Soviet era provides a good alternative to automobile travel. Unfortunately, Russia's train stations have become less safe than they were in the past.

Departures

Which platform does the train to…leave from?	**С какой платформы отходит поезд до…?** *s kah-koy plaht-for-mih aht-khoh-deet poh-eest dah…*
Is this the track [platform] to…?	**С этой платформы поезд на…?** *s eh-tie plaht-for-mih poh-eest nah…*
Where is track [platform]…?	**Где платформа…?** *gdyeh plaht-for-mah…*
Where do I change for…?	**Где мне делать пересадку на…?** *gdyeh mnyeh dyeh-laht' pee-ree-saht-koo nah…*

On Board

Can I sit here/open the window?	**Можно здесь сидеть/открывать окно?** *mo-zhno zdyes see-dyet'/at-krih-vat' ahk-noh*
Is this seat taken?	**Это место занято?** *eh-tah myes-tah zah-nee-tah*
I think that's my seat.	**Мне кажется, это моё место.** *mnyeh kah-zhih-tsah eh-tah mah-yoh myes-tah*
Here's my reservation.	**Вот моя бронь.** *Vot ma-yah brohn'*

YOU MAY HEAR…

Посадка заканчивается! *pah-saht-kah zah-kahn-chee-vah-ee-tsah*
All aboard!

Пожалуйста, предъявите билеты. *pah-zhahl-stah preed-yah-vee-tee bee-lyeh-tih*
Tickets, please.

Вам надо делать пересадку в… *vahm nah-dah dyeh-laht' pee-ree-saht-koo v…*
You have to change at…

Следующая остановка… *slyeh-doo-yoo-shchah-yah ahs-tah-nof-kah…*
Next stop…

Bus

Where's the bus station?	**Где автобусная станция?** gdyeh ahf·**toh**·boos·nah·yah <u>stahn</u>·tsih·yah
How far is it?	**Как далеко это?** kahk dah·lee·**koh** eh·tah
How do I get to…?	**Как мне доехать до…?** kahk mnyeh dah·**yeh**·khaht' dah…
Does the bus stop at…?	**Этот автобус останавливается в…?** <u>eh</u>·taht ahf·**toh**·boos ah·stah·<u>nahv</u>·lee·vah·ee·tsah v…
Could you tell me when to get off?	**Вы скажете мне, где выходить?** vih <u>skah</u>·zhih·tee mnyeh gdyeh vih·khah·<u>deet'</u>
Do I have to change buses?	**Мне нужно делать пересадку?** mnyeh <u>noozh</u>·nah <u>dyeh</u>·laht' pee·ree·<u>saht</u>·koo
Stop here, please!	**Остановите здесь, пожалуйста!** ah·stah·nah·<u>vee</u>·tee zdyes' pah·<u>zhahl</u>·stah

For Tickets, see page 18.

Buses offer a standard fare no matter how far you're going but you can't change buses on the same ticket. In big cities, a system of magnetized fare cards that can be used on buses and trolleybuses (electric buses powered by two overhead wires) as well as the metro (where such cards can be purchased) is in operation. In smaller cities you will need to purchase **талоны** tah·<u>loh</u>·nih (paper tickets that you have to stamp) from a conductor on the bus or from kiosks.

A popular alternative to buses are fixed-route taxis called **маршрутные такси** mahrsh·<u>root</u>·nih·yeh tahk·see or mini-buses, **маршрутки** mahrsh·<u>root</u>·kee, that follow a fixed route, usually the same as bus routes.

YOU MAY SEE...

АВТОБУСНАЯ ОСТАНОВКА *ahf·toh·boos·nah·yah ahs·tah·nof·kah*	bus stop
ОСТАНОВКА ПО ТРЕБОВАНИЮ *os·tah·nov·kah po tree·bo·vah·nee·yoo*	request stop
ВХОД/ВЫХОД *fkhot/vih·khaht*	enter/exit
ПРОКОМПОСТИРУЙТЕ ТАЛОН *prah·kahm·pah·stee·rooy·tyeh tah·lon*	stamp your ticket

Metro

Where's the nearest metro [underground] station?	**Где ближайшая станция метро?** *gdyeh blee·zhie·shah·yah stahn·tsih·yah meet·roh*
Could I have a map of the metro [underground]?	**Можно мне схему метро?** *mozh·nah mnyeh skhyeh·moo meet·roh*
Which line for...?	**По какой линии ехать до...?** *pah kah·koy lee·nee·ee yeh·khaht' dah...*
Which direction?	**В каком направлении?** *f kah·kom·nap·rah·vlye·nee·ee*
Where do I change for...?	**Где делать пересадку до...?** *gdyeh dyeh·laht' pee·ree·saht·koo dah...*
Is this the right train for...?	**Этот поезд идёт до...?** *eh·taht poh·eest ee·dyot dah...*
How many stops to...?	**Сколько остановок до ...?** *skol'·kah as·tah·noh·vahk doh*
Where are we?	**Где мы находимся?** *gdyeh mih nah·khoh·deem·syah*
For Tickets, see page 18.	

МЕТРО *meet·roh* (subway) is the fastest and most convenient way to get around town. Moscow, St. Petersburg and a few other major cities have subway systems. Moscow has the most extensive system; its older stations are sights worth visiting in their own right, featuring a blend of ornate neoclassicism and Socialist Realism. The subway operates from 6:00 a.m. to 1:00 a.m. There is a set fare regardless of the distance traveled. If you plan to use public transit a lot, you may decide to buy a pass (**единый билет** *yee·dee·niy bee·lyet*), valid for 8 days, 16 days or a month, for travel on the metro, bus, trolleybus and tram.

Boat & Ferry

When is the ferry to…?	**Когда паром до…?** *kahg·dah pah·rom dah…*	
Where are the life jackets?	**Где спасательные жилеты?** *gdyeh spah·sah·teel'·nih·ee zhih·lyeh·tih*	

For Tickets, see page 18.

> ### YOU MAY SEE…
>
> | | |
> |---|---|
> | **СПАСАТЕЛЬНАЯ ШЛЮПКА** *spah·sah·teel'·nah·yah shlyoop·kah* | life boat |
> | **СПАСАТЕЛЬНЫЙ ЖИЛЕТ** *spah·sah·teel'·niy zhih·lyeht* | life jacket |

Taxi

Where can I get a taxi?	**Где можно взять такси?** *gdyeh mozh·nah vzyaht' tahk·see*
Can you send a taxi?	**Не могли бы Вы прислать такси?** *nee mogh·lee bih vih pree·slat'tahk·see*

What is the number for a taxi?	**Как вызвать такси по телефону?** *kahk vihz•vaht' tahk•see pah tee•lee•foh•noo*
I'd like a taxi now/ for tomorrow at…	**Мне нужно такси сейчас/на завтра на…** *mnyeh noozh•nah tahk•see see•chahs/nah zahf•trah nah…*
Pick me up at (place/time)…	**Подъезжайте за мной к/в…** *pahd•yeh•zhie•tee zah mnoy k/v…*
Please take me to…	**Пожалуйста, отвезите меня…** *pah•zhahl•stah aht•vee•zee•tee mee•nyah…*
this address	**по этому адресу** *pah eh•tah•moo ahd•ree•soo*
the airport	**в аэропорт** *v ah•eh•rah•port*
the train station	**на вокзал** *nah vahg•zahl*
I'm late.	**Я опаздываю.** *yah ah•pahz•dih•vah•yoo*
Can you drive faster/slower?	**Не могли бы вы ехать быстрее/ медленнее?** *nee mahg•lee bih vih yeh•khaht' bihs•tryeh•yeh/myed•leen•nee•yeh*
Stop/Wait here.	**Остановитесь/Подождите здесь.** *ah•stah•nah•vee•tees'/pah•dahzh•dee•tee zdyes'*

YOU MAY HEAR…

Куда? *koo•dah*	Where to?
Какой адрес? *kah•koy ahd•rees*	What's the address?
Здесь положен дополнительный аэропортовый сбор/сбор за ночное время. *zdyes' po•lo•zhihn doh•pohl•nee• tyel'•nih ah•eh•rah•por•toh•viy sbohr/sbohr za noch•no•eh vreh•myah*	There's a nighttime/ airport surcharge.

How much will it cost?	**Сколько это будет стоить?** _skol'•kah eh•tah boo•deet stoh•eet'_
You said…rubles.	**Вы сказали…рублей.** _vih skah•zah•lee… roob•lyey_
Keep the change.	**Оставьте сдачу.** _ah•stahf'•tee zdah•choo_
A receipt, please.	**Можно чек, пожалуйста.** _mozh•nah chehk pah•zhahl•stah_

You'll find mainly private taxi services throughout Russia. It is common practice for Russians to hail private cars in the street, but foreigners, especially those who know little Russian and are unfamiliar with their surroundings, should exercise extreme caution. Before entering a private car, make sure that the driver understands where you want to go and agree on a price.

Warning: Never enter a car if somebody besides the driver is in it. Be especially careful after dark.

Bicycle & Motorbike

I'd like to hire…	**Я хотел _m_ /хотела _f_ бы взять напрокат…** _yah khah•tyel/khah•tyeh•lah bih vzyaht' nah•prah•kaht…_
a bicycle	**велосипед** _vee•lah•see•pyet_
a moped	**мопед** _mah•pyet_
a motorcycle	**мотоцикл** _mah•tah•tsihkl_
How much per day/week?	**Сколько стоит в день/неделю?** _skol'•kah stoh•eet v dyen'/nee•dyeh•lyoo_
Can I have a helmet/lock?	**Могу я получить шлем/замок?** _mah•goo yah pah•loo•cheet' shlyem/zah•mok_

Car Hire

Where can I rent a car?	**Где можно взять машину напрокат?** *gdyeh mozh·nah vzyaht' mah·shih·noo nah·prah·kaht*
I'd like to rent [hire]…	**Я хотел m /хотела f бы взять напрокат…** *yah khah·tyel/khah·tyeh·lah bih vzyaht' nah·prah·kaht…*
a cheap/small car	**недорогую/небольшую машину** *nih·do·ro·goo·yoo/nye·bol'·shoo·yoo mah·shih·noo*
a 2-/4-door car	**двух/четырёх дверную машину** *dvookh/chee·tih·ryokh dvyer·noo·yoo mah·shih·noo*
an automatic/manual car	**машину с автоматической/ручной трансмиссией** *mah·shih·noo s ahf·tah·mah·tee·chees·koy/rooch·noy trahns·mee·see·yey*
a car with air-conditioning	**машину с кондиционером** *mah·shih·noo s kahn·dee·tsih·ah·nyeh·rahm*
a car with a car seat	**машину с детским сидением** *mah·shih·noo s dyets·keem see·dyen'·yem*
How much…?	**Сколько…?** *skol'·kah…*
per day/week	**в день/неделю** *v dyen'/nee·dyeh·lyoo*
per kilometer	**за километр** *zah kee·lah·myetr*
for unlimited mileage	**за неограниченный пробег** *zah nee·ahg·rah·nee·cheen·niy prah·byek*
with insurance	**со страховкой** *sah strah·khof·kie*
Are there any special weekend rates?	**Есть особый тариф по выходным?** *yest' ah·soh·biy tah·reef pah vih·khahd·nihm*

Fuel Station

Where's the nearest fuel station?	**Где ближайшая заправочная станция?** *gdyeh blee·zhie·shah·yah zah·prah·vahch·nah·yah stahn·tsih·yah*

YOU MAY HEAR...

У Вас есть международное водительское удостоверение? *oo vahs yest' meezh•doo•nah•rod•nah•yeh vah•dee•teel'•skah•yeh oo•dahs•tah•vee•ryeh•nee•yeh*

Do you have an international driver's license?

Ваш паспорт, пожалуйста. *vahsh pahs•pahrt pah•zhahl•stah*

Your passport, please.

Вам нужна страховка? *vahm noozh•nah strah•khof•kah*

Do you want insurance?

Нужен залог... *noo•zhihn zah•log...*

There is a deposit of...

Распишитесь здесь. *rahs•pee•shih•tees' zdyes'*

Please sign here.

Fill it up, please.

Полный бак, пожалуйста. *pol•niy bahk pah•zhahl•stah*

...liters, please.

...литров бензина, пожалуйста. *...leet•rahf been•zee•nah pah•zhahl•stah*

I'll pay in cash/ by credit card.

Я заплачу наличными/по кредитной карточке. *yah zah•plah•choo nah•leech•nih•mee/ pah kree•deet•nie kahr•tahch•kyeh*

YOU MAY SEE...

бензин А-98 *been•zeen ah dee•vyah•nos•tah voh•seem'* super

бензин А-93 *been•zeen ah dee•vyah•nos•tah tree* regular

дизельное топливо *dee•zeel'•nah•yeh top•lee•vah* diesel

Asking Directions

Is this the right road to…?	**Это дорога на…?** _eh·tah dah·roh·gah nah…_
How far is it to…?	**Далеко до…отсюда?** _dah·lee·koh dah… aht·syoo·dah_
Where's…?	**Где…?** _gdyeh…_
…Street	**улица…** _oo·lee·tsah…_
this address	**этот адрес** _eh·taht ahd·rees_
the highway [motorway]	**шоссе** _shahs·seh_
Can you show me on the map?	**Можете показать мне на карте?** _moh·zhih·tee pah·kah·zaht' mnyeh nah kahr·tee_
I'm lost.	**Я заблудился m /заблудилась f.** _yah zah·bloo·deel·syah/zah·bloo·dee·lahs'_

YOU MAY HEAR…

прямо _pryah·mah_	straight ahead
слева _slyeh·vah_	on the left
справа _sprah·vah_	on the right
на углу/за углом _nah oo·gloo/zah oo·glohm_	on/around the corner
напротив _nah·proh·teef_	opposite
позади _pah·zah·dee_	behind
рядом с _ryah·dahm s_	next to
после _pos·lee_	after
север/юг _syeh·veer/yook_	north/south
восток/запад _vahs·tok/zah·paht_	east/west
у светофора _oo svee·tah·foh·rah_	at the traffic light
на перекрестке _nah pee·ree·kryost·kee_	at the intersection

YOU MAY SEE...

	ОБГОН ЗАПРЕЩЕН *ahb·gon zah·pree·shchon*	no passing
STOP	**СТОП** *stop*	stop
	ОДНОСТОРОННЕЕ ДВИЖЕНИЕ *ahd·nah·stah·ron·nyeh·yeh dvee·zheh·nee·yeh*	one-way street
	УСТУПИ ДОРОГУ *oos·too·pee dah·roh·goo*	yield [give way]
	ВЪЕЗД ЗАПРЕЩЕН *vyezd zah·pree·shchon*	no entry
	СТОЯНКА ЗАПРЕЩЕНА *stah·yahn·kah zah·pree·shchee·nah*	no parking
	ОПАСНЫЙ ПОВОРОТ *ah·pahs·niy pah·vah·rot*	dangerous curve
	ПЕШЕХОДНЫЙ ПЕРЕХОД *pee·shih·khod·niy pee·ree·khot*	pedestrian crossing
50	**ОГРАНИЧЕНИЕ СКОРОСТИ** *ah·grah·nee·cheh·nee·yeh skoh·rahs·tee*	maximum speed limit

Parking

Can I park here?	**Здесь можно поставить машину?** *zdyes' mozh·nah pah·stah·veet' mah·shih·noo*
Where is the nearest parking garage/parking lot [car park]?	**Здесь рядом есть крытая стоянка/ автостоянка?** *zdyes' ryah·dahm yest' krih·tah·yah stah·yahn·kah/ ahf·tah·stah·yahn·kah*

Where's the parking meter?	**Где счётчик времени стоянки?** *gdyeh shchot-cheek vreh-meh-nee stah-yahn-kee*
How much...?	**Сколько...?** *skol'-kah...*
per hour	**в час** *f chahs*
per day	**в день** *v dyen'*
overnight	**за ночь** *zah nahch*

Parking is usually unrestricted, except in central areas of Moscow and St. Petersburg, where parking meters and no-parking zones can be found. Illegally parked cars are subject to clamping and towing.

Breakdown & Repair

My car broke down/won't start.	**У меня сломалась/не заводится машина.** *oo mee-nyah slah-mah-lahs'/nee zah-voh-dee-tsah mah-shih-nah*
Can you fix it?	**Можно починить?** *mozh-nah pah-chee-neet'*
When will it be ready?	**Когда будет готово?** *kahg-dah boo-deet gah-toh-vah*
How much will it cost?	**Сколько это будет стоить?** *skol'-kah eh-tah boo-deet stoh-eet'*
I have a puncture/ flat tyre (tire).	**У меня проколота шина/спущено колесо** *oo meh-nya proh-koh-loh-tah shee-nah/ spoo-shchyeh-noh koh-leh-soh*

Accidents

| There has been an accident. | **Произошла авария.** *prah-ee-zah-shlah ah-vah-ree-yah* |
| Call an ambulance/ the police. | **Вызовите скорую помощь/милицию.** *vih-zah-vee-tee skoh-roo-yoo poh-mahshch'/ mee-lee-tsih-yoo* |

Places to Stay

ESSENTIAL

Can you recommend a hotel?	**Можете порекомендовать гостиницу?** _moh•zhih•tee pah•ree•kah•meen•dah•vaht' gahs•tee•nee•tsoo_
I have a reservation.	**У меня заказ.** _oo mee•nyah zah•kahs_
My name is...	**Меня зовут...** _mee•nyah zah•voot..._
Do you have a room...?	**У вас есть номер...?** _oo vahs yest' noh•meer..._
for one/two	**на одного/двоих** _nah ahd•nah•voh/dvah•eekh_
with a bathroom	**с ванной** _s vahn•nie_
with air-conditioning	**с кондиционером** _s kahn•dee•tzih•ah•nyeh•rahm_
For tonight.	**На эти сутки.** _nah eh•tee soot•kee_
For two nights.	**На два дня.** _nah dvah dnyah_
For one week.	**На неделю.** _nah nee•dyeh•lyoo_
How much?	**Сколько?** _skol'•kah_
Do you have anything cheaper?	**Есть что-нибудь подешевле?** _yest' shtoh•nee•boot' pah•dee•shev•lee_
When's check-out?	**Во сколько надо освободить номер?** _vah skol'•kah nah•dah ah•svah•bah•deet' noh•meer_
Can I leave this in the safe?	**Можно оставить это в сейфе?** _mozh•nah ah•stah•veet' eh•tah f sey•fee_
Can I leave my bags?	**Можно я оставлю сумки?** _mozh•nah yah ah•stahv•lyoo soom•kee_
Can I have the bill/a receipt?	**Можно счёт/чек?** _mozh•nah shchot/chehk_
I'll pay in cash/by credit card.	**Я заплачу наличными/по кредитной карточке.** _yah zah•plah•choo nah•leech•nih•mee/ pah kree•deet•noy kahr•tahch•kee_

Because of the many rules governing foreigners in Russia, it is easiest to make travel, housing and visa arrangements through a tour or travel agency. A Russian visa can be obtained once you have either a hotel reservation or an official invitation (**приглашение** *pree·glah·sheh·nee·yeh*) from a friend, business associate or relative in Russia.

Wherever you stay, you will need to make sure you are given an official registration paper, which you will need to relinquish when you exit the country.

If you stay in a hotel, the staff will take your passport from you while they process this registration. Be sure to obtain a receipt for your passport and carry it with you, as you can be stopped by the police and fined for not having a passport with you. If you stay with friends or relatives, you will need to obtain this registration from **ОВИР** *ah·veer* (the Department of Visas and Registration) within 72 hours of your arrival.

Somewhere to Stay

Can you recommend...	**Можете порекомендовать... ?** *moh·zhih·tee pah·ree·kah·meen·dah·vaht'*
a hotel	**гостиницу** *gahs·tee·nee·tsoo*
a hostel	**общежитие** *ahp·shchee·zhih·tee·yeh*
a campsite	**палаточный лагерь** *pah·lah·toch·niy lah·geer'*
a bed and breakfast	**гостиницу типа «ночлег и завтрак»** *gahs·tee·nee·tsoo tee·pah noch·lyeg ee zavt·rahk*
What is it near?	**Что находится рядом?** *shtoh nah·khoh·dee·tsah ryah·dahm*
How do I get there?	**Как туда добраться?** *kahk too·dah dah·brah·tsah*

If at all possible, arrange to be met at the airport by a representative from your hotel. Some travel agencies, such as Intourist, will meet you when you exit customs. If you are not being met, try to use public transportation to get to your hotel. Be very cautious about getting into a taxi.

Intourist no longer holds a monopoly on accommodations in Russia, and in major cities an increasing number of new or newly renovated hotels are now jointly operated with Western companies. These first-class ventures offer a new, if pricey, option for tourists. If you are on an Intourist package tour you can state your hotel preference, but the final arrangements rest with Intourist.

Hotels also usually have service bureaus (**бюро обслуживания** *byoo·roh ahp·sloo·zhih·vah·nee·yah*) manned by multilingual staff, who provide information, arrange outings and excursions, make reservations and provide general assistance.

At the Hotel

I have a reservation.	**У меня заказ.** *oo mee·nyah zah·kahs*
My name is…	**Моя фамилия…** *mee·nyah zah·voot…*
Do you have a room…?	**У вас есть номер…?** *oo vahs yest' noh·meer…*
with a bathroom [toilet]/shower	**с ванной/душем** *s vahn·nie/doo·shehm*
with air-conditioning	**с кондиционером** *s kahn·dee·tsih·ah·nyeh·rahm*
that's smoking/ non-smoking	**для курящих/некурящих** *dlyah koo·ryah·shcheekh/nee·koo·ryah·shcheekh*
For…	**На…** *nah…*
tonight.	**эти сутки.** *eh·tee soot·kee*
two nights.	**два дня.** *dvah dnyah*
one week.	**неделю.** *nee·dyeh·lyoo*
Does the hotel have…?	**В гостинице есть…?** *v gahs·tee·nee·tseh yest'…*
a computer	**компьютер** *kahm·pyoo·ter*
an elevator [lift]	**лифт** *leeft*
(wireless) internet service	**(беспроводной) интернет** *(bees·prah·vahd·noy) een·ter·net*
room service	**обслуживание номеров** *ahp·sloo·zhih·vah·nee·yeh nah·mee·rof*
a gym	**спортзал** *sport·zahl*

a pool	**бассейн** *bah•seyn*
I need...	**Мне нужно...** *mnyeh noozh•nah...*
an extra bed	**ещё одну кровать** *ee•shchoh ahd•noo krah•vaht'*
a cot	**раскладушку** *rahs•klah•doosh•koo*
a crib [child's cot]	**детскую кроватку** *dyets•koo•yoo krah•vaht•koo*

YOU MAY HEAR...

Ваш паспорт/Вашу кредитную карточку, пожалуйста. *vahsh pahs•pahrt/vah•shoo pah•zhahl•stah kree•deet•noo•yoo kahr•tahch•koo*
Your passport/Your credit card, please.

Заполните бланк. *zah•pol•nee•tyeh blahnk*
Fill out this form.

распишитесь здесь. *rahs•pee•shih•tyes' zdyes'*
Sign here.

Price

How much per night/week?	**Сколько в сутки/неделю?** *skol'•kah f soot•kee/nee•dyeh•lyoo*
Does the price include breakfast/ sales tax [VAT]?	**Цена включает завтрак/НДС?** *tsih•nah klyoo•chah•eet zahf•trahk/en•deh•es*
Are there any discounts?	**Есть скидки?** *yest' skih•dkih*

Preferences

Can I see the room?	**Могу я посмотреть номер?** *mah•goo yah pos•maht•ret' noh•mehr*
I'd like a...room.	**Мне нужен номер...** *mneh noo•zhyen noh•mehr*
better	**лучше** *loo•chshye*
bigger	**больше** *bol'•shye*

cheaper	**дешевле** deh·*shyev*·leh
quieter	**тише** *tih*·shye
I'll take it.	**Я сниму его.** yah snee·moo·eh·*voh*
No, I won't take it.	**Я не буду его снимать.** yah neh *boo*·doo ehvoh *snih*·maht'

Questions

Where's…?	**Где…?** gdyeh…
the bar	**бар** bahr
the toilets	**туалет** too·ah·*lyet*
the elevator [lift]	**лифт** leeft
Can I have…?	**Можно мне…?** *mozh*·nah mnyeh…
a blanket	**одеяло** ah·dee·*yah*·lah
an iron	**утюг** oo·*tyook*
the room key/ key card	**ключ/ключ-карта от номера** klyooch/klyooch *kahr*·tah ot *noh*·meh·rah
a pillow	**подушку** pah·*doosh*·koo
soap	**мыло** *mih*·lah

YOU MAY SEE…

ОТ СЕБЯ/НА СЕБЯ aht see·*byah*/nah see·*byah*	push/pull
ТУАЛЕТ too·ah·*lyet*	restroom [toilet]
ДУШ doosh	shower
ЛИФТ leeft	elevator [lift]
ЛЕСТНИЦА *lyes*·nee·tsah	stairs
ПРАЧЕЧНАЯ *prah*·cheech·nah·yah	laundry
НЕ БЕСПОКОИТЬ nyeh bees·pah·*koh*·eet'	do not disturb
АВАРИЙНЫЙ ВЫХОД ah·vah·*reey*·niy *vih*·khaht	emergency exit
ВЫХОД *vih*·khaht	exit
БУДИЛЬНИК boo·*deel*'·neek	wake-up call

toilet paper	**туалетную бумагу** _too·ah·lyet·noo·yoo_
	boo·mah·goo
a towel	**банное полотенце** _bahn·nah·yeh_
	pah·lah·tyen·tseh
Do you have an adapter for this?	**У вас есть адаптер для этого?** _oo vahs yest'_ _ah·dahp·ter dlyah eh·tah·vah_
How do I turn on the lights?	**Как мне включить свет?** _kahk mnyeh_ _fklyoo·cheet' svyet_
Wake me at…	**Разбудите меня в…** _rahz·boo·dee·tee_ _mee·nyah v…_
Could I have my things from the safe?	**Можно взять вещи из сейфа?** _mozh·nah_ _vzyaht' vyeh·shchee ees sey·fah_
Is there mail/ a message for me?	**Есть почта/сообщение для меня?** _yest'_ _poch·tah/sah·ahp·shchyeh·nee·yeh dlyah mee·nyah_
Do you have a laundry service?	**У Вас есть прачечная?** _oo vahs yest'_ _prah·cheech·nah·yah_

Problems

There's a problem.	**Есть проблема.** _yest' prah·blyeh·mah_
I've lost my key/key card.	**Я потерял** _m_ **/потеряла** _f_ **ключ/электронный** **ключ.** _yah pah·tee·ryahl/pah·tee·ryah·lah_ _klyooch/ee·leek·tron·niy klyooch_
I've locked myself out of my room.	**Я случайно захлопнул** _m_ **/захлопнула** _f_ **дверь.** _yah sloo·chie·nah zah·khlop·nool/_ _zah·khlop·noo·lah dvyer'_
There's no hot water/toilet paper.	**Нет горячей воды/туалетной бумаги.** _nyet gah·ryah·chey vah·dih/too·ah·lyet·nie_ _boo·mah·gee_
The room is dirty.	**В комнате грязно.** _f kom·nah·tyeh gryahz·nah_
There are bugs in. our room.	**У нас в комнате насекомые.** _oo nahs f_ _kom·nah·tyeh nah·see·koh·mih·yeh_

The…has broken down.	**…не работает.**	…nee rah•boh•tah•yet
Can you fix…?	**Можно починить…?**	mozh•nah pah•chee•neet'…
the air-conditioning	**кондиционер**	kahn•dee•tsih•ah•nyer
the fan	**вентилятор**	veen•tee•lyah•tahr
the heat [heating]	**отопление**	ah•tahp•lyeh•nee•yeh
the light	**свет**	svyet
the TV	**телевизор**	tee•lee•vee•zahr
the toilet	**туалет**	too•ah•lyet
I'd like to move to another room.	**Я хотел m /хотела f бы другую комнату.**	yah khah•tyel/khah•tyeh•lah bih droo•goo•yoo kom•nah•too

---

While 220 volt AC tends to be standard in Russia, you'll still find 110-120 volt AC in some places. Russian outlets differ from Western ones, but large hotels often have outlets that will take Western plugs. Since suitable adapters are sometimes hard to find in Russia, especially outside major cities, it is prudent to travel with one. If you are traveling with electronics built to support multiple voltages, you may want to bring a surge protector suitable for Russian outlets. If your electronics do not support 220 volt current, you will need both an adapter and a step-down transformer.

Checking Out

When's check-out?	**Во сколько надо освободить комнату?** vah skol'•kah nah•dah ah•svah•bah•deet' kom•nah•too
Could I leave my bags here until…?	**Можно мне оставить вещи здесь до…?** mozh•nah mnyeh ah•stah•veet' vyeh•shchee zdyes' dah…

Can I have an itemized bill/ a receipt?	**Можно детальный счёт/чек?** _mozh_•nah _dee_•_tahl'_•niy shchot/chehk
I think there's a mistake in this bill.	**Мне кажется, в счёте ошибка.** mnyeh _kah_•zhee•tsah v _shchoh_•tee ah•_shihp_•kah
I'll pay in cash/by credit card.	**Я заплачу наличными/по кредитной карточке.** yah zah•plah•_choo_ nah•_leech_•nih•mee/ pah kree•_deet_•nie _kahr_•tahch•kyeh

Tips of 10-20% are generally appropriate in restaurants and taxis, depending on the level of service. Porters and maids will certainly expect and appreciate a dollar or two (or the ruble equivalent) for each bag they carry or day that they clean.

As anywhere else, generous tippers will often get better service than those who tip poorly or not at all. Tour guides and their drivers, especially if they have gone 'above and beyond' to get you into restaurants and museums, will expect to be compensated somewhat above the agreed rate.

Renting

I've reserved an apartment/a room.	**Я заказывал** *m* **/заказывала** *f* **квартиру/комнату.** *yah zah-kah-zih-vahl/ zah-kah-zih-vah-lah kvahr-tee-roo/kom-nah-too*
My name is…	**Меня зовут…** *mee-nyah zah-voot…*
Can I have the key/key card?	**Можно получить ключ/электронный ключ?** *mozh-nah pah-loo-cheet' klyooch/ ee-leek-tron-niy klyooch*
Are there…?	**Есть…?** *yest'…*
dishes and utensils	**посуда** *pah-soo-dah*
pillows	**подушки** *pah-doosh-kee*
sheets	**простыни** *proh-stih-nee*
towels	**полотенца** *pah-lah-tyen-tsah*
When/Where do I put out the bins?	**Когда/Куда выносить мусор?** *kahg-dah/ koo-dah vih-nah-seet' moo-sahr*
…is broken.	**…не работает.** *…nee rah-boh-tah-yet*
How does…work?	**Как работает…?** *kahk rah-boh-tah-yet…*
the air-conditioner	**кондиционер** *kahn-dee-tsih-ah-nyer*
the dishwasher	**посудомоечная машина** *pah-soo-dah-moh-eech-nah-yah mah-shih-nah*
the freezer	**морозильная камера** *mah-rah-zeel'-nah-yah kah-mee-rah*
the heater	**обогреватель** *ah-bah-gree-vah-teel'*
the microwave	**микроволновка** *meek-rah-vahl-nof-kah*
the refrigerator	**холодильник** *khah-lah-deel'-neek*
the stove	**плита** *plee-tah*
the washing machine	**стиральная машина** *stee-rahl'-nah-yah mah-shih-nah*

Domestic Items

I need…	**Мне нужно…** mnyeh _noozh_•nah…
an adapter	**адаптер** ah•_dahp_•ter
aluminum [kitchen] foil	**фольга** fahl'•_gah_
a bottle opener	**открывалка** aht•krih•_vahl_•kah
a broom	**веник** _vyeh_•neek
a can opener	**консервный нож** kahn•_syerv_•niy nosh
cleaning supplies	**моющие средства** _moh_•yoo•shchee•yeh _sryet_•stvah
a corkscrew	**штопор** _shtoh_•pahr
detergent	**стиральный порошок** stee•_rahl'_•niy pah•rah•_shok_
dishwashing liquid	**жидкость для мытья посуды** _zhiht_•kahst' dlyah mih•_tyah_ pah•_soo_•dih
bin bags	**мешки для мусора** meesh•_kee_ dlyah _moo_•sah•rah
a light bulb	**лампочка** _lahm_•pahch•kah
matches	**спички** _speech_•kee
a mop	**швабра** _shvahb_•rah
napkins	**салфетки** sahl•_fyet_•kee

paper towels	**бумажные полотенца** *boo·mahzh·nih·ee pah·lah·tyen·tsah*
I need...	**Мне нужно...** *mnyeh noozh·nah...*
plastic wrap [cling film]	**продуктовая плёнка** *prah·dook·toh·vah·yah plyon·kah*
a plunger	**вантуз** *vahn·toos*
scissors	**ножницы** *nozh·nee·tsih*
a vacuum cleaner	**пылесос** *pih·lee·sos*

For In the Kitchen, see page 78.

At the Hostel

Do you have any places left for tonight?	**Есть свободные места на сегодня?** *yest' svah·bod·nih·yeh mee·stah nah see·vod·nyah*
Can I have...?	**Можно мне...?** *mozh·nah mnyeh...*
a single/double room	**одноместный/двухместный номер** *ahd·nah·myes·niy/dvookh·myes·niy noh·meer*
a blanket	**одеяло** *ah·dee·yah·lah*
a pillow	**подушку** *pah·doosh·koo*
sheets	**простыни** *proh·stih·nee*
a towel	**полотенце** *pah·lah·tyen·tseh*
Do you have lockers?	**У Вас есть запирающиеся шкафчики?** *oo vahs yest' zah·pee·rah·yoo·shcheeyeh·sya shkaf·chee·kee*
What time do you lock up?	**Во сколько закрывается вход?** *vah skol'·kah zah·krih·vah·ee·tsah fkhot*

Спутник *spoot·neek* (Sputnik), the Russian youth travel association, organizes group tours for students with accommodation in **молодёжная турбаза** *mah·lah·dyozh·nah·yah toor·bah·zah* (youth hostels).

| Do I need a membership card? | **Нужна ли мне членская карта?** *noozh•nah lee mneh chlehn•skaya kahr•tah* |
| Here's my international student card. | **Вот мой международный студенческий билет.** *vot moy meezh•doo•nah•rod•niy stoo•dehn•chyes•keey bee•lyet* |

Going Camping

Can I camp here?	**Здесь можно разбить лагерь?** *zdyes' mozh•nah rahz•beet' lah•geer'*
Is there a campsite near here?	**Здесь есть кемпинг поблизости?** *zdyes' yest' kehm•peenk pah•blee•zahs•tee*
What is the charge per day/week?	**Сколько стоит в день/неделю?** *skol'•kah stoh•eet v dyen'/nee•dyeh•lyoo*
Are there…?	**Есть…?** *yest'…*
cooking facilities	**кухня** *kookh•nyah*
electrical outlets	**электроточки** *ee•lyek•trah•toch•kee*
laundry facilities	**прачечная** *prah•cheech•nah•yah*
showers	**душ** *doosh*
tents for hire	**палатки напрокат** *pah•laht•kee nah•prah•kaht*
Where can I empty the chemical toilet?	**Куда мне выбросить содержимое химического туалета?** *koo•dah mnyeh vih•brah•seet' sah•deer•zhih•mah•yeh khee•mee•chees•kah•vah too•ah•lyeh•tah*

For Domestic Items, see page 47.

YOU MAY SEE…

ПИТЬЕВАЯ ВОДА *peet'•ee•vah•yah vah•dah*	drinking water
СТОЯНКА ЗАПРЕЩЕНА *stah•yahn•kah zah•pree•shchee•nah*	no camping
КОСТРЫ ЗАПРЕЩЕНЫ *kahst•rih zah•pree•shchee•nih*	no fires

Communications

ESSENTIAL

Where's an internet cafe?	**Где находится интернет-кафе?** *gdyeh nah·khoh·dee·tsah een·ter·net kah·feh*
Can I access the internet here/ check e-mail?	**Здесь можно войти в Интернет/ проверить электронную почту?** *zdyes' mozh·nah vie·tee v een·ter·net/prah·vyeh·reet' ee·leek·tron·noo·yoo poch·too*
How much per half hour/hour?	**Сколько за полчаса/час?** *skol'·kah zah pol·chee·sah/chahs*
How do I connect/ log on?	**Как мне подключиться/зарегистрироваться?** *kahk mnyeh paht·klyoo·chee·tsah/ zah·ree·gee·stree·rah·vah·tsah*
I'd like a phone card, please.	**Телефонную карточку, пожалуйста.** *tee·lee·fon·noo·yoo kahr·tahch·koo pah·zhahl·stah*
Can I have your phone number?	**Можно Ваш номер телефона?** *mozh·nah vahsh noh·meer tee·lee·foh·nah*
Here's my number/ e-mail address.	**Вот мой номер/адрес электронной почты.** *vot moy noh·meer/ahd·rees ee·leek·tron·nie poch·tih*
Call me.	**Звоните.** *zvah·nee·tee*
E-mail me.	**Напишите мне по электронной почте.** *nah·pee·shih·tee mnyeh pah ee·leek·tron·nie poch·tyeh*
Hello. This is…	**Алло. Это…** *ah·loh eh·tah…*
I'd like to speak to…	**Я хотел *m* /хотела *f* бы поговорить с…** *yah khah·tyel/khah·tyeh·lah bih pah·gah·vah·reet' s…*
Repeat that, please.	**Повторите, пожалуйста.** *pahf·tah·ree·tee pah·zhahl·stah*

I'll call back later.	**Я перезвоню попозже.** *yah*
	pee•ree•zvah•nyoo pah•pozh•zheh
Bye.	**До свидания.** *dah svee•dah•nee•yah*
Where is the	**Где здесь ближайшая почта/главпочтамт?**
nearest/main post	*gdyeh zdyes' blee•zhie•shah•yah poch•tah/*
office?	*glahf•pahch•tamt*
I'd like to send this	**Я хотел m /хотела f бы отправить это**
to…	**в…** *yah khah•tyel/khah•tyeh•lah bih*
	aht•prah•veet' eh•tah v…

Online

Where's an internet	**Где находится интернет-кафе?** *gdyeh*
cafe?	*nah•khoh•dee•tsah een•ter•net kah•feh*
Does it have	**Есть беспроводной Интернет?** *yest'*
wireless internet?	*bees•prah•vahd•noy een•ter•net*
What is the WiFi	**Какой пароль от WiFi?** *kah•koy pah•rol' ot WiFi*
password?	
Is the WiFi free?	**WiFi бесплатный?** *WiFi behs•plaht•niy*
Do you have bluetooth?	**У Вас есть bluetooth?** *oo vas yest' bluetooth*
How do I turn the	**Как мне включить/выключить**
computer on/off?	**компьютер?** *kahk mnyeh fklyoo•cheet'/*
	vih•klyoo•cheet' kahm•pyoo•ter
Can I…?	**Я смогу…?** *yah smah•goo…*
access the internet	**войти в Интернет здесь** *vie•tee*
here	*v een•ter•net zdyes'*
check e-mail	**проверить электронную почту**
	prah•vyeh•reet' ee•leek•tron•noo•yoo poch•too
print	**распечатать** *rahs•pee•chah•taht'*
plug in/charge my	**подключить/зарядить ноутбук/iPhone/iPad/**
laptop/iPhone/	**BlackBerry?** *pod•klyoo•cheet'/zah•rya•deet'*

iPad/BlackBerry?	*notebook /iPhone/iPad/BlackBerry*
access Skype?	**войти в Skype?** *voy•tee v Skype*
How much per hour/half hour?	**Сколько за час/полчаса?** *skol'•kah zah chahs/pol•chah•sah*
How do I...?	**Как мне...?** *kahk mnyeh...*
connect/ disconnect	**подключиться/отключиться** *paht•klyoo•chee•tsah/aht•klyoo•chee•tsah*
log on/off	**войти/выйти** *vie•tee/viy•tee*
type this symbol	**напечатать этот символ** *nah•pee•chah•taht/ eh•taht seem•vahl*
What's your e-mail?	**Какой у вас адрес электронной почты?** *kah•koy oo vahs ahd•rees ee•leek•tron•nie poch•tih*
My e-mail is...	**Мой адрес электронной почты...** *moy ahd•rees ee•leek•tron•nie poch•tih...*
Do you have a scanner?	**У Вас есть сканер?** *oo vas est' skah•nehr*

Social Media

Are you on Facebook/Twitter?	**Вы есть в Facebook/Twitter?** *vih est' v Facebook/Twitter*
What's your user name?	**Какое у Вас имя пользователя?** *kah•koh•eh oo vas ee•mya pol'•zo•vah•tyeh•lya*
I'll add you as a friend.	**Я добавлю Вас в друзья.** *yah doh•bahv•lyoo vas v drooz'•ya*
I'll follow you on Twitter.	**Я присоединюсь к Вам в Twitter.** *yah pree•soh•eh•dee•nyus' k vam v Twitter*
Are you following...?	**Вы присоединились...?** *vih pree•soh• eh•dee•nee•lees'*
I'll put the pictures on Facebook/Twitter.	**Я выложу фотографии на Facebook/Twitter.** *yah vih lah•zhoo•fo•to•grah•fee•ee na Facebook/Twitter*
I'll tag you in the pictures.	**Я отмечу Вас на фотографиях.** *yah ot•meh•choo vas na foh•to•grah•fee•yakh*

YOU MAY SEE...

ЗАКРОЙТЕ *zah-kroy-tee*	close
УДАЛИТЕ *oo-dah-lee-tee*	delete
ЭЛЕКТРОННАЯ ПОЧТА *ee-leek-tron-nah-yah poch-tah*	e-mail
ВЫХОД *vih-khaht*	exit
СПРАВКА *sprahf-kah*	help
МГНОВЕННЫЙ ОБМЕН СООБЩЕНИЯМИ *mgnah-vyen-niy ahb-myen sah-ahp-shchyeh-nee-yah-mee*	instant messenger
ИНТЕРНЕТ *een-ter-net*	internet
ВХОД В СИСТЕМУ *fhot f sees-tyeh-moo*	login
НОВОЕ (СООБЩЕНИЕ) *noh-vah-yeh (sah-ahp-shchyeh-nee-yeh)*	new (message)
ВКЛ/ВЫКЛ *fkl/vihkl*	on/off
ОТКРЫТЬ *aht-kriht'*	open
РАСПЕЧАТАТЬ *rahs-pee-chah-taht'*	print
СОХРАНИТЬ *sah-khrah-neet'*	save
ОТПРАВИТЬ *aht-prah-veet'*	send
ИМЯ ПОЛЬЗОВАТЕЛЯ/ПАРОЛЬ *ee-myah pol'-zah-vah-tee-lyah/pah-rol'*	username/ password
БЕСПРОВОДНОЙ ИНТЕРНЕТ *bees-prah-vahd-noy een-ter-net*	wireless internet

Phone

A phone card/ prepaid phone, please.	**Телефонную карточку/оплаченный телефон, пожалуйста.** *tee-lee-fon-noo-yoo kahr-tahch-koo/ ah-plah-cheen-niy tee-lee-fon pah-zhahl-stah*
How much?	**Сколько?** *skol'-kah*
Where's the pay phone?	**Где есть таксофон?** *gdeh est' tah-xo-fohn*

What's the area/country code for…?	**Какой код города/страны для…?** kah‑koy kot goh‑rah‑dah/strah‑nih dlyah…
What's the number for Information?	**Какой номер справочной службы?** kah‑koy noh‑meer sprah‑vahch‑nie sloozh‑bih
I'd like the number for…	**Мне нужен номер…** mnyeh noo‑zhihn noh‑meer…
I'd like to call collect [reverse the charges].	**Я хочу позвонить за счет абонента [удержать оплату].** yah kho‑choo poz‑voh‑neet' zah shchot ah‑boh‑nehn‑tah [oo‑dehr‑zhat' op‑lah‑too]
My phone doesn't work here.	**Мой телефон здесь не работает.** moy tee‑lee‑fon zdyes' nee rah‑boh‑tah‑eet
What network are you on?	**К какой сети Вы подключены?** k kah‑koy sye‑tee vih pod‑klyoo‑cheh‑nih
Is it 3G?	**Это 3G?** eh‑tah 3G
I have run out of credit/minutes.	**У меня закончились единицы/минуты.** oo meh‑nya zah‑kohn‑chee‑lees' eh‑dee‑nee‑tsih/mee‑noo‑tih
Can I buy some credit?	**Могу я приобрести единицы?** moh‑goo yah pree‑obrye‑stee ye‑dee‑nee‑tsih
Do you have a phone charger?	**У Вас есть зарядное устройство для телефона?** u vas est' zah‑ryad‑no‑he oost‑roy‑stvoh dlya teh‑leh‑foh‑nah
Can I have your number?	**Можно Ваш номер телефона?** mozh‑nah vahsh noh‑meer tee‑lee‑foh‑nah
Here's my number.	**Вот мой телефон.** vot moy tee‑lee‑fon
Call me.	**Звоните.** zvah‑nee‑tee
Text me.	**Пришлите СМС.** pree‑shlee‑tee es‑em‑es
I'll call you.	**Я позвоню Вам.** yah pah‑zvah‑nyoo vahm
I'll text you.	**Я пришлю Вам СМС.** yah pree‑shlyoo vahm es‑em‑es

For Numbers, see page 157.

Telephone Etiquette

Hello. This is…	**Алло. Это…** ah·*loh* eh·tah…
I'd like to speak to…	**Я хотел *m*/хотела *f* бы поговорить с…** yah khah·*tyel*/khah·*tyeh*·lah bih pah·gah·vah·*reet's*…
Extension…	**Добавочный номер…** dah·*bah*·vahch·niy *noh*·meer…
Speak louder/more slowly, please.	**Говорите громче/медленнее, пожалуйста.** gah·vah·*ree*·tee *grom*·cheh/*myed*·leen·nee·yeh pah·*zhahl*·stah

YOU MAY HEAR…

Кто говорит? ktoh gah·vah·*reet*	Who's calling?
Подождите, пожалуйста. pah·dah·*zhdee*·tee pah·*zhahl*·stah	Hold on, please.
Соединяю. sah·ee·dee·*nyah*·yoo	I'll put you through.
Боюсь, что его/её нет. bah·*yoos'* shtoh yee·*voh*/yee·*yoh* nyet	I'm afraid he's/she's not in.
Он/Она не может подойти к телефону. on/ah·*nah* nee *moh*·zhiht pah·die·*tee* k tee·lee·*foh*·noo	He/She can't come to the phone.
Хотите оставить сообщение? khah·*tee*·tee ah·*stah*·veet' sah·ahp·*shcheh*·nee·yeh	Would you like to leave a message?
Перезвоните позже/через десять минут. pee·ree·zvah·*nee*·tee *pozh*·zheh/*cheh*·reez dyeh·seet' mee·*noot*	Call back later/in 10 minutes.
Он/Она может перезвонить Вам? on/ah·*nah moh*·zhiht pee·ree·zvah·*neet'* vahm	Can he/she call you back?
Можно Ваш номер телефона? *mozh*·nah vahsh *noh*·meer tee·lee·*foh*·nah	What's your number?

Repeat that, please.	**Повторите, пожалуйста.** pahf·tah·_ree_·tee pah·_zhahl_·stah
I'll call back later.	**Я перезвоню попозже.** yah pee·ree·zvah·_nyoo_ pah·_pozh_·zheh
Bye.	**До свидания.** dah svee·_dah_·nee·yah

For Business Travel, see page 134.

Fax

Can I send/receive a fax here?	**Я могу здесь получить/отправить факс?** yah mah·_goo_ zdyes' pah·loo·_cheet'_/aht·_prah_·veet' fahks
What's the fax number?	**Какой номер факса?** kah·_koy_ noh·meer fahk·sah
Fax this to…	**Отправьте это по факсу, номер…** aht·_prahf'_·tee _eh_·tah pah _fahk_·soo noh·meer…

Post

Where's the post office/mailbox?	**Где почта/почтовый ящик?** gdyeh _poch_·tah/pahch·_toh_·viy yah·shcheek
A stamp for this postcard/letter, please.	**Дайте марку на эту открытку/это письмо, пожалуйста.** _die_·tee _mahr_·koo nah _eh_·too aht·_kriht_·koo/_eh_·tah pees'·_moh_ pah·_zhahl_·stah
How much?	**Сколько?** _skol_'·kah
I want to send this package by airmail/express.	**Я хочу послать эту посылку авиа/экспресс почтой.** yah khah·_choo_ pah·_slaht'_ _eh_·too pah·_sihl_·koo _ah_·vee·ah/eeks·_press_ poch·toy
A receipt, please.	**Дайте чек, пожалуйста.** _die_·_tee_ chek pah·_zhahl_·stah

YOU MAY HEAR...

Пожалуйста, заполните таможенную	Please fill out
декларацию. *pah·zhahl·stah zah·pol·nee·tee*	the customs
tah·moh·zhihn·noo·yoo dee·klah·rah·tsih·yoo	declaration form.
Какая стоимость? *kah·kah·yah*	What's the value?
stoh·ee·mahst'	
Что там? *shtoh tahm*	What's inside?

The main post offices in Moscow and St. Petersburg offer round-the-clock service. Other post offices are generally open Monday through Saturday from 8:00 a.m. to 7:00 p.m. and Sunday from 9:00 a.m. to 7:00 p.m. Major hotels have their own postal and telephone services. Both incoming and outgoing international mail is slow, so allow plenty of time. While DHL has the greatest presence in Russia among Western express shipping companies, FedEx, UPS and other companies also provide service to and from Russia.

Food & Drink

Курягa Шоколадная

Урюк от сердечных болезней

Урюк Чайный ароматный

Eating Out

ESSENTIAL

Can you recommend a good restaurant/bar?	**Можете посоветовать хороший ресторан/ бар?** <u>moh</u>·zhih·tee pah·sah·<u>vyeh</u>·tah·vaht' khah·<u>roh</u>·shiy ree·stah·<u>rahn</u>/bahr
Is there a traditional Russian/an inexpensive restaurant near here?	**Здесь есть традиционный русский/ недорогой ресторан поблизости?** zdyes' yest' trah·dee·tsih·<u>on</u>·niy <u>roos</u>·keey/nee·dah·rah·<u>goy</u> ree·stah·<u>rahn</u> pah·<u>blee</u>·zahs·tee
A table for…, please.	**Столик на…, пожалуйста.** <u>stoh</u>·leek nah…pah·<u>zhahl</u>·stah
Could we sit…?	**Можно нам сесть…?** <u>mozh</u>·nah nahm syehst'…
here/there	**здесь/там** zdyehs'/tahm
outside	**на улице** nah <u>oo</u>·lee·tseh
in a non-smoking area	**где не курят** gdyeh nee <u>koo</u>·ryaht
I'm waiting for someone.	**Я кое-кого жду.** yah <u>koh</u>·ee kah·<u>voh</u> zhdoo
Where are the toilets?	**Где туалет?** gdyeh too·ah·<u>lyeht</u>
A menu, please.	**Меню, пожалуйста.** mee·<u>nyoo</u> pah·<u>zhahl</u>·stah
What do you recommend?	**Что вы посоветуете?** shtoh vih pah·sah·<u>vyeh</u>·too·ee·tee
I'd like…	**Я хотел m /хотела f бы…** yah khah·<u>tyel</u>/ khah·<u>tyeh</u>·lah bih…
Some more…, please.	**Можно ещё…, пожалуйста.** <u>mozh</u>·nah ee·<u>shchoh</u>…pah·<u>zhahl</u>·stah
Enjoy your meal!	**Приятного аппетита!** pree·<u>yaht</u>·nah·vah ah·pee·<u>tee</u>·tah

The check [bill], please.	**Счёт, пожалуйста.** *shchoht pah-zhahl-stah*
Is service included?	**Счёт включает обслуживание?** *shchot fklyoo-chah-eet ahp-sloo-zhih-vah-nee-yeh*
Can I pay by credit card?	**Можно платить кредитной карточкой?** *mozh-nah plah-teet' kree-deet-noy kahr-tahch-kie*
Can I have a receipt?	**Можно чек?** *mozh-nah chek*
Thank you!	**Спасибо!** *spah-see-bah*

Where to Eat

Can you recommend...?	**Вы можете порекомендовать...?** *vih moh-zhih-tee pah-ree-kah-meen-dah-vaht'...*
a restaurant	**ресторан** *ree-stah-rahn*
a bar	**бар** *bahr*
a cafe	**кафе** *kah-feh*
a fast-food place	**кафе быстрого обслуживания** *kah-feh bihs-trah-vah ahp-sloo-zhih-vah-nee-yah*
a cheap restaurant	**недорогой ресторан** *neh-doh-roh-goy rehs-toh-rahn*
an expensive restaurant	**дорогой ресторан** *doh-roh-goy rehs-toh-rahn*
a restaurant with a good view	**ресторан с хорошим видом из окна** *rehs-toh-rahn s kho-roh-sheem vee-dohm eez ohk-nah*
an authentic/ a non-touristy restaurant	**национальный/не туристический ресторан** *nah-tsee-oh-nahl' niy/neh too-rees-tee-chehs-kiy reh-stoh-rahn*
a blini bar	**блинную** *bleen-noo-yoo*

A vast array of fast-food options have sprung up in Russia's
major cities, and, in addition to international fast-food chains,
many home-grown restaurants that serve traditional Russian food
can be found, such as Russkoe Bistro, Yolki-Palki Taverns and Mu-Mu.

Reservations & Preferences

I'd like to reserve a table...	**Я хотел *m*/хотела *f* бы заказать столик...** yah khah·*tyel*/khah·*tyeh*·lah bih zah·kah·*zaht'* *stoh*·leek...
for two	**на двоих** nah dvah·*eekh*
I'd like to reserve a table...	**Я хотел *m*/хотела *f* бы заказать столик...** yah khah·*tyel*/khah·*tyeh*·lah bih zah·kah·*zaht'* *stoh*·leek...
for this evening	**на сегодня на вечер** nah see·*vod*·nyah nah *vyeh*·cheer
for tomorrow at...	**на завтра на...** nah *zahf*·trah nah...
A table for two, please.	**Столик на двоих, пожалуйста.** *stoh*·leek nah dvah·*eekh* pah·*zhahl*·stah
We have a reservation.	**У нас заказ.** oo nahs zah·*kahs*
My name is...	**Меня зовут...** mee·*nyah* zah·*voot*...

Can we sit...?	**Можем мы сесть ...?** _moh_•zhehm mih sehst'
here/there	**здесь/там** zdyes'/tahm
outside	**снаружи** snah•_roo_•zhih
in a non-smoking area	**в некурящем зале** v nye•koo•_rya_•shcheem _zah_•leh
by the window	**возле окна** _voz_•leh okh•_nah_
in the shade	**в тени** v teh•_nee_
in the sun	**на солнце** nah _sohln_•tseh
Where is the restroom [toilet]?	**Где туалет?** gdyeh too•ah•_lyet_

YOU MAY HEAR...

У вас заказан столик? oo vahs zah•_kah_•zahn _stoh_•leek	Do you have a reservation?
Сколько? _skol'_•kah	How many?
Для курящих или некурящих? dlyah koo•_ryah_•shcheekh ee•lee nee•koo•_ryah_•shcheekh	Smoking or non-smoking?
Будете заказывать? _boo_•dee•tee zah•_kah_•zih•vaht"	Are you ready to order?
Что вы желаете? shtoh vih zhih•_lah_•ee•tee	What would you like?
Я бы рекомендовал m /рекомендовала f yah bih ree•kah•meen•dah•_vahl_/ ree•kah•meen•dah•_vah_•lah	I recommend...
Приятного аппетита! pree•_yaht_•nah•vah ah•pee•_tee_•tah	Enjoy your meal!

How to Order

| Waiter!/Waitress! | **Официант!/Девушка!** ah•fee•tsih•_ahnt_/ _dyeh_•voosh•kah |

We're ready to order.	**Мы готовы сделать заказ.** *mih gah•toh•vih*
	zdyeh•laht' zah•kahs
May I see the wine	**Можно посмотреть карту вин?** *mozh•nah*
list?	*pah•smah•tryet' kahr•too veen*
I'd like...	**Я хотел *m* /хотела *f* бы...** *yah khah•tyel/*
	khah•tyeh•lah bih...
a bottle of...	**бутылку...** *boo•tihl•koo...*
a carafe of...	**графин...** *grah•feen...*
a glass of...	**бокал...** *bah•kahl...*
The menu, please.	**Меню, пожалуйста.** *mee•nyoo pah•zhahl•stah*
Do you have...?	**У вас есть...?** *oo vahs yest'...*
a menu in English	**меню на английском** *mee•nyoo nah*
	ahn•gleeys•kahm
a fixed-price menu	**комплексное меню** *kom•pleeks•nah•yeh mee•nyoo*
a children's menu	**детское меню** *dyets•kah•yeh mee•nyoo*
What do you	**Что вы посоветуете?** *shtoh vih*
recommend?	*pah•sah•vyeh•too•ee•tee*
What's this?	**Что это?** *shtoh eh•tah*
What's in it?	**Что туда входит?** *shtoh too•dah fkhoh•deet*
Is it spicy?	**Это острое?** *eh•tah os•trah•yeh*
I'd like...	**Я хотел *m* /хотела *f* бы...** *yah khah•tyel/*
	khah•tyeh•lah bih...
More...please.	**Можно ещё...пожалуйста.** *mozh•nah*
	yee•shchoh...pah•zhahl•stah
With/Without...	**С/Без...** *s/byes...*
I can't have...	**Мне нельзя есть...** *mnyeh neel'•zyah yest'...*
rare	**с кровью** *s krov'•yoo*
medium	**средне прожаренный** *sryed•nee prah•zhah•ree•niy*
well-done	**хорошо прожаренный** *khah•rah•shoh*
	prah•zhah•ree•niy
It's to go [take away].	**Это с собой.** *eh•tah s sah•boy*

63

YOU MAY SEE...

НАЦЕНКА nah·<u>tsen</u>·kah	cover charge
КОМПЛЕКСНЫЙ МЕНЮ <u>kom</u>·plyeks·niy меню	fixed-price menu
МЕНЮ ДНЯ mee·<u>nyoo</u> dnyah	menu of the day
ОБСЛУЖИВАНИЕ (НЕ) ВКЛЮЧЕНО	service (not)
ahp·<u>sloo</u>·zhih·vah·nee·yeh (nee) fklyoo·chee·<u>noh</u>	included
БЛЮДО ДНЯ <u>blyoo</u>·dah dnyah	specials

Cooking Methods

baked	**печеный** pee·<u>choh</u>·niy	
boiled	**варёный** vah·<u>ryoh</u>·niy	
braised	**тушёный** too·<u>shoh</u>·niy	
breaded	**панированный** pah·nee·<u>roh</u>·vah·niy	
creamed	**со сливками** soh <u>sleev</u>·kah·mee	
diced	**нарезанный мелкими кубиками**	
	nah·<u>ryeh</u>·zah·niy <u>myel</u>·kee·mee <u>koo</u>·bee·kah·mee	
filleted	**филе** fee·<u>lyeh</u>	
fried	**жареный** <u>zhah</u>·ree·niy	
grilled	**жареный на** гриле <u>zhah</u>·ree·niy nah <u>gree</u>·lee	
poached	**отварной** aht·vahr·<u>noy</u>	
roasted	**запечёный** zah·pee·<u>choh</u>·nih	
sautéed	**соте** sah·<u>teh</u>	
smoked	**копчёный** kahp·<u>choh</u>·niy	
steamed	**паровой** pah·rah·<u>voy</u>	
stewed	**тушёный** too·<u>shoh</u>·niy	
stuffed	**фаршированный** fahr·shih·<u>roh</u>·vah·niy	

Dietary Requirements

I'm diabetic.	**Я диабетик.** yah dee•ah•<u>byeh</u>•teek
I'm lactose intolerant.	**У меня непереносимость лактозы.** oo mee•<u>nyah</u> nee•pee•ree•nah•<u>see</u>•mahst' lahk•<u>toh</u>•zih
I'm vegetarian.	**Я вегетарианец.** yah vee•gee•tah•ree•<u>ah</u>•neets
I'm vegan.	**Я вегетарианец.** yah vee•gee•tah•ree•<u>ah</u>•neets
I'm allergic to…	**У меня аллергия на…** oo mee•<u>nyah</u> ah•leer•<u>gee</u>•yah nah…
I can't eat…	**Мне нельзя есть…** mnyeh neel'•<u>zyah</u> yest'…
dairy	**молочные продукты** mah•<u>loch</u>•nih•yeh prah•<u>dook</u>•tih
gluten	**растительный белок** rahs•<u>tee</u>•tyel'•niy bee•<u>lok</u>
nuts	**орехи** ah•<u>ryeh</u>•khee
pork	**свинину** svee•<u>nee</u>•noo
shellfish	**раков** <u>rah</u>•kahf
spicy foods	**острую пищу** <u>os</u>•troo•yoo pee•shchoo
wheat	**пшеничную муку** pshih•<u>neech</u>•noo•yoo moo•<u>koo</u>
Is it halal/kosher?	**Это халяль/кошерное?** <u>eh</u>•tah khah•<u>lyahl</u>/ kah•<u>sher</u>•nah•yeh
Do you have…?	**У Вас есть…?** oo vas est'

skimmed milk	**обезжиренное молоко** oh-bez-_zhee_-reh-noh-ye moh-loh-_koh_
whole milk	**цельное молоко** _tsehl_-noye moh-loh-_koh_
soya milk	**соевое молоко** _soh_-yeh-voh-ye moh-loh-_koh_

Dining with Children

Do you have children's portions?	**У вас есть детские порции?** oo vahs yest' _dyets_-kee-yeh _por_-tsih-ee
A highchair/child's seat, please.	**Высокий детский стульчик/Детское сидение, пожалуйста.** vih-_soh_-keey _dyets_-keey stool'-cheek/_dyets_-kah-yeh see-_dyeh_-nee-yeh pah-_zhahl_-stah
Where can I feed/ change the baby?	**Где мне покормить/переодеть ребёнка?** gdyeh mnyeh pah-kahr-_meet_/pee-ree-ah-_dyet_ ree-_byon_-kah
Can you warm this?	**Вы можете подогреть это** vih _moh_-zhih-tee pah-dah-_gryet_' eh-tah

For Traveling with Children, see page 136.

How to Complain

How much longer will our food be?	**Сколько ещё ждать?** _skol_'-kah ee-_shchoh_ zhdaht'
We can't wait any longer.	**Мы не можем больше ждать.** mih nee _moh_-zhem _bol_'-sheh zhdaht'
We're leaving.	**Мы уходим.** mih oo-_khoh_-deem
I didn't order this.	**Это не то, что я заказывал** m / **заказывала** f. _eh_-tah nee toh shtoh yah zah-_kah_-zih-vahl/zah-_kah_-zih-vah-lah
I ordered…	**Я просил** m /**просила** f… yah prah-_seel_/ prah-_see_-lah…

I can't eat this.	**Это невозможно есть.** _eh·tah nee·vahz·<u>mozh</u>·nah yest'_
This is too...	**Это слишком...** _eh·tah <u>slee</u>·shkam..._
cold/hot	**холодное/горячее** _khah·<u>lod</u>·nah·yeh/ gah·<u>ryah</u>·chee·yeh_
salty/spicy	**солёное/острое** _sah·<u>lyoh</u>·nah·yeh/<u>os</u>·trah·yeh_
tough/bland	**жёсткое/мягкое** _<u>zhost</u>·kah·yeh/<u>myahkh</u>·kah·yeh_
This isn't clean/ fresh.	**Это грязное/несвежее.** _eh·tah <u>gryahz</u>·nah·yeh/nee·<u>svyeh</u>·zhih·yeh_

Paying

The check [bill], please.	**Счёт, пожалуйста.** _shchot pah·<u>zhahl</u>·stah_
We'd like to pay separately.	**Мы будем платить отдельно.** _mih <u>boo</u>·deem plah·<u>teet'</u> ahd·<u>dyel'</u>·nah_
It's all together.	**Всё вместе.** _fsyoh <u>vmyes</u>·tee_
Is service included?	**Счёт включает обслуживание?** _shchot fklyoo·<u>chah</u>·eet ahp·<u>sloo</u>·zhih·vah·nee·yeh_
What's this amount for?	**А это за что?** _ah eh·tah zah shtoh_
I didn't have that.	**Я это не заказывал _m_/заказывала _f_.** _yah eh·tah nee zah·<u>kah</u>·zih·vahl/zah·<u>kah</u>·zih·vah·lah_
I had...	**У меня было...** _oo mee·<u>nyah</u> <u>bih</u>·lah..._
Can I pay by credit card?	**Можно платить кредитной карточкой?** _<u>mozh</u>·nah plah·<u>teet'</u> kree·<u>deet</u>·nie <u>kahr</u>·tahch·kie_
Can I have an itemized bill/a receipt?	**Можно детальный счёт/чек?** _<u>mozh</u>·nah dee·<u>tahl'</u>·niy shchot/chek_
That was a very good meal.	**Всё было очень вкусно.** _fsyoh <u>bih</u>·lah <u>oh</u>·cheen' <u>fkoos</u>·nah_
I've already paid.	**Я уже оплатил.** _yah oo·<u>zheh</u> oplah·teel_

Meals & Cooking

The country's geographic, climatic and ethnic variety is reflected in a rich and varied cuisine. Russians have a sweet tooth and are very fond of desserts and pastries, as well as their excellent ice cream. Eating plays an important part in Russian social life, and it is while dining that you'll find Russians at their most hospitable. Don't forget to wish your table companions a hearty appetite: **Приятного аппетита!** *pree·yaht·nah·vah ah·pee·tee·tah*. At the end of a meal Russians will often thank those who dined with them. The proper response is **На здоровье!** *nah zdah·rov'·yeh*.

Breakfast

boiled egg	**вареное яйцо**	*vah·ryoh·nah·yeh yie·tsoh*
bread	**хлеб**	*khlyep*
fried eggs	**яичница**	*yah·eesh·nee·tsah*
fruit juice	**фруктовый сок**	*frook·toh·viy sok*
grapefruit juice	**грейпфрутовый сок**	*greyp·froo·tah·viy sok*
ham and eggs	**яичница с ветчиной**	*yah·eesh·nee·tsah s veet·chee·noy*
honey	**мёд**	*myot*
jam	**джем**	*dzhem*
oatmeal	**овсянка**	*ahf·syahn·kah*
orange juice	**апельсиновый сок**	*ah·peel'·see·nah·viy sok*
scrambled eggs	**яичница-болтунья**	*yah·eesh·nee·tsah bahl·toon'·yah*
toast	**тост**	*tost*
yogurt	**йогурт**	*yoh·goort*

Appetizers

assorted meat	**ассорти мясное** *ah·sahr·tee myahs·noh·yeh*
assorted fish	**ассорти рыбное** *ah·sahr·tee rihb·nah·yeh*
caviar	**икра** *eek·rah*
ham	**ветчина** *veet·chee·nah*
herring	**сельдь** *syel't'*
mushrooms	**грибы** *gree·bih*
hot pancake filled with cheese (Georgian dish)	**хачапури** *khah·chah·poo·ree*
pancakes...	**блины...** *blee·nih...*
with caviar	**с икрой** *s eek·roy*
with jam	**с вареньем** *s vah·ryen'·yem*
with salmon	**с сёмгой** *s syom·gie*
with sheep's cheese	**с брынзой** *s brihn·zie*
with sour cream	**со сметаной** *sah smee·tah·nie*
paté (mostly liver)	**паштет** *pahsh·tyet*
pie	**пирог** *pee·rok*
sausage	**колбаса** *kahl·bah·sah*
shrimp [prawns]	**креветки** *kree·vyet·kee*
spiced herring	**кильки** *keel'·kee*
sturgeon	**осетрина** *ah·seet·ree·nah*

Appetizers are often divided into hot and cold. If you want to indicate that a particular item will be an appetizer, just indicate that it is **На закуску** *nah zah·koos·koo*.

Блины *blee·nih* (pancakes) are often made with yeast and stuffed with different fillings. Smaller and thicker than western pancakes, they are usually served with sour cream (**сметана** *smee·tah·nah*) and/or butter (**масло** *mahs·lah*).

Soup

beet soup (borsch)	**борщ** *borshch*
beet soup with extra bacon	**московский** *mahs·kof·skeey*
chicken soup	**суп из курицы** *soop ees koo·ree·tsih*
cold beet soup	**холодник** *khah·lahd·neek*
cold soup made from kvass, cucumbers, eggs, onions and sour cream	**окрошка** *ah·krosh·kah*
fish soup	**уха** *oo·khah*
spicy Georgian soup made with mutton and rice	**харчо** *khahr·choh*
mushroom soup	**грибной суп** *greeb·noy soop*
pea soup	**гороховый суп** *gah·roh·khah·viy soop*
potato soup	**картофельный** *kahr·toh·feel'·niy soop*
soup made with salted cucumbers and olives	**солянка** *sah·lyahn·kah*
thick soup made with cabbage or sauerkraut	**щи** *shchee*

| Uzbek mutton soup with bacon and tomatoes | **шурпа** *shoor•pah* |
| Ukrainian beet soup with garlic | **украинский борщ** *oo•krah•een•skeey borshch* |

Fish & Seafood

carp	**карп** *kahrp*
crab	**краб** *krahp*
halibut	**палтус** *pahl•toos*
herring	**сельдь** *syel't'*
lobster	**омар** *ah•mahr*
mackerel	**макрель** *mahk•ryel'*
oysters	**устрицы** *oos•tree•tsih*
pike perch fried in butter/poached	**судак жареный в тесте/отварной** *soo•dahk zhah•ree•niy f tyes•tee/aht•vahr•noy*
shrimp [prawns]	**креветки** *kree•vyet•kee*
salmon	**сёмга** *syom•gah*
sprats	**шпроты** *shproh•tih*
trout	**форель** *fah•ryel'*
tuna	**тунец** *too•nyets*
sturgeon...	**осетрина...** *ah•seet•ree•nah...*
served with a white sauce	**под белым соусом** *pahd byeh•lihm soh•oo•sahm*
poached	**по-русски** *pah roos•kee*
steamed	**паровая** *pah•rah•vah•yah*

Meat & Poultry

beef	**говядина** *gah•vyah•dee•nah*
beef stroganoff	**бефстроганов** *beef•stroh•gah•nahf*
braised beef with aromatic vegetables	**говядина тушёная** *gah•vyah•dee•nah too•shoh•nah•yah*

cabbage stuffed with meat and rice	**голубцы** *gah·loop·tsih*
chicken	**курица** *koo·ree·tsah*
chopped meat in a savory sauce	**азу** *ah·zoo*
duck	**утка** *oot·kah*
duck roasted with apples	**утка тушёная с яблоками** *oot·kah too·shoh·nah·yah s yahb·lah·kah·mee*
goose	**гусь** *goos'*
lamb	**молодая баранина** *mah·lah·dah·yah bah·rah·nee·nah*
lamb kebabs	**шашлык** *shahsh·lihk*
liver	**печёнка** *pee·chon·kah*
pork	**свинина** *svee·nee·nah*
rabbit	**кролик** *kroh·leek*
stuffed breast of chicken	**котлеты по-киевски** *kaht·lyeh·tih pah kee·eef·skee*
stuffed pasta	**пельмени** *peel'·myeh·nee*
turkey	**индейка** *een·dyey·kah*
veal	**телятина** *tee·lyah·tee·na*

Vegetables & Staples

beans	**фасоль** *fah·sol'*
beet	**свёкла** *svyok·lah*
bread	**хлеб** *khlyep*
cabbage	**капуста** *kah·poos·tah*
carrots	**морковь** *mahr·kof'*
cauliflower	**цветная капуста** *tsveet·nah·yah kah·poos·tah*
cucumber	**огурец** *ah·goo·ryets*
eggplant [aubergine]	**баклажан** *bahk·lah·zhahn*
mushrooms	**грибы** *greeb·ih*
noodles	**лапша** *lahp·shah*

onion	**лук** *look*
pasta	**макароны** *mah·kah·roh·nih*
stuffed pasta	**пельмени** *peel'·myeh·nee*
small pastries with various sweet or savoury fillings	**пирожки** *pee·rahsh·kee*
peas	**горох** *gah·rokh*
pepper	**перец** *pyeh·reets*
porridge	**каша** *kah·shah*
potato	**картофель** *kahr·toh·feel'*
rice	**рис** *rees*
spaghetti	**спагетти** *spah·gyeh·tee*
sweet corn	**сладкая кукуруза** *slaht·kah·yah koo·koo·roo·zah*
tomato	**помидор** *pah·mee·dor*
zucchini [courgette]	**молодой кабачок** *mah·lah·doy kah·bah·chok*

Fruit

apple	**яблоко** *yahb·lah·kah*
apricot	**абрикос** *ab·ree·kos*
banana	**банан** *bah·nahn*
cherry	**черешня** *chee·ryesh·nyah*
currants	**смородина** *smah·roh·dee·nah*
gooseberry	**крыжовник** *krih·zhov·neek*
grapes	**виноград** *vee·nah·graht*
lemon	**лимон** *lee·mon*
melon	**дыня** *dih·nyah*
orange	**апельсин** *ah·peel'·seen*
peach	**персик** *pyer·seek*
pear	**груша** *groo·shah*
pineapple	**ананас** *ah·nah·nahs*
plum	**слива** *slee·vah*

| strawberry | **клубника** *kloob·nee·kah* |
| watermelon | **арбуз** *ahr·boos* |

Cheese

baked sour milk, often served chilled	**ряженка** *ryah·zhihn·kah*
...cheese	**сыр...** *sihr...*
Latvian	**латвийский** *laht·veey·skeey*
Poshekhonsky	**пошехонский** *pah·shih·khon·skeey*
Russian	**российский** *rah·seey·skeey*
sharp ewe's milk cheese	**брынза** *brihn·zah*
fresh white cheese or spread	**сырок** *sih·rok*
white unsalted cheese similar to cottage cheese	**творог** *tvah·rok*

Dessert

apple baked in pastry	**яблоко в тесте** *yahb·lah·kah f tyes·tee*
cottage cheese pastry	**ватрушка** *vah·troosh·kah*
Ukrainian dumplings filled with white cheese	**вареники** *vah·ryeh·nee·kee*
fruit compote	**компот** *kahm·pot*
fruit jelly-like drink	**кисель** *kee·syel'*
...ice cream	**...мороженое** *...mah·roh·zhih·nah·yeh*
chocolate	**шоколадное** *shah·kah·lad·nah·yeh*
fruit	**фруктовое** *frook·toh·vah·yeh*
vanilla	**ванильное** *vah·neel'·nah·yeh*

pie…	**пирог…** *pee·rok…*	
with cottage cheese	**с творогом** *s tvah·rah·gom*	
with fruit	**с фруктами** *s frook·tah·mee*	
with lemon	**с лимоном** *s lee·moh·nahm*	
rice pudding	**рисовый пудинг** *ree·sah·viy poo·deenk*	
small apple	**оладьи с яблоками** *ah·lahd'·yee s*	
pancakes	*yahb·lah·kah·mee*	
small pancakes	**блинчики с вареньем** *bleen·chee·kee s*	
served with jam	*vah·ryen'·yem*	
sponge roll	**рулет** *roo·lyet*	
whipped cream	**взбитые сливки** *vzbee·tih·yeh sleef·kee*	
yeast cake	**ромовая баба** *roh·mah·vah·yah bah·bah*	
saturated in liquor		
white cheese	**сырники со сметаной** *sihr·nee·kee sah*	
fritters served with	*smee·tah·nie*	
sour cream		

Sauces & Condiments

mustard	**горчица** *gahr·chee·tsah*
pepper	**перец** *pyeh·reets*
salt	**соль** *sol'*
sugar	**сахар** *sah·khahr*
ketchup	**кетчуп** *Keht·choop*

At the Market

Where are the trolleys/ baskets?	**Где здесь тележки/корзинки?** *gdyeh zdyes' tee·lyesh·kee/kahr·zeen·kee*
Where is…?	**Где…?** *gdyeh…*
I'd like some of that/those.	**Дайте, пожалуйста, вон то/те.** *die·tee pah·zhahl·stah von toh/tyeh*
Can I taste it?	**Можно это попробовать?** *mozh·nah eh·tah pah·proh·bah·vaht'*

I'd like...	**Дайте, пожалуйста,...** _die_·tee pah·_zhahl_·stah...
a kilo/half-kilo of...	**кило/полкило...** kee·_loh_/pol·kee·_loh_...
a liter/half-liter of...	**литр/пол-литра...** leetr/pol·_leet_·rah...
a piece of...	**кусочек...** koo·_soh_·cheek...
a slice of...	**ломтик...** _lom_·teek...
More./Less.	**Побольше./Поменьше.** pah·_bol'_·sheh/ pah·_myen'_·sheh
How much?	**Сколько?** _skol'_·kah
Where do I pay?	**Куда платить?** koo·_dah_ plah·_teet'_
A bag, please.	**Пакет, пожалуйста.** pah·_kyet_ pah·_zhahl_·stah
I'm being helped.	**Меня уже обслуживают.** mee·_nyah_ oo·_zheh_ ahp·_sloo_·zhih·vah·yoot

For Conversion Tables, see page 163.

Measurements in Russia are metric — and that applies to the weight of food too. If you tend to think in pounds and ounces, it's worth brushing up on what the metric equivalent is before you go shopping for fruit and veg in markets and supermarkets. Five hundred grams, or half a kilo, is a common quantity to order, and that converts to just over a pound (17.65 ounces, to be precise).

YOU MAY HEAR...

Я вас слушаю. yah vahs _sloo_·shah·yoo	Can I help you?
Что вы хотите? shtoh vih khah·_tee_·tee	What would you like?
Что ещё? shtoh ee·_shchoh_	Anything else?
Это...рублей. _eh_·tah...roob·_lyey_	That's...rubles.

Today, Russia's cities feature supermarkets very much like those in western Europe and the United States. The business and tourism districts of Moscow and St. Petersburg now feature small stores very much like the American convenience store, where you can buy a drink and snack.

YOU MAY SEE...

ГОДЕН ДО... _goh•deen dah..._	best if used by...
КАЛОРИЙ _kah•loh•reey_	calories
ОБЕЗЖИРЕННЫЙ _ah•beezh•zhih•ree•niy_	fat free
ХРАНИТЬ В ХОЛОДИЛЬНИКЕ _khrah•neet' f khrah•lah•deel'•nee•kee_	keep refrigerated
МОЖЕТ СОДЕРЖАТЬ СЛЕДЫ... _moh•zhiht sah•deer•zhaht' slee•dih..._	may contain traces of...
РЕАЛИЗОВАТЬ ДО... _ree•ah•lee•zah•vaht' dah..._	sell by...
ВЕГЕТАРИАНСКОЕ ПИТАНИЕ _vee•gee•tah•ree•ahn•skah•yeh pee•tah•nee•yeh_	suitable for vegetarians

In the Kitchen

bottle opener	**открывалка** aht·krih·_vahl_·kah
bowl	**миска** _mees_·kah
can opener	**консервный нож** kahn·_syerv_·niy nosh
corkscrew	**штопор** _shtoh_·pahr
cup	**чашка** _chahsh_·kah
fork	**вилка** _veel_·kah
frying pan	**сковорода** skah·vah·rah·_dah_
glass	**стакан** stah·_kahn_
knives	**ножи** nah·_zhih_
measuring cup/ spoon	**мерная чашка/ложка** _myer_·nah·yah _chahsh_·kah/_losh_·kah
napkin	**бумажные салфетки** boo·_mahzh_·nih·yeh sahl·_fyet_·kee
plate	**тарелка** tah·_ryel_·kah
pot	**высокая кастрюля** vih·_soh_·kah·yah kahs·_tryoo_·lyah
saucepan	**кастрюля** kahs·_tryoo_·lyah
spatula	**лопаточка** lah·_pah_·tahch·kah
spoons	**ложки** _losh_·kee

Drinks

ESSENTIAL

May I see the wine list/drink menu?	**Можно посмотреть карту вин/меню напитков?** _mozh_·nah pah·smah·_tryet' kahr_·too veen/mee·_nyoo_ nah·_peet_·kahf
What do you recommend?	**Что вы порекомендуете?** shtoh vih pah·ree·kah·meen·_doo_·ee·tee

I'd like a bottle/ glass of red/white wine.	**Я хотел _m_/хотела _f_ бы бутылку/бокал красного/белого вина.** _yah khah·tyel/ khah·tyeh·lah bih boo·tihl·koo/bah·kahl krahs·nah·vah/byeh·lah·vah vee·nah_
The house wine, please.	**Вино ресторана, пожалуйста.** _vee·noh ree·stah·rah·nah pah·zhahl·stah_
Another bottle/ glass, please.	**Ещё одну бутылку/один бокал, пожалуйста.** _yee·shchoh ahd·noo boo·tihl·koo/ah·deen bah·kahl pah·zhahl·stah_
I'd like a local beer.	**Я хотел _m_/хотела _f_ бы местного пива.** _yah khah·tyel/khah·tyeh·lah bih myes·nah·vah pee·vah_
Let me buy you a drink.	**Позвольте вам предложить что-нибудь выпить.** _pahz·vol'·tee vahm preed·lah·zhiht' shtoh·nee·boot' vih·peet'_
Cheers!	**За ваше здоровье!** _za vah·sheh zdah·rov'·yeh_
A coffee/tea, please.	**Кофе/Чай, пожалуйста.** _koh·fye/chie pah·zhahl·stah_
Black.	**Чёрный.** _chor·niy_
With...	**С...** _s..._
milk	**молоком** _mah·lah·kom_
sugar	**сахаром** _sah·khah·rahm_
artificial sweetener	**заменителем сахара** _zah·mee·nee·tee·lyem sah·khah·rah_
..., please.	**..., пожалуйста.** _...pah·zhahl·stah_
Juice	**Сок** _sok_
Soda	**Содовую** _soh·dah·voo·yoo_
Sparkling/Still water	**Воду с газом/без газа** _voh·doo z gah·zahm/beez gah·zah_
Is the tap water safe to drink?	**Безопасно ли пить воду из крана?** _bee·zah·pahs·nah lee peet' voh·doo ees krah·nah_

Non-alcoholic Drinks

apple/orange juice	**яблочный/апельсиновый сок** _yahb·lahch·niy/ah·peel'·<u>see</u>·nah·viy sok_
coffee...	**кофе...** <u>koh</u>·fyeh...
black	**чёрный** <u>chor</u>·niy
decaffeinated	**без кафеина** bees kah·fee·<u>ee</u>·nah
with milk	**с молоком** s mah·lah·<u>kom</u>
iced tea	**чай со льдом** chie sah l'dom
kvass, soft drink made from yeast	**квас** kvahss
lemonade	**лимонад** lee·mah·<u>naht</u>
milk	**молоко** mah·lah·<u>koh</u>
milk shake	**молочный коктейль** mah·<u>loch</u>·niy kahk·<u>teyl'</u>
mineral water	**минеральная вода** mee·nee·<u>rahl'</u>·nah·yah vah·<u>dah</u>
soda	**содовая** <u>soh</u>·dah·vah·yah
tea	**чай** chie
water	**вода** vah·<u>dah</u>

Stores and kiosks in large towns and cities are full of imported and locally produced soft drinks, fruit juice and mineral water. Ice cream cafes offer something called **коктейль** kahk·<u>teyl'</u> (cocktail), a non-alcoholic drink made from fruit juice or lemonade, to which ice cream and sometimes whipped cream is added.

Квас kvahs is a popular traditional Russian soft drink and a good thirst quencher in the summer. Kvass, which looks like beer, is made from black bread and yeast.

YOU MAY HEAR...

Вам принести что-нибудь попить? *vahm pree·nees·tee shtoh·nee·boot' pah·peet'* — Can I get you a drink?

С молоком/сахаром? *s mah·lah·kom/sah·khah·rahm* — With milk/sugar?

Воду с газом или без газа? *voh·doo z gah·zahm ee·lee beez gah·zah* — Sparkling or still water?

Aperitifs, Cocktails & Liqueurs

brandy (cognac)	**коньяк** *kahn'·yahk*	
gin	**джин** *dzhihn*	
liqueur	**ликёр** *lee·kyor*	
rum	**ром** *rom*	
sherry	**херес** *khyeh·rees*	
vodka	**водка** *vot·kah*	
whisky	**виски** *vees·kee*	

Russian vodka is world famous. Kremlevskaya, Stolichnaya, Moskovskaya and some other brands are well-known internationally. Make sure you buy alcohol from a licensed seller, in order to avoid purchasing a low-quality counterfeit.

Beer

Moscow beer	**московское**	mahs•_kof_•skah•ye
Russian beer	**жигулёвское**	zhih•goo•_lyof_•skah•ye
Riga beer	**рижское**	_reesh_•skah•yeh
dark/light	**темное/светлое**	_tyom_•noh•ye/_sveht_•loye
local/imported	**местное/импортное**	_mehst_•noh•ye/ _eem_•port•noye
bottled/draft	**в бутылках/разливное**	v boo•_tihl_•kahkh/ rahz•leev•_noh_•eh
non-alcoholic	**безалкогольное**	behz•ahl•koh•_gohl'_ noh•eh

Wine

champagne	**шампанское**	sham•_pahn_•sko•ye
dry	**сухое**	soo•_khoh_•yeh
sparkling wine (like champagne)	**игристое**	eeg•_rees_•tah•yeh
red wine	**красное вино**	_krahs_•nah•yeh vee•_noh_
rosé wine	**розовое вино**	_roh_•zah•vah•yeh vee•_noh_
sweet	**сладкое**	_slaht_•kah•yeh
white wine	**белое вино**	_byeh_•lah•yeh vee•_noh_

International brands of wine are available throughout Russia. It is sometimes easier to find French, Californian and Italian wines than to find old favorites from Georgia.

Russian sparkling wine is a popular drink. Dry, it can accompany almost any meal; sweet, it is usually enjoyed after meals or with dessert. Quality and price vary for wine with the same label. In general, it is better to buy alcohol in a liquor store than from a kiosk or street vendor.

On the Menu

aperitif	**аперитив**	_ah•pee•ree•teef_
apple	**яблоко**	_yahb•lah•kah_
apple baked in pastry	**яблоко в тесте**	_yahb•lah•kah f tyes•tee_
apricot	**абрикос**	_ahb•ree•kos_
artificial sweetener	**заменитель сахара**	_zah•mee•nee•teel' sah•khah•rah_
chopped meat in a savory sauce	**азу**	_ah•zoo_

bacon	**грудинка** groo·_deen_·kah
banana	**банан** bah·_nahn_
beans	**фасоль** fah·_sol'_
beef stroganoff	**бефстроганов** beef·_stroh_·gah·nahf
beef	**говядина** gah·_vyah_·dee·nah
beer	**пиво** _pee_·vah
beet [beetroot]	**свёкла** _svyok_·lah
beet soup (borsch)	**борщ** borshch
braised beef with aromatic vegetables	**говядина тушёная с кореньями** gah·_vyah_·dee·nah too·_shoh_·nah·yah s kah·_ryen'_·yah·mee
brandy	**бренди** _bren_·dee
bread	**хлеб** khlyep
butter	**масло** _mahs_·lah
cabbage	**капуста** kah·_poos_·tah
cake (large)	**торт** tort
cake (small)	**пирожное** pee·_rozh_·nah·yeh
carrots	**морковь** mahr·_kof'_
caviar	**икра** eek·_rah_
cereal	**каша** _kah_·shah
champagne	**шампанское** shahm·_pahn_·skah·yeh
cheese	**сыр** sihr
cherry	**вишня** _veesh_·nyah
stuffed breast of chicken	**котлеты по-киевски** kaht·_lyeh_·tih pah _kee_·eef·skee
chicken soup	**суп из курицы** soop ees _koo_·ree·tsih
chicken	**курица** _koo_·ree·tsah
chocolate	**шоколад** shah·kah·_laht_
chop	**отбивная** aht·beev·_nah_·yah
chopped meat	**рубленое мясо** _roob_·lee·nah·yeh _myah_·sah
coffee	**кофе** _koh_·fyeh

cold cuts [charcuterie]	**мясная закуска** myahs·*nah*·yah zah·*koos*·kah
cold soup made from kvass, cucumbers, eggs, onions and sour cream	**окрошка** ah·*krosh*·kah
cornmeal	**кукурузная мука** koo·koo·*rooz*·nah·yah moo·*kah*
cottage cheese tart	**ватрушка** vaht·*roosh*·kah
cottage cheese	**творог** tvah·*rok*
crab	**краб** krahp
crabmeat	**мясо краба** *myah*·sah *krah*·bah
cracker	**крекер** *kryeh*·kyer
cream	**сливки** *sleef*·kee
cucumber	**огурец** ah·goo·*ryets*
cumin	**тмин римский** tmeen *reem*·skeey
currants	**смородина** smah·*roh*·dee·nah
duck	**утка** *oot*·kah
dumpling	**клёцка** *klyots*·kah
egg	**яйцо** *yie*·tsoh
eggplant [aubergine]	**баклажан** bahk·lah·*zhahn*
fish soup	**уха** oo·*khah*
fish	**рыба** *rih*·bah
fresh white cheese	**сырок** sih·*rok*
fritter	**оладья** ah·*lahd'*·yah
fruit compote	**компот** kahm·*pot*
fruit jelly	**кисель** kee·*syel'*
fruit	**фрукты** *frook*·tih
garlic sauce	**чесночный соус** chees·*noch*·niy *soh*·oos
garlic	**чеснок** chees·*nok*

gin	**джин** *dzhihn*
ginger	**имбирь** *eem·beer'*
goat cheese	**сыр из козьего молока** *sihr ees koz'·yeh·vah mah·lah·kah*
goat	**козлятина** *kahz·lyah·tee·nah*
cabbage stuffed with rice and meat	**голубцы** *gah·loop·tsih*
goose	**гусь** *goos'*
gooseberry	**крыжовник** *krih·zhov·neek*
grapefruit	**грейпфрут** *greyp·froot*
grapefruit juice	**сок из грейпфрута** *sok eez greyp·froo·tah*
grapes	**виноград** *vee·nahg·raht*
halibut	**палтус** *pahl·toos*
ham	**ветчина** *veet·chee·nah*
hamburger	**гамбургер** *gahm·boor·geer*
herbs	**травы** *trah·vih*
herring	**сельдь** *syel't'*
honey	**мёд** *myot*
ice (cube)	**кубик льда** *koo·beek l'dah*
ice cream	**мороженое** *mah·roh·zhih·nah·yeh*
jam	**варенье** *vah·ryen'·yeh*
jelly	**желе** *zhih·lyeh*
juice	**фруктовый сок** *frook·toh·viy sok*
kidney	**почка** *poch·kah*
lamb	**молодая баранина** *mah·lah·dah·yah bah·rah·nee·nah*
lamb kebabs	**шашлык** *shahsh·lihk*
lemon	**лимон** *lee·mon*
lemonade	**лимонад** *lee·mah·naht*
liqueur	**ликёр** *lee·kyor*
liver	**печень** *pyeh·cheen'*

lobster	**омар**	*ah·<u>mahr</u>*
mackerel	**макрель**	*mahk·<u>ryel'</u>*
meat	**мясо**	*<u>myah</u>·sah*
melon	**дыня**	*<u>dih</u>·nyah*
milk shake	**молочный коктейль**	*mah·<u>loch</u>·niy kahk·<u>teyl'</u>*
milk	**молоко**	*mah·lah·<u>koh</u>*
mineral water	**минеральная вода**	*mee·nee·<u>rahl'</u>·nah·yah vah·<u>dah</u>*

mushroom	**гриб**	*greep*
mustard	**горчица**	*gahr·<u>chee</u>·tsah*
mutton	**баранина**	*bah·<u>rah</u>·nee·nah*
noodles	**лапша**	*lahp·<u>shah</u>*
nuts	**орехи**	*ah·<u>ryeh</u>·khee*
olive	**оливка**	*ah·<u>leef</u>·kah*
onions	**лук**	*look*
orange juice	**апельсиновый сок**	*ah·peel'·<u>see</u>·nah·viy sok*
orange liqueur	**апельсиновый ликёр**	*ah·peel'·<u>see</u>·nah·viy lee·<u>kyor</u>*
orange	**апельсин**	*ah·peel'·<u>seen</u>*
oyster	**устрица**	*<u>oost</u>·ree·tsah*
pancakes	**блины**	*blee·<u>nih</u>*
pasta	**макароны**	*mah·kah·<u>roh</u>·nih*
pastry	**кондитерские изделия**	*kahn·<u>dee</u>·teer·skee·yeh eez·<u>dyeh</u>·lee·yah*
pâté	**паштет**	*pahsh·<u>tyet</u>*
peach	**персик**	*<u>pyer</u>·seek*
peanut	**арахис**	*ah·<u>rah</u>·khees*
pear	**груша**	*<u>groo</u>·shah*
peas	**горошек**	*gah·<u>roh</u>·shek*
pepper	**перец**	*<u>pyeh</u>·reets*

pie or tart served with a variety of fruit or cheese fillings	**пирог** _pee·rok_	
pike perch fried in batter	**судак жареный в тесте** _soo·dahk zhah·ree·niy f tyes·tee_	
pike perch poached	**судак отварной** _soo·dahk aht·vahr·noy_	
pineapple	**ананас** _ah·nah·nahs_	
plum	**слива** _slee·vah_	
pork	**свинина** _svee·nee·nah_	
potato chips [crisps]	**чипсы** _cheep·sih_	
potatoes	**картофель** _kahr·toh·feel'_	
rabbit	**кролик** _kroh·leek_	
red currant	**красная смородина** _krahs·nah·yah smah·roh·dee·nah_	
rice pudding	**рисовый пудинг** _ree·sah·viy poo·deenk_	
rice	**рис** _rees_	
roast beef	**ростбиф** _rost·beef_	
roast duck with apples	**утка тушёная с яблоками** _oot·kah too·shoh·nah·yah s yahb·lah·kah·mee_	
roast pork with plums	**жаркое из свинины с черносливом** _zhahr·koh·yeh ees svee·nee·nih s cheer·nah·slee·vahm_	
roast	**жаркое** _zhahr·koh·yeh_	
roll	**булочка** _boo·lahch·kah_	
rum	**ром** _rom_	
Russian soft drink	**квас** _kvahs_	
salmon	**лосось** _lah·sos'_	
salt	**соль** _sol'_	
sauce	**соус** _soh·oos_	
sausage	**колбаса** _kahl·bah·sah_	

shellfish	**моллюски** *mah·lyoos·kee*
sherry	**херес** *kheh·rees*
shrimp	**креветка** *kree·vyet·kah*
small apple pancakes	**оладьи с яблоками** *ah·lahd'·yee s yahb·lah·kah·mee*
small pancakes with jam	**блинчики с вареньем** *bleen·chee·kee s vah·ryen'·yem*
snack	**лёгкая закуска** *lyokh·kah·yah zah·koos·kah*
soup	**суп** *soop*
sour cream	**сметана** *smee·tah·nah*
spaghetti	**спагетти** *spah·gyeh·tee*
spices	**приправы** *pree·prah·vih*
spicy Georgian soup made with mutton and rice	**харчо** *khahr·choh*
spirits	**спиртные напитки** *speert·nih·yeh nah·peet·kee*
sponge roll	**рулет** *roo·lyet*
steak	**бифштекс** *beef·shteks*
strawberries	**клубника** *kloob·nee·kah*
stuffed pasta	**пельмени** *peel'·myeh·nee*
sturgeon poached	**осетрина по-русски** *ah·seet·ree·nah pah roos·kee*
sturgeon served with a white sauce	**осетрина под белым соусом** *ah·seet·ree·nah pahd byeh·lihm soh·oo·sahm*
sturgeon steamed	**осетрина паровая** *ah·seet·ree·nah pah·rah·vah·yah*
sugar	**сахар** *sah·khahr*
sweet corn	**сладкая кукуруза** *slaht·kah·yah koo·koo·roo·zah*
syrup	**сироп** *see·rop*
tea	**чай** *chie*

thick soup made with cabbage or sauerkraut	**щи** *shchee*
toast	**тост** *tost*
tomato	**помидор** *pah·mee·<u>dor</u>*
trout	**форель** *fah·<u>ryel'</u>*
tuna	**тунец** *too·<u>nyets</u>*
turkey	**индейка** *een·<u>dyey</u>·kah*
Uzbek soup made with mutton, bacon and tomato	**шурпа** *shoor·<u>pah</u>*
vanilla	**ваниль** *vah·<u>neel'</u>*
veal	**телятина** *tee·<u>lyah</u>·tee·nah*
vegetables	**овощи** *<u>oh</u>·vah·shchee*
vodka	**водка** *<u>vot</u>·kah*
water	**вода** *vah·<u>dah</u>*
watermelon	**арбуз** *arh·<u>boos</u>*
wheat	**пшеница** *pshih·<u>nee</u>·tsah*
whipped cream	**взбитые сливки** *<u>vzbee</u>·tih·yeh <u>sleef</u>·kee*
whisky	**виски** *<u>vees</u>·kee*
wine	**вино** *vee·<u>noh</u>*
yeast cake saturated in liquor	**ромовая баба** *<u>roh</u>·mah·vah·yah <u>bah</u>·bah*
yogurt	**йогурт** *<u>yoh</u>·goort*
zucchini [courgette]	**цуккини** *tsoo·<u>kee</u>·nee*

People

Conversation

ESSENTIAL

Hello./Hi!	**Здравствуйте./Привет!** <u>zdrah</u>·stvooy·tee/ pree·<u>vyet</u>
How are you?	**Как дела?** kahk dee·<u>lah</u>
Fine, thanks.	**Спасибо, хорошо.** spah·<u>see</u>·bah khah·rah·<u>shoh</u>
Excuse me!	**Извините!** eez·vee·<u>nee</u>·tee
Do you speak English?	**Вы говорите по-английски?** vih gah·vah·<u>ree</u>·tee pah ahn·<u>gleey</u>·skee
What's your name?	**Как Вас зовут?** kahk vahz zah·<u>voot</u>
My name is...	**Меня зовут...** mee·<u>nyah</u> zah·<u>voot</u>...
Pleased to meet you.	**Очень приятно.** <u>oh</u>·cheen′ pree·<u>yaht</u>·nah
Where are you from?	**Откуда вы приехали?** aht·<u>koo</u>·dah vih pree·<u>yeh</u>·khah·lee
I'm from the U.S./U.K.	**Я из США/Великобритании.** yah ees seh sheh <u>ah</u>/vee·lee·kah·bree·<u>tah</u>·nee·ee
What do you do?	**Ваша профессия?** <u>vah</u>·shah prah·<u>fyeh</u>·see·yah
I work for...	**Я работаю в...** yah rah·<u>boh</u>·tah·yoo v...
I'm a student.	**Я студент.** yah stoo·<u>dyehnt</u>
I'm retired.	**Я на пенсии.** yah nah <u>pyehn</u>·see·ee
Do you like...?	**Вы любите...?** vih <u>lyoo</u>·bee·tee...
Goodbye.	**До свидания.** dah svee·<u>dah</u>·nee·yah
See you later.	**Увидимся.** oo·<u>vee</u>·deem·syah

It is polite to address people you know by their first name and patronymic, derived from the father's name. So, Nikolay, whose father's name is Ivan, would be called Nikolay Ivanovich; Natalia, whose father's name is Alexander, would be called Natalia Alexandrovna.

Like many other languages, Russian has two forms of the pronoun you: the informal (singular) **ты** *tih* and the formal (plural) **вы** *vih*. **Ты** is used between members of the same family, close friends and to address young children; **вы** *vih* is the polite form of address when you are talking to a person you do not know well or who is older or senior to you. When you are addressing more than one person, **вы** must always be used.

The pre-revolutionary **господин** *gahs·pah·deen* (Mr.) and **госпожа** *gahs·pah·zhah* (Mrs. or Miss) has re-entered usage in Russia.

Language Difficulties

Do you speak English?	**Вы говорите по-английски?** *vih gah·vah·ree·tee pah ahn·gleey·skee*
Does anyone here speak English?	**Кто-нибудь говорит по-английски?** *ktoh nee·bood' goh·voh·reet poh ahn·gleey·skee*
I don't speak Russian.	**Я не говорю по-русски.** *yah nyeh gah·vah·ryoo pah·roos·kee*
I don't speak much Russian.	**Я плохо говорю по-русски.** *yah ploh·khah gah·vah·ryoo pah·roos·kee*
Speak slowly, please.	**Говорите медленнее, пожалуйста.** *gah·vah·ree·tee myed·lee·nee·yeh pah·zhahl·stah*
Repeat that, please.	**Повторите, пожалуйста.** *pahf·tah·ree·tee pah·zhahl·stah*

Excuse me?	**Простите?** prah·_stee_·tee
What was that?	**Что такое?** shtoh tah·_koh_·yeh
Can you spell it?	**Вы можете это написать?** vih _moh_·zheh·teh _eh_·toh nah·pee·_saht'_
Write it down, please.	**Напишите, пожалуйста.** nah·pee·_shih_·tee pah·_zhahl_·stah
Translate this for me, please.	**Переведите мне это, пожалуйста.** pee·ree·vee·_dee_·tee mnyeh _eh_·tah pah·_zhahl_·stah
What does this/ that mean?	**Что это/то значит?** shtoh _eh_·tah/toh _znah_·cheet
I (don't) understand.	**Я (не) понимаю.** yah (nee) pah·nee·_mah_·yoo
Do you understand?	**Вы понимаете?** vih pah·nee·_mah_·ee·tee

YOU MAY HEAR...

| **Я плохо говорю по-английски.** yah _ploh_·khah gah·vah·_ryoo_ pah·ahn·_gleey_·skee | I speak only a little English. |
| **Я не говорю по-английски.** yah _nee_ gah·vah·_ryoo_ pah·ahn·_gleey_·skee | I don't speak English. |

Making Friends

Hello./Hi!	**Здравствуйте./Привет!** _zdrah_·stvooy·tee/ pree·_vyet_
Good morning.	**Доброе утро.** _doh_·brah·yeh _oot_·rah
Good afternoon.	**Добрый день.** _doh_·briy dyen'
Good evening.	**Добрый вечер.** _doh_·briy _vyeh_·cheer
My name is...	**Меня зовут...** mee·_nyah_ zah·_voot_...
What's your name?	**Как Вас зовут?** kahk vahz zah·_voot_
I'd like to introduce you to...	**Хочу познакомить Вас с...** khah·_choo_ pah·znah·_koh_·meet' vahs s...

Nice to meet you.	**Очень приятно.** _oh_•cheen' pree•_yaht_•nah
How are you?	**Как дела?** kahk dee•_lah_
Fine, thanks.	**Спасибо, хорошо.** spah•_see_•bah khah•rah•_shoh_
And you?	**А как вы?** ah kahk vih

> At first meeting **Здравствуйте!** _zdrah_•stvooy•tee (Hello!) is
> the preferred greeting; you can use the informal **Здравствуй!**
> _zdrah_•stvooy to address children. **Привет!** pree•_vyet_ (Hi!) is less
> formal and may sound rude if used in the wrong context.

Travel Talk

I'm here...	**Я здесь...** yah zdyes'...
on business	**в командировке** f kah•mahn•dee•_rof_•kyeh
on vacation [holiday]	**в отпуске** v _ot_•poos•kyeh
studying	**учусь** oo•_choos'_
I'm staying for...	**Я здесь на...** yah zdyes' nah...
I've been here...	**Я здесь уже...** yah zdyes' oo•_zheh_...
a day	**день** dyen'
a week	**неделю** nee•_dyeh_•lyoo
a month	**месяц** _myeh_•syahts
Where are you from?	**Откуда вы?** aht•_koo_•dah vih
I'm from...	**Я из...** yah eez...

For Numbers, see page 157.

Personal

| Who are you with? | **С кем вы?** s kyem vih |
| I'm on my own. | **Я один** _m_ /**одна** _f_. yah ah•_deen_/ahd•_nah_ |

I'm with…	**Я с…** yah s…
my husband/wife	**моим мужем/моей женой** mah·eem moo·zhihm/mah·yey zhee·noy
my boyfriend/ girlfriend	**моим другом/моей подругой** mah·eem droo·gahm/mah·yey pah·droo·gie
I'm with…	**Я с…** yah s…
a friend/friends	**другом/друзьями** droo·gahm/drooz'·yah·mee
a colleague/ colleagues	**коллегой/коллегами** kah·lyeh·gie/ kah·lyeh·gah·mee
When's your birthday?	**Когда Ваш день рождения?** kahg·dah vahsh dyen' rahzh·dyeh·nee·yah
How old are you?	**Сколько Вам лет?** skol'·kah vahm lyet
I'm…	**Мне…** mnyeh…
I'm…	**Я…** yah…
single	**холост** m **/не замужем** f yah khoh·lahst/ nee zah·moo·zhihm
in a relationship	**с партнёром** s pahrt·nyoh·rahm
engaged	**Я помолвлен** m **/помолвлена** f yah pah·mohl·vlen/pah·mohl·vle·nah
married	**женат** m **/замужем** f zhih·naht/ zah·moo·zhihm
divorced	**разведён** m **/разведена** f rahz·vee·dyon/ rahz·vee·dee·nah
separated	**не живу с женой** m **/мужем** f nee zhih·voo s zhih·noy/moo·zhihm
I'm widowed.	**Я вдовец** m **/вдова** f. yah vdah·vyets/ vdah·vah
Do you have children/ grandchildren?	**У Вас есть дети/внуки?** oo vahs yest' dyeh·tee/vnoo·kee

For Numbers, see page 157.

Work & School

What do you do?	**Ваша профессия?**	_vah_·shah prah·_fyeh_·see·yah
What are you studying?	**Что вы изучаете?**	shtoh vih ee·zoo·_chah_·ee·tee
I'm studying…	**Я изучаю…**	yah ee·zoo·_chah_·yoo…
I…	**Я…**	yah
work full-/	**работаю полный/неполный день**	
part-time	rah·_boh_·tah·yu _pohl_·niy/neh·_pohl_·niy dehn'	
am unemployed	**Я безработный** *m*/**безработная** *f* yah	
	bez·rah·_boht_·nee/bez·rah·_boht_·na·yah	
work at home	**работаю дома** rah·_boh_·tah·yu _doh_·mah	
Who do you work for?	**Где вы работаете?** gdyeh vih rah·_boh_·tah·ee·tee	
I work for…	**Я работаю в…** yah rah·_boh_·tah·yoo v…	
Here's my business card.	**Вот моя визитка.** vot mah·yah vee·_zeet_·kah	

For Business Travel, see page 134.

Weather

What is the weather forecast?	**Какой прогноз погоды?** kah·_koy_ prahg·_nos_ pah·_goh_·dih	
What beautiful/ terrible weather!	**Какая чудесная/ужасная погода!** kah·_kah_·yah choo·_dyes_·nah·yah/ oo·_zhahs_·nah·yah pah·_goh_·dah	
It's cool./warm.	**Прохладно./Тепло.** prah·_khlahd_·nah/teep·_loh_	
It's hot./cold.	**Жарко./Холодно.** _zhahr_·kah/_hoh_·lahd·nah	
It's rainy./sunny.	**Дождливо./Солнечно.** dahzh·_dlee_·vah/ _sol_·neech·nah	
It's snowy/icy.	**Идёт снег./Гололёд.** ee·_dyot_ snyek/ gah·lah·_lyot_	
Do I need a jacket?	**Нужно надевать куртку?** _noozh_·nah nah dee·_vaht'_ _koort_·koo	
Do I need an umbrella?	**Нужно брать зонт?** _noozh_·nah braht' zont	

For Temperature, see page 164.

Romance

ESSENTIAL

Would you like to go out for a drink/meal?	**Не хотите выпить/поесть где-нибудь?** nee khah·_tee_·tee vih·peet'/pah·_yest'_ gdyeh·nee·boot'
What are your plans for tonight/tomorrow?	**Какие у вас планы на сегодняшний вечер/завтра?** kah·_kee_·yeh oo vahs _plah_·nih nah see·_vod_·neesh·neey vyeh·cheer/_zahf_·trah
Can I have your number?	**Можно Ваш номер телефона?** _mozh_·nah vahsh _noh_·meer tee·lee·_foh_·nah
Can I join you?	**Можно к Вам присоединиться?** _mozh_·nah k vahm pree·sah·ee·dee·_nee_·tsah
Let me buy you a drink.	**Позвольте вам предложить что-нибудь выпить.** pahz·_vol'_·tee vahm preed·lah·_zheet'_ _shtoh_·nee·boot' vih·peet'
I like you.	**Вы мне нравитесь.** vih mnyeh _nrah_·vee·tees'
I love you.	**Я Вас люблю.** yah vahs lyoob·_lyoo_

The Dating Game

Would you like to…?	**Хотите…?** khah·_tee_·tee…
go out for coffee	**выпить кофе где-нибудь** vih·peet' koh·fyeh gdyeh·nee·boot'
go for a drink	**пойти выпить где-нибудь** pie·tee vih·peet' gdyeh·nee·boot'
go for a meal	**пойти поесть где-нибудь** pie·tee pah·_yest'_ gdyeh·nee·boot'
What are your plans for…?	**Какие у вас планы на…?** kah·_kee_·yeh oo vahs _plah_·nih nah…

98

today	**сегодня** *seh·vohd·nya*
tonight	**сегодняшний вечер** *see·vod·neesh·neey vyeh·cheer*
tomorrow	**завтра** *zahf·trah*
this weekend	**эти выходные** *eh·tee vih·khahd·nih·yeh*
Where would you like to go?	**Куда вы хотите пойти?** *koo·dah vih khah·tee·tee pie·tee*
I'd like to go to…	**Я хотел m /хотела f бы пойти в…** *yah khah·tyel m/khah·tyeh·lah f bih pie·tee v…*
Do you like…?	**Вы любите…?** *vih lyoo·bee·tee…*
Can I have your number/e-mail?	**Можно Ваш номер телефона/ электронный адрес?** *mozh·nah vahsh noh·meer tee·lee·foh·nah/ee·leek·tron·niy ahd·rees*
Are you on facebook/Twitter?	**Вы есть в facebook/Twitter?** *vih est' v facebook/Twitter*
Can I join you?	**Можно к Вам присоединиться?** *mozh·nah k vahm pree·sah·ee·dee·nee·tsah*
You're very attractive.	**Вы прекрасно выглядите.** *vih pree·krahs·nah vih·glee·dee·tee*
Shall we go somewhere quieter?	**Пойдём куда-нибудь в тихое место?** *pie·dyom koo·dah·nee·boot' f tee·khah·yeh myes·tah*

For Communications, see page 50.

Accepting & Rejecting

Thank you! I'd love to.	**Спасибо! Я с удовольствием.** *spah·see·bah yah s oo·dah·vol'·stvee·yem*
Where shall we meet?	**Где встретимся?** *gdyeh fstryeh·teem·syah*
I'll meet you at the bar/your hotel.	**Встретимся в баре/вашем отеле.** *fstryeh·teem·syah v bah·ryeh/vah·shem ah·teh·lee*

I'll come by at...	**Я зайду в...** yah zayh·_doo_ v...
Thank you, but I'm busy.	**Спасибо, но я занят** m **/занята** f**.**
	spah·_see_·bah noh yah _zah_·nyaht/zah·nyah·_tah_
I'm not interested.	**Меня это не интересует.** mee·_nyah_ _eh_·tah
	nee een·tee·ree·_soo_·eet
Leave me alone.	**Оставьте меня в покое.** ah·_stahf'_·tee
	mee·_nyah_ f pah·_koh_·yeh
Stop bothering me!	**Перестаньте мне надоедать!**
	pee·ree·_stahn'_·tee mnyeh nah·dah·ee·_daht'_

Getting Intimate

Can I hug/kiss you?	**Можно тебя обнять/поцеловать?** _mozh_·nah
	tee·_byah_ ahb·_nyaht'_/pah·tsih·lah·_vaht'_
Yes.	**Да.** dah
No.	**Нет.** nyet
Stop!	**Перестань!** pee·ree·_stahn'_
I love you.	**Я Вас люблю.** yah vahs lyoob·_lyoo_

Sexual Preferences

Are you gay?	**Ты гей** m **/лесбиянка** f**?** tih gyey/
	lez·bee·_yahn_·kah
I'm...	**Я...** yah...
heterosexual	**гетеросексуал** gyeh·teh·rah·sek·soo·_ahl_
homosexual	**гомосексуал** goh·mah·sek·soo·_ahl_
bisexual	**бисексуал** bee·sek·soo·_ahl_
Do you like men/	**Вам нравятся мужчины/женщины?** vam
women?	_nrah_·vyat·sya moo·_zhchee_·nih/_zhehn_·shchee·nih

Leisure Time

Sightseeing

ESSENTIAL

Where's the tourist information office?	**Где турбюро?** *gdyeh toor·byoo·roh*
What are the main points of interest?	**Какие главные достопримечательности?** *kah·kee·yeh glahv·nih·yeh dah·stah·pree·mee·chah·teel'·nahs·tee*
Do you have tours in English?	**У вас есть экскурсии на английском?** *oo vahs yehst' ehks·koor·see·ee nah ahn·gleey·skahm*
Can I have a map/ guide?	**Можно мне карту/путеводитель?** *mozh·nah mnyeh kahr·too/poo·tee·vah·dee·teel*

Tourist Information

Do you have any information on…?	**У Вас есть информация по…?** *oo vahs yest' een·fahr·mah·tsih·yah pah…*
Can you recommend…?	**Вы можете порекомендовать…?** *vih moh·zhih·tee pah·ree·kah·meen·dah·vaht'…*
a boat trip	**водную экскурсию** *vod·noo·yoo eks·koor·see·yoo*
an excursion	**экскурсию** *eks·koor·see·yoo*
a sightseeing tour	**обзорную экскурсию** *ahb·zor·noo·yoo eks·koor·see·yoo*

Intourist hotels have **бюро обслуживания** byoo·_roh_ ahp·_sloo_·zhih·vah·nee·yah (service bureaus) manned by multilingual staff who provide information, arrange outings and excursions, make reservations and give general assistance. Other useful sources of information are the tourist information offices, English-language newspapers, *The Moscow Times* and *Where in St. Petersburg?*, found in many hotels and at kiosks.

On Tour

I'd like to go on the tour to…	**Я хотел** *m* **/хотела** *f* **бы поехать на экскурсию в…** yah khah·_tyel_/khah·_tyeh_·lah bih pah·_yeh_·khaht' nah eks·_koor_·see·yoo v…
When's the next tour?	**Когда будет следующая поездка?** kahg·_dah_ _boo_·deht _sleh_·doo·yu·shchah·ya poh·_yehzd_·kah
Are there tours in English?	**Есть экскурсии на английском?** yest' eks·_koor_·see·ee nah ahn·_gleey_·skahm
Is there an English guide book/audio guide?	**Есть путеводитель/аудиокнига на английском языке?** est' poo·teh·voh·_dee_·tehl'/ ah·oo·dee·oh·_knee_·gah nah ahng·_leey_·skohm yaz·_ihkeh_
What time do we leave/return?	**Во сколько отправляемся/возвращаемся?** vah _skol'_·kah aht·prahv·_lyah_·eem·syah/ vahz·vrah·_shchah_·eem·syah
We'd like to have a look at the…	**Нам хотелось бы посмотреть…** nahm khah·_tyeh_·las' bih pah·smah·_tryet'_…
Can we stop here…?	**Можно здесь остановиться, чтобы…?** _mozh_·nah zdyes' ah·stah·nah·_vee_·tsah _shtoh_·bih…
to take photographs	**пофотографировать** pah·fah·tah·grah·_fee_·rah·vaht'

to buy souvenirs	**купить сувениры** koo·<u>peet'</u> soo·vee·<u>nee</u>·rih
to use the restroom [toilet]	**сходить в туалет** skhah·<u>deet'</u> f too·ah·<u>lyet</u>
Is there access for the disabled?	**Есть условия для инвалидов?** yest' oos·<u>loh</u>·vee·yah dlyah een·vah·<u>lee</u>·dahf

For Tickets, see page 18.

Seeing the Sights

Where is…?	**Где…?** gdye…
the battleground	**место сражения** <u>myes</u>·tah srah·<u>zheh</u>·nee·yah
the botanical garden	**ботанический сад** bah·tah·<u>nee</u>·chees·keey saht
the castle	**замок** <u>zah</u>·mahk
the downtown area	**центр города** tsentr <u>goh</u>·rah·dah
the fountain	**фонтан** fahn·<u>tahn</u>
the library	**библиотека** bee·blee·ah·<u>tyeh</u>·kah
the market	**рынок** <u>rih</u>·nahk
the museum	**музей** moo·<u>zey</u>
the old town	**старый город** <u>stah</u>·riy <u>goh</u>·raht
the opera house	**опера** <u>oh</u>·peh·rah
the palace	**дворец** dvah·<u>ryets</u>
the park	**парк** pahrk

the ruins	**руины** *roo·een·y*
the shopping area	**торговый район** *tahr·goh·viy rah·yon*
the town square	**центральная площадь** *tsihn·trahl'·nah·yah ploh·shchaht'*
Show me on the map	**Покажите мне на карте.** *pah·kah·zhih·tee mnyeh nah kahr·tye*
It's...	**Это...** *eh·tah...*
amazing	**удивительно** *oo·dee·vee·tehl'·noh*
beautiful	**прекрасно** *pree·krahs·nah*
boring	**скучно** *skoosh·nah*
It's...	**Это...** *eh·tah...*
interesting	**интересно** *een·tee·ryes·nah*
magnificent	**великолепно** *vee·lee·kah·lyep·nah*
romantic	**романтично** *rah·mahn·teech·nah*
strange	**странно** *strah·noh*
terrible	**ужасно** *oo·zhahs·nah*
ugly	**безобразно** *bee·zah·brahz·nah*
I (don't) like it.	**Мне это (не) нравится.** *mnyeh eh·tah (nee) nrah·vee·tsah*

For Asking Directions, see page 34.

Religious Sites

Where's...?	**Где...?** *gdyeh...*
the Catholic/ Protestant church	**церковь католическая/протестантская** *tser·kahf' kah·toh·lee·che·ska·ya/pro·tye·stahn·ska·ya*
the mosque	**мечеть** *mee·chet'*
the shrine	**обитель** *ah·bee·teel'*
the synagogue	**синагога** *see·nah·goh·gah*
the temple	**храм** *khrahm*
What time is mass/ the service?	**Когда будет месса/служба?** *kahg·dah boo·deet myes·sah/sloozh·bah*

Shopping

ESSENTIAL

Where is the shop/mall?	**Где магазин/торговый центр?** *gdyeh mah·gah·zeen/tahr·goh·viy tsehntr*
I'm just looking.	**Я просто смотрю.** *yah proh·stah smah·tryoo*
Can you help me?	**Можете мне помочь?** *moh·zhih·tee mnyeh pah·mohch*
I'm being helped.	**Меня уже обслуживают.** *mee·nyah oo·zheh ahp·sloo·zhih·vah·yoot*
How much?	**Сколько?** *skol'·kah*
That one.	**Вон то.** *vohn toh*
That's all, thanks.	**Это всё, спасибо.** *eh·tah fsyoh spah·see·bah*
Where do I pay?	**Куда платить?** *koo·dah plah·teet'*
I'll pay in cash/by credit card.	**Я заплачу наличными/по кредитной карточке.** *yah zah·plah·choo nah·leech·nih·mee/pah kree·deet·noy kahr·tahch·kee*
A receipt, please.	**Чек, пожалуйста.** *chehk pah·zhahl·stah*

Shopping in Moscow and St. Petersburg now looks very much like shopping in New York and London, at least in the city centers and malls. Moscow does its serious shopping in the mega-stores along the outer ring-road, where names like Ikea and Marks & Spencer can be found. The Tyoply Stan mega mall claims to be Europe's busiest shopping center. Both cities also offer thriving and rich open-air markets, for example, Moscow's Izmailovsky Market, near Partizanskaya metro station, or St. Petersburg's market, near the Nevsky Prospect metro station. These are great places to pick up souvenirs.

At the Shops

Where is…?	**Где…?** gdyeh…
the antiques store	**антикварный магазин** ahn·tee·<u>kvahr</u>·niy mah·gah·<u>zeen</u>
the bakery	**булочная** <u>boo</u>·lahch·nah·yah
the bank	**банк?** bahnk
the bookstore	**книжный магазин** <u>kneezh</u>·niy mah·gah·<u>zeen</u>
Where is…?	**Где…?** gdyeh…
the clothing store	**магазин одежды** mah·gah·<u>zeen</u> ah·dyezh·dih
the delicatessen	**гастроном** gah·stroh·<u>nohm</u>
the department store	**универмаг** oo·nee·veer·<u>mahk</u>
the gift shop	**магазин подарков** mah·gah·<u>zeen</u> poh·<u>dahr</u>·kohv
the jeweler	**ювелирный магазин** yoo·vee·<u>leer</u>·niy mah·gah·<u>zeen</u>
the liquor store [off-license]	**винный магазин** <u>veen</u>·niy mah·gah·<u>zeen</u>
the market	**рынок** <u>rih</u>·nahk
the music store	**музыкальный магазин** moo·zih·<u>kahl'</u>·niy mah·gah·<u>zeen</u>
the pastry store	**кондитерская** kahn·<u>dee</u>·teer·skah·yah
the pharmacy	**аптека** ahp·<u>tyeh</u>·kah
the shoe store	**обувной магазин** ah·boov·<u>noy</u> mah·gah·<u>zeen</u>
Where is…?	**Где…?** gdyeh…
the shopping mall	**торговый центр** tahr·<u>goh</u>·viy tsehntr
the souvenir store	**магазин сувениров** mah·gah·<u>zeen</u> soo·vee·<u>nee</u>·rahf
the supermarket	**универсам** oo·nee·veer·<u>sahm</u>
the tobacconist	**табачный киоск** tah·<u>bahch</u>·niy kee·<u>osk</u>
the toy store	**магазин игрушек** mah·gah·<u>zeen</u> ee·<u>groo</u>·shek

107

Ask an Assistant

What are the hours of operation?	**В какие часы работает?** *f kah·kee·yeh chah·sih rah·boh·tah·yet*
Where is…?	**Где…?** *gdyeh…*
the cashier [cash desk]	**касса** *kahs·sah*
the escalator	**эскалатор** *es·kah·lah·tahr*
the elevator [lift]	**лифт** *leeft*
the fitting room	**примерочная** *pree·myeh·rahch·nah·yah*
the store directory	**перечень отделов** *pyeh·ree·cheen' ahd·dyeh·lahf*
Help me, please.	**Помогите мне, пожалуйста.** *pah·mah·gee·tee mnyeh pah·zhahl·stah*
I'm just looking.	**Я просто смотрю.** *yah proh·stah smah·tryoo*
I'm being helped.	**Меня уже обслуживают.** *mee·nyah oo·zheh ahp·sloo·zhih·vah·yoot*
Do you have…?	**У Вас есть…?** *oo vahs yest'…*
Where is…?	**Где…?** *gdyeh…*
Could you show me…?	**Можете мне показать…?** *moh·zhih·tee mnyeh pah·kah·zaht'…*
Can you ship/wrap it?	**Вы можете доставить/завернуть это?** *vih moh·zhih·tee dah·stah·veet'/zah·veer·noot' eh·tah*
How much?	**Сколько?** *skol'·kah*
That's all, thanks.	**Это всё, спасибо.** *eh·tah fsyoh spah·see·bah*

For Clothes & Accessories, see page 116.

For Meals & Cooking, see page 68.

For Souvenirs, see page 120.

YOU MAY HEAR...

Я вас слушаю. *yah vahs sloo•shah•yoo* Can I help you?
Одну минуту. *ahd•noo mee•noo•too* One moment.
Что вы хотите? *shtoh vih khah•tee•tee* What would you like?
Что ещё? *shtoh ee•shchoh* Anything else?

YOU MAY SEE...

ОТКРЫТО/ЗАКРЫТО *aht•krih•tah/* open/closed
zah•krih•toh
ЗАКРЫТО НА ОБЕД *zah•krih•toh nah ah•byed* closed for lunch
ПРИМЕРОЧНАЯ *pree•meh•rah•chnah•ya* fitting room
КАССА *kah•sah* cashier
ТОЛЬКО НАЛИЧНЕ *tohl'•koh nah•lich•nih•ee* cash only
ПРИНИМАЮТСЯ КРЕДИТНЫЕ КАРТЫ credit cards accepted
pree•nee•mah•yoot•sah kreh•deet•nihye kahr•tih
ЧАСЫ РАБОТЫ *chah•sih rah•bohty* business hours
ВЫХОД *vih•khaht* exit

Personal Preferences

I'd like something…	**Я хочу что-нибудь…** *yah khah•choo shtoh•nee•boot'…*	
cheap/expensive	**дешёвое/дорогое** *dee•shoh•vah•yeh/ dah•rah•goh•yeh*	
larger/smaller	**побольше/поменьше** *pah•bol'•sheh/ pah•myen'•sheh*	
from this region	**из этого региона** *eez eh•tah•vah reh•gih•oh•nah*	
around… rubles	**примерно… рублей** *pree•mehr•noh … roob•lyey*	

Is it real?	**Это настоящее?** _eh·tah_ nahs·tah·_yah_·shchee·yeh
Could you show me this/that?	**Можете показать мне это/вон то?** _moh_·zhih·tee pah·kah·_zaht'_ mnyeh _eh_·tah/von toh
That's not quite what I want.	**Это не совсем то, что я хочу.** _eh_·tah nee sahf·_syem_ toh shtoh yah khah·_choo_
I don't like it.	**Это мне не нравится.** _eh_·tah mnyeh nee _nrah_·vee·tsah
That's too expensive.	**Это слишком дорого.** _eh_·tah _sleesh_·kahm _doh_·rah·gah
I'd like to think about it.	**Надо подумать.** _nah_·dah pah·_doo_·maht'
I'll take it.	**Я возьму это.** yah vahz'·_moo_ _eh_·tah

Paying & Bargaining

How much?	**Сколько?** _skol'_·kah
I'll pay...	**Я заплачу...** yah zah·plah·_choo_...
in cash	**наличными** nah·_leech_·nih·mee

YOU MAY HEAR...

Как будете платить? kahk _boo_·dee·tee plah·_teet'_	How are you paying?
Кредитная карта не принята. kreh·_deet_·nah·ya _kahr_·tah neh _pree_·nya·tah	Your credit card has been declined.
Только наличные, пожалуйста. _tol'_·kah nah·_leech_·nih·yeh pah·_zhahl_·stah	Cash only, please.
удостоверение личности пожалуйста. oo·dahs·ta·_veer_·en·ye leech·nus·tee pah·_zhahl_·stah	ID, please.
У Вас есть деньги мельче? oo vahs yest' _dyen'_·gee _myel'_·cheh	Do you have any smaller change?

While credit cards are increasingly common in Russia and fairly safe to use, especially in large and mid-sized cities, you should avoid using them in places that do not inspire complete confidence.

by credit card	**по кредитной карточке** pah kree-_deet_-noy _kar_-tach-kee
by traveler's cheque	**дорожным чеком** dah-_rozh_-nihm _cheh_-kahm
A receipt, please.	**Можно чек, пожалуйста.** _mozh_-nah chehk pah-_zhahl_-stah
That's too much.	**Это слишком дорого.** _eh_-tah _sleesh_-kahm _doh_-rah-gah
I'll give you…	**Я дам вам…** yah dahm vahm…
I only have…rubles.	**У меня только…рублей.** oo mee-_nyah_ tol'-kah…roob-_lyey_
Is that your best price?	**Это ваша последняя цена?** _eh_-tah _vah_-shah pahs-_lyed_-nee-yah tsih-_nah_
Can you give me a discount?	**Вы можете дать мне скидку?** vih _moh_-zhih-tee daht' mnyeh _skeet_-koo

Making a Complaint

I'd like…	**Я хотел _m_ /хотела _f_ бы…** yah khah-_tyel_/ khah-_tyeh_-lah bih…
to exchange this	**обменять это** ahb-mee-_nyaht'_ _eh_-tah
to return this	**возвратить это** vahz-vrah-_teet'_ _eh_-tah
a refund	**возврат денег** vahz-_vraht_ _dye_-neek
to see the manager	**увидеть менеджера** oo-_vee_-deet' _myeh_-ned-zhih-rah

Services

Can you recommend…?	**Вы можете порекомендовать…?** vih <u>moh</u>•zhih•tee pah•ree•kah•meen•dah•<u>vaht'</u>…
a barber	**парикмахерскую** pah•reek•<u>mah</u>•kheer•skoo•yoo
a dry cleaner	**химчистку** kheem•<u>cheest</u>•koo
a hairdresser	**парикмахерскую** pah•reek•<u>mah</u>•kheer•skoo•yoo
a laundromat [launderette]	**прачечную** <u>prah</u>•cheech•noo•yoo
a nail salon	**маникюрный салон** mah•nee•<u>kyoor</u>•niy sah•<u>lon</u>
a spa	**спа** spah
a travel agency	**бюро путешествий** byoo•<u>roh</u> poo•tee•<u>shest</u>•veey
Can you…this?	**Вы можете это…?** vih <u>moh</u>•zhih•tee <u>eh</u>•tah…
alter	**переделать** pee•ree•<u>dyeh</u>•lat'
clean	**почистить** pah•<u>chees</u>•teet'
mend	**заштопать** zah•<u>shtoh</u>•paht'
press	**погладить** pah•<u>glah</u>•deet'
When will it be ready?	**Когда будет готово?** kahg•<u>dah</u> <u>boo</u>•deet gah•<u>toh</u>•vah

Hair & Beauty

I'd like…	**Я хотел** *m* **/хотела** *f* **бы…** *yah khah·tyel/ khah·tyeh·lah bih…*
an appointment for today/tomorrow	**записаться на сегодня/завтра** *zah·pee·sah·tsah nah see·vod·nyah/zahf·trah*
some colour/ highlights	**покрасить волосы/сделать мелирование** *pah·kra·seet' voh·loh·sih/sdeh·laht' meh·lee·roh·vah·nee·yeh*
my hair styled/ blow-dried	**модельную стрижку/укладку феном** *mah·del'·noo·yoo/ook·lahd·koo·feh·nohm streesh·koo*
a haircut	**постричься** *pah·streech·syah*
an eyebrow/ bikini wax	**восковую эпиляцию бровей/зоны бикини** *vos·kah·voo·yoo eh·pee·lyah·tsih·yoo brah·vyey/zoh·nih bee·kee·nee*
a facial	**чистку лица** *cheest·koo lee·tsah*
a manicure/ pedicure	**маникюр/педикюр** *mah·nee·kyoor/ pee·dee·kyoor*
a (sports) massage	**(спортивный) массаж** *(spahr·teev·niy) mahs·sahsh*
a trim	**подравнивание** *pahd·rahv·nee·vah·nee·yeh*
Don't cut it too short.	**Не слишком коротко.** *nee sleesh·kahm koh·raht·kah*
Shorter here.	**Здесь покороче.** *zdyes' pah·kah·roh·cheh*
Do you do…?	**Вы делаете…?** *vih dyeh·lah·ee·tee…*
acupuncture	**иглотерапию** *eeg·lah·tee·rah·pee·yoo*
aromatherapy	**ароматерапию** *ah·roh·mah·tee·rah·pee·yoo*
oxygen treatment	**кислородотерапию** *kees·lah·roh·dah·tee·rah·pee·yoo*
Is there a sauna?	**Есть сауна?** *yest' sah·oo·nah*

Natural approaches to health and beauty include herb remedies and **баня** _bah•nyah_ (Russian steam bath); these are deeply ingrained in Russian traditional folk medicine. Today these approaches have been combined with modern spa and wellness resources. Even outside of Moscow and St. Petersburg you will find a variety of day and overnight spas. Most hotels offer facials, massage and a number of other day spa services right on the premises. It is customary to tip from 10-20% depending on your satisfaction with services provided.

Antiques

How old is this?	**Какой возраст этой вещи?** _kah•koy voz•rahst eh•tie vyeh•shchee_
Do you have anything from the…period?	**У Вас есть что-нибудь на период с …?** _oo vahs yest' shtoh•nee•boot' nah peh•ree•ot s_
Do I have to fill out any forms?	**Нужно заполнить формы?** _noozh•nah zah•pohl•neet' fohr•mih_
Will I have problems with customs?	**Могут быть проблемы на таможне?** _moh•goot biht' prah•blyeh•mih nah tah•mozh•nee_
Is there a certificate of authenticity?	**Есть сертификат подлинности?** _yest' seer•tee•fee•kaht pod•lyeen•nahs•tee_
Can you ship/wrap it?	**Вы можете доставить/упаковать?** _vih moh•zhih•tye dah•stah•veet'/oo•pah•kah•vaht'_

Clothing

I'd like…	**Я хотел _m_ /хотела _f_ бы…** _yah khah•tyel m/ khah•tyeh•lah f bih…_
Can I try this on?	**Можно это примерить?** _mozh•nah eh•tah pree•myeh•reet'_

It doesn't fit.	**Не подходит.** nee paht‑<u>khoh</u>‑deet
It's too big/small.	**Слишком велико/мало.** <u>sleesh</u>‑kahm vee‑lee‑<u>koh</u>/mah‑<u>loh</u>
It's too short/long.	**Слишком коротко/длинно.** <u>sleesh</u>‑kahm <u>koh</u>‑raht‑kah/<u>dleen</u>‑nah
It's too tight/loose.	**Слишком туго/слабо.** <u>slee</u>‑shkohm <u>too</u>‑goh/<u>slah</u>‑boh
Do you have this in size…?	**У Вас есть размер…?** oo vahs yest' rahz‑<u>myer</u>…
Do you have this in a bigger/smaller size?	**У Вас есть это большего/меньшего размера?** oo vahs yest' eh‑tah <u>bol</u>'‑shee‑vah/<u>myen</u>'‑shee‑vah rahz‑<u>myeh</u>‑rah

For Numbers, see page 157.

YOU MAY HEAR…

That looks great on you.	**Вам очень идет** vahm <u>oh</u>‑chen' eed‑<u>yoht</u>
How does it fit?	**Как Вам нравится?** kahk vahm <u>nrah</u>‑vee‑tsya
We don't have your size.	**У нас нет Вашего размера.** oo nahs neht <u>vah</u>‑sheh‑vah‑rahz‑meh‑rah

YOU MAY SEE…

МУЖСКАЯ ОДЕЖДА moosh‑<u>skah</u>‑yah ah‑<u>dyezh</u>‑dah	men's clothing
ЖЕНСКАЯ ОДЕЖДА <u>zhen</u>‑skah‑yah ah‑<u>dyezh</u>‑dah	women's clothing
ДЕТСКАЯ ОДЕЖДА <u>dyets</u>‑kah‑yah ah‑<u>dyezh</u>‑dah	children's clothing

Colors

I'm looking for something in…	**Я ищу что-нибудь…** yah ee·<u>shchoo</u> <u>shtoh</u>·nee·boot'…
beige	**бежевое** <u>byeh</u>·zhih·vah·yeh
black	**чёрное** <u>chor</u>·nah·yeh
blue	**синее** <u>see</u>·nee·yeh
brown	**коричневое** kah·<u>reech</u>·nee·vah·yeh
green	**зелёное** zee·<u>lyoh</u>·nah·yeh
gray	**серое** <u>syeh</u>·rah·yeh
orange	**оранжевое** ah·<u>rahn</u>·zhih·vah·yeh
pink	**розовое** <u>roh</u>·zah·vah·yeh
purple	**фиолетовое** fee·ah·<u>lyeh</u>·tah·vah·yeh
red	**красное** <u>krahs</u>·nah·yeh
white	**белое** <u>byeh</u>·lah·yeh
yellow	**жёлтое** <u>zhol</u>·tah·yeh

Clothes & Accessories

a backpack	**рюкзак** ryook·<u>zahk</u>
a belt	**ремень** ree·<u>myen'</u>
a bikini	**бикини** bee·<u>kee</u>·nee
a blouse	**блузка** <u>bloos</u>·kah
a bra	**бюстгальтер** byoost·<u>gahl</u>·teer
briefs [underpants]	**трусы** <u>troo</u>·sih
a coat	**пальто** pahl'·<u>toh</u>
a dress	**платье** <u>plaht'</u>·yeh
a hat	**шапка** <u>shahp</u>·kah
a jacket	**пиджак** peed·<u>zhahk</u>
jeans	**джинсы** <u>dzhihn</u>·sih
pajamas	**пижама** pee·<u>zhah</u>·mah
pants [trousers]	**брюки** <u>bryoo</u>·kee
pantyhose [tights]	**колготки** kahl·<u>got</u>·kee

a purse [handbag]	**сумка** <u>soom</u>·kah
a raincoat	**плащ** plahshch
a scarf	**шарф** shahrf
a shirt	**рубашка** roo·<u>bahsh</u>·kah
shorts	**шорты** <u>shor</u>·tih
a skirt	**юбка** <u>yoop</u>·kah
socks	**носки** nahs·<u>kee</u>
a suit	**костюм** kahs·<u>tyoom</u>
sunglasses	**солнечные очки** <u>sol</u>·neech·nih·yeh ahch·<u>kee</u>
a sweater	**пуловер** poo·<u>loh</u>·veer
a sweatshirt	**свитер** <u>svee</u>·tehr
swimming trunks	**плавки** <u>plahf</u>·kee
a swimsuit	**купальник** koo·<u>pahl'</u>·neek
a T-shirt	**майка** <u>mie</u>·kah
a tie	**галстук** <u>gahls</u>·took
underwear	**нижнее бельё** <u>neezh</u>·nee·yeh bee·<u>lyoh</u>

Fabric

I'd like…	**Я хотел** *m* **/хотела** *f* **бы…** yah khah·<u>tyel</u>/ khah·<u>tyeh</u>·lah bih…
cotton	**хлопок** <u>khloh</u>·pahk
denim	**джинс** dzhihns
lace	**кружева** kroo·zhih·<u>vah</u>
leather	**кожа** <u>koh</u>·zhah
linen	**лен** lyon
silk	**шёлк** sholk
wool	**шерсть** sherst'
Is it machine washable?	**Это можно стирать в машине?** <u>eh</u>·tah <u>mozh</u>·nah stee·<u>raht'</u> v mah·<u>shih</u>·nyeh

Shoes

I'd like...	**Я хотел m /хотела f бы...** yah khah·*tyel*/ khah·*tyeh*·lah bih...
high-heeled/flat shoes	**туфли на высоком/низком каблуке** *toof*·lee nah vih·*soh*·kahm/*nees*·kahm kahb·loo·*kyeh*
boots	**сапоги** sah·pah·*gee*
loafers	**мокасины** mah·kah·*see*·nih
sandals	**сандалии** sahn·*dah*·lee·ee
shoes	**туфли** *toof*·lee
slippers	**тапочки** *tah*·pahch·kee
sneakers	**кроссовки** krah·*sof*·kee
In size...	**Размер...** rahz·*myer*...

For Numbers, see page 157.

Sizes

small (S)	**малый** *mah*·liy
medium (M)	**средний** *sryed*·neey
large (L)	**большой** bahl'·*shoy*
extra large (XL)	**очень большой** *oh*·cheen' bahl'·*shoy*
petite	**маленький** *mah*·leen'·keey
plus size	**для полных** dlyah *pol*·nihkh

Newsagent & Tobacconist

Do you sell English-language books/newspapers?	**Есть в продаже английские книги/газеты?** yest' f prah·<u>dah</u>·zheh ahn·<u>gleey</u>·skee·yeh <u>knee</u>·gee/gah·<u>zyeh</u>·tih
I'd like…	**Дайте…** <u>die</u>·tee…
candy	**конфеты** kohn·<u>feh</u>·tih
chewing gum	**жевательную резинку** zhih·<u>vah</u>·teel·'noo·yoo ree·<u>zeen</u>·koo
a chocolate bar	**плитку шоколада** <u>pleet</u>·koo shoh·koh·<u>lah</u>·dah
cigars	**сигары** see·<u>gah</u>·rih
a pack/carton of cigarettes	**пачку/блок сигарет** <u>pahch</u>·koo/blok see·gah·<u>ryet</u>
a lighter	**зажигалку** zah·zhih·<u>gahl</u>·koo
a magazine	**журнал** zhoor·<u>nahl</u>
matches	**спички** <u>speech</u>·kee
a newspaper	**газету** gah·<u>zyeh</u>·too
a pen	**ручку** <u>rooch</u>·koo
a road/town map of…	**карту автомобильных дорог/города…** <u>kahr</u>·too ahf·tah·mah·<u>beel</u>'·nihkh dah·<u>rok</u>/ <u>goh</u>·rah·dah…
stamps	**марки** <u>mahr</u>·kee

Photography

I'm looking for…camera.	**Я ищу…фотоаппарат.** yah ee·<u>shchoo</u>… fah·tah·ah·pah·<u>raht</u>
an automatic	**автоматический** ahf·tah·mah·<u>tee</u>·chees·keey
a digital	**цифровой** tsihf·rah·<u>voy</u>
a disposable	**одноразовый** ahd·nah·<u>rah</u>·zah·viy
I'd like…	**Я хотел *m*/хотела *f* бы…** yah khah·<u>tyel</u>/ khah·<u>tyeh</u>·lah bih…
a battery	**батарейку** bah·tah·<u>ryey</u>·koo

digital prints	**цифровые фотографии** tsihf·rah·vih·yeh fah·tah·grah·fee·ee
a memory card	**карту памяти** kahr·too pah·myah·tee
Can I print digital photos here?	**Здесь можно напечатать цифровые фотографии?** zdyes' mozh·nah nah·pee·chah·taht' tsihf·rah·vih·yeh fah·tah·grah·fee·ee

Souvenirs

amber	**янтарь** yeen·tahr'
balalaika (traditional musical instrument)	**балалайка** bah·lah·lie·ka
caviar	**икра** eek·rah
chess set	**шахматы** shahkh·mah·tih
fur hat	**меховая шапка** mee·khah·vah·yah shahp·kah
key ring	**брелок** bree·lok
nesting doll	**матрёшка** maht·ryosh·kah
Palekh box	**палехская шкатулка** pah·leekh·skah·yah shkah·tool·kah
postcard	**открытка** aht·kriht·kah
poster	**плакат** plah·kaht
rug from Tekin	**текинский ковер** tee·keen·skeey kah·vyor
samovar	**самовар** sah·mah·vahr
shawl	**шаль** shahl'
souvenir guide	**альбом** ahl'·bom
tea towel	**кухонное полотенце** koo·khahn·nah·yeh pah·lah·tyen·tseh
T-shirt	**майка** mie·kah
wood carving	**резьба по дереву** reez'·bah pah dyeh·ree·voo
wooden spoons	**деревянные ложки** dee·ree·vyan·nih·yeh losh·kee
Can I see this/that?	**Можно посмотреть это/вон то?** mozh·nah pah·smah·tryet' eh·tah/von toh

It's the one in the window/display case.	**Это то, что на витрине/стеллаже.** _eh_·tah toh shtoh nah vee·_tree_·nyeh/stee·lah·_zheh_
I'd like…	**Я хотел m /хотела f бы…** yah khah·_tyel_/ khah·_tyeh_·lah bih…
a battery	**батарейку** bah·tah·_ryey_·koo
a bracelet	**браслет** brahs·_lyet_
a brooch	**брошь** brosh
earrings	**серьги** _syer'_·gee
a necklace	**ожерелье** ah·zhih·_ryel'_·yeh
a ring	**кольцо** kal'·_tsoh_
a watch	**часы** chah·_sih_
copper	**медь** myet'
crystal (quartz)	**хрусталь** khroo·_stahl'_
diamond	**брильянт** breel'·_yahnt_
white/yellow gold	**белое/желтое золото** _byeh_·lah·yhe/ _zhol_·tah·yeh _zoh_·lah·tah
pearl	**жемчуг** _zhem_·chook
pewter	**олово** _oh_·lah·vah
platinum	**платину** _plah_·tee·noo
sterling silver	**чистое серебро** _chees_·tah·yeh see·reeb·_roh_
Is this real?	**Это настоящее?** _eh_·tah nah·stah·_yah_·shchee·yeh
Can you engrave it?	**Вы можете сделать на нем гравировку?** vih _moh_·zhih·tee _zdyeh_·laht' nah nyom grah·vee·_rof_·koo

In the past shops called **Подарки** pah·*dahr*·kee (gifts) were the traditional places for Russians to buy souvenirs. There are similar departments in almost every department store nowadays. Worth a visit, these stores carry everything from crystal & jewelry to toiletries. Favorite gifts for Russians are flowers, chocolate, wine, cognac and crystal. Visitors take home matreshkas (nesting dolls), lacquered wood boxes, scarves, jewelry, etc.

Sport & Leisure

ESSENTIAL

When's the game?	**Во сколько игра?** vah *skohl'*·kah eeg·*rah*
Where's…?	**Где…?** gdyeh…
the beach	**пляж** plyahsh
the park	**парк** pahrk
the pool	**бассейн** bah·*syeyn*
Is it safe to swim/ dive here?	**Здесь не опасно плавать/нырять?** zdyehs' nee ah·*pahs*·nah plah·vaht'/nih·*ryaht'*
Can I hire golf clubs?	**Я могу взять напрокат клюшки для гольфа?** yah mah·*goo* vzyaht' nah·prah·*kaht* *klyoosh*·kee dlyah *gohl'*·fah
How much per hour?	**Сколько стоит в час?** *skohl'*·kah *stoh*·eet f chahs
How far is it to…?	**Далеко до…отсюда?** dah·lee·*koh* dah… aht·*syoo*·dah
Can you show me on the map?	**Можете показать мне на карте?** *moh*·zhih·tyeh pah·kah·*zaht'* mnyeh nah *kahr*·tyeh

Watching Sport

When's…?	**Когда…?** kahg·_dah_…
the baseball game	**бейсбольный матч** beys·_bohl_'·niy mahtch
the basketball game	**баскетбольный матч** bahs·keed·_bol_'·niy mahtch
the boxing match	**боксёрский матч** bahk·_syor_·skeey mahtch
the cricket game	**игра в крикет** eeg·_rah_ v kree·_kyet_
the cycling race	**велогонка** vyeh·lah·_gon_·kah
the golf tournament	**турнир по гольфу** toor·_neer_ pah _gol_'·foo
the soccer [football] game	**футбольный матч** foot·_bol_'·niy mahtch
the tennis match	**теннисный матч** _teh_·nees·niy mahtch
the volleyball game	**волейбольный матч** vah·leey·_bol_'·niy mahtch
Which teams are playing?	**Какие команды играют?** kah·_kee_·yeh kah·_mahn_·dih ee·_grah_·yoot
Where's…?	**Где…?** gdyeh…
the horse track	**ипподром** eep·pah·_drom_
the racetrack	**автодром** ahf·tah·_drom_
the stadium	**стадион** stah·dee·_on_
Where can I place a bet?	**Где я могу сделать ставку?** gdyeh yah mah·_goo zdyeh_·laht' _stahf_·koo

---

The most popular sports in Russia are ice hockey, skiing and skating in winter, and soccer, volleyball and horseback riding in summer. Water sports, especially swimming, are very popular all year round, as are hunting and fishing.

A turkish-style public bath (**баня** _bah_·nyah) is a very popular form of relaxation and a fun way to meet people.

Playing Sport

Where's…?	**Где…?**	_gdyeh_…
the golf course	**поле для гольфа**	_poh•lyeh dlyah gol'•fah_
the gym	**спортзал**	_sport•zahl_
the park	**парк**	_pahrk_
the tennis courts	**теннисные корты**	_teh•nees•nih•yeh kor•tih_
How much…?	**Сколько стоит…?**	_skohl'•kah stoh•eet_…
per day	**в день**	_v dyen'_
per hour	**в час**	_f chahs_
per game	**за игру**	_zah eeg•roo_
per round	**за круг**	_zah krook_
Can I hire…?	**Я могу взять напрокат…?**	_yah mah•goo vzyaht' nah•prah•kaht_…
golf clubs	**клюшки для гольфа**	_klyoosh•kee dlyah gohl'•fah_
equipment	**снаряжение**	_snah•ree•zheh•nee•yeh_
a racket	**ракетку**	_rah•kyet•koo_

At the Beach/Pool

Where's the beach/pool?	**Где пляж/бассейн?** gdyeh plyahsh/bah·<u>seyn</u>
Is there…?	**Здесь есть…?** zdyes' yest'…
a kiddie pool	**детский бассейн** <u>dyets</u>·keey bah·<u>seyn</u>
an indoor/ outdoor pool	**закрытый/открытый бассейн** zah·<u>krih</u>·tiy/aht·<u>krih</u>·tiy bah·<u>seyn</u>
a lifeguard	**спасатель** spah·<u>sah</u>·teel'
Is it safe…?	**Здесь не опасно…?** zdyes' nee ah·<u>pahs</u>·nah…
to swim	**плавать** <u>plah</u>·vaht'
to dive	**нырять** nih·<u>ryat'</u>
for children	**для детей** dlyah dee·<u>tyey</u>
I want to hire…	**Я хочу взять напрокат…** yah khah·<u>choo</u> vzyat' nah·prah·<u>kaht</u>…
a deck chair	**шезлонг** shez·<u>lonk</u>
diving equipment	**водолазное снаряжение** voh·doh·<u>lahz</u>·noh·ye snah·rya·<u>zheh</u>·nee·ye
a jet-ski	**водный мотоцикл** <u>vod</u>·niy mah·tah·<u>tsihkl</u>
a motorboat	**моторную лодку** mah·<u>tor</u>·noo·yoo <u>lot</u>·koo
a rowboat	**лодку** <u>lot</u>·koo
snorkeling equipment	**сняряжение для подводного плавания** snah·rya·<u>zheh</u>·nee·ye dlya pohd·<u>vohd</u>·navah <u>plah</u>·vahn'ya
I want to hire…	**Я хочу взять напрокат…** yah khah choo vzyat' nah prah kaht…
a surfboard	**доску для серфинга** dahs·<u>koo</u> dlyah <u>ser</u>·feen·gah
a towel	**полотенце** pah·lah·<u>tyen</u>·tseh
an umbrella	**зонт** zont
water skis	**водные лыжи** <u>vod</u>·nih·yeh <u>lih</u>·zhih
a windsurfer	**виндсерфер** vind·<u>syer</u>·fehr

For Traveling with Children, see page 136.

Although the Russian summer is short, it can be hot. During the warmer months, Russians head to local lakes and rivers to swim or to a number of popular resorts on the Black Sea. The tourist infrastructure that went into decline after the fall of the Soviet Union is gradually being updated and the Black Sea coast is becoming an appealing international vacation destination, especially the town of Sochi, host of the 2014 Winter Olympics.

Winter Sports

A lift pass for a day/five days, please.	**Абонемент на подъемник на день/пять дней, пожалуйста.** ah·bah·nee·<u>ment</u> nah pahd'·<u>yom</u>·neek nah dyen'/pyat' dnyey pah·<u>zhahl</u>·stah
I want to hire…	**Я хотел *m* /хотела *f* бы взять напрокат… yah** khah·<u>tyel</u>/khah·tyeh·<u>lah</u> bih vzyat' nah·prah·<u>kaht</u>…
boots	**лыжные ботинки** <u>lihzh</u>·nih·ee bah·<u>teen</u>·kee
a helmet	**шлем** shlyem
poles	**лыжные палки** <u>lihzh</u>·nih·ee <u>pahl</u>·kee
skis	**лыжи** <u>lih</u>·zhih
a snowboard	**сноуборд** <u>snoh</u>·oo·bort
snowshoes	**снегоступы** snee·gah·<u>stoo</u>·pih
These are too big/small.	**Это слишком велико/мало.** <u>eh</u>·tah <u>sleesh</u>·kahm vee·lee·<u>koh</u>/mah·<u>loh</u>
Are there lessons?	**Есть уроки?** yest' oo·<u>roh</u>·kee
I'm a beginner.	**Я новичок.** ya noh·vee·<u>chohck</u>
I'm experienced.	**Я опытный лыжник.** yah <u>oh</u>·piht·niy <u>lizh</u>·neek
A trail [piste] map, please.	**Схему трассы, пожалуйста.** <u>skhyeh</u>·moo <u>trah</u>·sih pah·<u>zhahl</u>·stah

Skiing, particularly cross-country, is a popular sport in Russia. Moscow even has two downhill ski slopes, one in Krylatskoye and one in Bitsevsky Park. Adventurous tourists can find guided skiing adventures in remote areas of the taiga, while others can rent skis in city parks, such as Moscow's Sokolniki and Bitsevsky. Skating is also very popular. There are ice rinks in large parks and squares. Russians also enjoy traditional horse-drawn sleighs.

YOU MAY SEE...

ПОДЪЁМНИК phad·yom·neek	drag lift
ВАГОН ПОДВЕСНОЙ ДОРОГИ vah·gon pahd·vees·noy dah·roh·gee	cable car
ПОДВЕСНОЙ ПОДЪЁМНИК pahd·vees·noy phad·yom·neek	chair lift
ДЛЯ НАЧИНАЮЩИХ dlyah nah·chee·nah·yoo·shcheekh	novice
ДЛЯ ОПЫТНЫХ dlyah oh·piht·nihkh	intermediate
ДЛЯ МАСТЕРОВ dlyah mahs·tee·rof	expert
ТРАССА ЗАКРЫТА trah·sah zah·krih·tah	trail [piste] closed

Out in the Country

I'd like a map of...	**Я хотел** m **/хотела** f **бы карту...** yah khah·tyel/khah·tyeh·lah bih kahr·too...
this region	**этого района** eh·tah·vah rah·yoh·nah
the walking routes	**пешеходных маршрутов** pee·shee·khod·nihkh mahrsh·roo·tahf

the bike routes	**велосипедных маршрутов**
	vee·lah·see·pyed·nihkh mahrsh·roo·tahf
the trails	**трасс** *trahs*
Is it easy/difficult?	**Он легкий/сложный?** *on lyokh·keey/slozh·niy*
Is it far/steep?	**Он длинный/крутой?** *on dleen·niy/kroo·toy*
How far is it to…?	**Какое расстояние до…?** *kah·koh·yeh*
	rah·stah·yah·nee·yeh dah…
Can you show me	**Можете показать мне на карте?** *moh·zhih·tee*
on the map?	*pah·kah·zaht' mnyeh nah kahr·tyeh*
I'm lost.	**Я заблудился** *m* **/заблудилась** *f* **.** *yah*
	zah·bloo·deel·syah/zah·bloo·dee·lahs'
Where's…?	**Где…?** *gdyeh…*
the bridge	**мост** *most*
the cave	**пещера** *pee·shchyeh·rah*
the cliff	**обрыв** *ah·brihf*
the farm	**ферма** *fyer·mah*
the field	**поле** *poh·leh*
the forest	**лес** *lyes*
the hill	**холм** *khohlm*
the lake	**озеро** *oh·zee·rah*
the mountain	**гора** *gah·rah*
the nature preserve	**заповедник** *zah·pah·vyed·neek*
the overlook	**смотровая площадка** *smah·trah·vah·yah*
	plah·shchaht·kah
the park	**парк** *pahrk*
the path	**тропинка** *trah·peen·kah*
the peak	**пик** *peek*
the picnic area	**площадка для пикника** *plah·shchaht·kah*
	dlyah peek·nee·kah
the pond	**пруд** *prood*
the river	**река** *ree·kah*

the sea	**море** _moh_·ryeh
the thermal spring	**минеральный источник** mee·nee·_rahl'_·nihy ees·_toch_·neek
the stream	**течение** tye·_chye_·nyeh
the valley	**долина** dah·_lee_·nah
the vineyard	**виноградник** vee·noh·_grahd_·nik
the waterfall	**водопад** vah·dah·_paht_

Going Out

ESSENTIAL

What is there to do in the evenings?	**Что здесь можно делать по вечерам?** shtoh zdyehs' _mozh_·nah _dyeh_·laht' pah vee·chee·_rahm_
Do you have a program of events?	**У Вас есть программа мероприятий?** oo vahs yehst' prah·_grah_·mah mee·rah·pree·_yah_·teey
What's playing at the movies [cinema] tonight?	**Что идёт в кинотеатре сегодня вечером?** shtoh ee·_dyot_ f kee·nah·tee·_aht_·ree see·_vohd_·nyah _vyeh_·chee·rahm
Where's…?	**Где…?** gdyeh…
the downtown area	**центр города** tsehntr _goh_·rah·dah
the bar	**бар** bahr
the dance club	**дискотека** dees·kah·_tyeh_·kah
Is there a cover charge?	**Нужно платить за вход?** _noozh_·nah plah·_teet'_ zah fkhot

Most Russian restaurants have traditionally featured music and dancing, and Russians are less shy than others about getting out of their chairs and letting loose. Women do not wait for an invitation; it is not uncommon to see women dancing together or friends dancing as a group.

Moscow and St. Petersburg are developing solid reputations among young jet-setters as first-class party cities with a number of exclusive nightclubs. Many nightclubs and dance clubs are located in popular hotels and casinos.

Entertainment

Can you recommend...?	**Вы можете порекомендовать...?** *vih moh·zhih·tee pah·ree·kah·meen·dah·vaht'...*
a concert	**концерт** *kahn·tsert*
a movie	**фильм** *feel'm*
an opera	**оперу** *oh·pee·roo*
a play	**пьесу** *pyeh·soo*

When does it start/end?	**Когда начинается/заканчивается?** *kahg·dah nah·chee·nah·ee·tsah/ zah·kahn·chee·vah·ee·tsah*
What's the dress code?	**Какая форма одежды?** *kah·kah·yah for·mah ah·dyezh·dih*
I like...	**Я люблю...** *yah lyoob·lyoo...*
classical music	**классическую музыку** *klah·see·chees·koo·yoo moo·zih·koo*
folk music	**народную музыку** *nah·rod·noo·yoo moo·zih·koo*
jazz	**джаз** *dzhahs*
pop music	**поп-музыку** *pop·moo·zih·koo*
rap	**рэп** *rep*

For Tickets, see page 18.

There is extensive English-language information available on the internet about the schedules of performances at the Bolshoi Theater in Moscow and the Mariinsky Theater in St. Petersburg. Both theaters offer free courier service that can deliver tickets to your hotel or apartment.

YOU MAY HEAR...

Выключите Ваши мобильные телефоны, пожалуйста. *vih·klyoo·chee·tee vah·shee mah·beel'·nih·ee tee·lee·foh·nih pah·zhahl·stah*

Turn off your cell [mobile] phones, please

Nightlife

What is there to do in the evenings?	**Что здесь можно делать по вечерам?** *shtoh zdyehs' mozh·nah dyeh·laht' pah vee·chee·rahm*
Can you recommend...?	**Вы можете порекомендовать...?** *vih moh·zhih·tee pah·ree·kah·meen·dah·vaht'...*
a bar	**бар** *bahr*
a cabaret	**ресторан с эстрадным выступлением** *reh·stah·rahn s ehst·rahd·nihm vihs·toop·lehnyehm*
a casino	**казино** *kah·zee·noh*
a dance club	**дискотеку** *dees·kah·tyeh·koo*
a gay club	**гейклуб** *gyey·kloop*
a jazz club	**джазовый клуб** *dzhah·zoh·viy kloob*
a club with Russian music	**клуб с русской музыкой** *kloob s roos·koy moo·zih·koy*
a nightclub	**ночной клуб** *nahch·noy kloop*
Is there live music?	**Там есть живая музыка?** *tahm yest' zhih·vah·yah moo·zih·kah*
How do I get there?	**Как туда добраться?** *kahk too·dah dah·brah·tsah*
Is there a cover charge?	**Нужно платить за вход?** *noozh·nah plah·teet' zah fkhot*
Let's go dancing.	**Пойдём танцевать.** *pie·dyom tahn·tsih·vaht'*
Is this area safe at night?	**В этом районе ночью безопасно?** *v etohm rah·yoh·neh nohch'·yu beh·zoh·pahs·noh*

Special Requirements

Business Travel

ESSENTIAL

I'm here on business.	**Я здесь по делам.** yah zdyehs' pah dee-_lahm_
Here's my business card.	**Вот моя визитка.** voht mah-_yah_ vee-_zeet_-kah
Can I have your card?	**Можно Вашу визитку?** _mozh_-nah _vah_-shoo vee-_zeet_-koo
I have a meeting with…	**У меня встреча с…** oo mee-_nyah_ _fstreh_-chah s…
Where's…?	**Где…?** gdyeh…
the business center	**бизнес-центр** _beez_-nehs tsehntr
the convention hall	**конференц-зал** kahn-fee-_ryehnts_ zahl
the meeting room	**комната для встреч** _kohm_-nah-tah dlyah fstrehch

On Business

I'm here to attend…	**Я приехал** m /**приехала** f **на…** yah pree-_yeh_-khahl/pree-_yeh_-khah-lah nah…
a seminar	**семинар** see-mee-_nahr_
a conference	**конференцию** kahn-fee-_ryen_-tsih-yoo
a meeting	**деловую встречу** dee-lah-_voo_-yoo _fstreh_-choo
My name is…	**Меня зовут…** mee-_nyah_ zah-_voot_…
May I introduce my colleague…	**Разрешите представить моего** m /**мою** f **коллегу…** rahz-ree-_shih_-tee preet-_stah_-veet' mah-ee-_voh_/mah-_yoo_ kah-_lyeh_-goo…
Pleasure to meet you.	**Был рад** m /**Была рада** f **встретиться с вами.** bihl rahd/bih-_lah_ _rah_-dah _fstryeh_-tee-tsah s _vah_-mee
I'm sorry I'm late.	**Извините за опоздание.** eez-vee-_nee_-tee zah ah-pahz-_dah_-nee-yeh

I have a meeting/an appointment with …	**У меня встреча с…** *oo meh•nya vstreh•chah s*
I need an interpreter.	**Мне нужен переводчик.** *mnyeh noo•zhihn pee•ree•vot•cheek*
You can reach me at the…Hotel.	**Вы можете найти меня в гостинице…** *vih moh•zhih•tee nie•tee mee•nyah v gahs•tee•nee•tseh…*
I'm here until…	**Я буду здесь до…** *yah boo•doo zdyes' dah…*
I need to…	**Мне нужно… mnyeh noozh•nah…**
make a call	**позвонить** *pah•zvah•neet'*
make a photocopy	**сделать копию** *zdyeh•laht' koh•pee•yoo*
send an e-mail	**послать электронное сообщение** *pah•slaht' ee•leek•tron•nah•yeh sah•ahp•shcheh•nee•yeh*
send a fax	**послать факс** *pah•slaht' fahks*
send a package (overnight)	**отправить (срочную) посылку** *aht•prah•veet' (sroch•noo•yoo) pah•sihl•koo*
It was a pleasure to meet you.	**Был рад m/Была рада f встретиться с вами.** *bihl rahd/bih•lah rah•dah fstryeh•tee•tsah s vah•mee*

For Communications, see page 50.

Russian business interactions are generally curt and matter-of-fact, without niceties such as 'at your earliest convenience' or 'please feel free to.' As a result, when translated literally, Russian business conversations can sound rude and demanding. Keep in mind that cultural differences like these may lead to unnecessary misunderstandings.

YOU MAY HEAR...

У Вас назначена встреча? *oo vahs nahz·nah·chee·nah fstreh·chah*

Do you have an appointment?

С кем? *s kyem*

With whom?

Он/Она на встрече. *on/ah·nah nah fstreh·cheh*

He/She is in a meeting.

Одну минуту, пожалуйста. *ahd·noo mee·noo·too pah·zhahl·stah*

One moment, please.

Присаживайтесь. *pree·sah·zhih·vie·tees'*

Have a seat.

Не желаете что-нибудь выпить? *nee zhih·lah·ee·tee shtoh·nee·boot' vih·peet'*

Would you like something to drink?

Спасибо за визит. *spah·see·bah zah vee·zeet*

Thank you for coming.

Traveling with Children

ESSENTIAL

Is there a discount for children?

Есть скидка для детей? *yest' skeet·kah dlyah dee·tyey*

Can you recommend a babysitter?

Вы можете порекомендовать няню? *vih moh·zhih·tee pah·ree·kah·men·dah·vaht' nyah·nyoo*

Could we have a child's seat/ highchair?

Можно детский/высокий стульчик? *mozh·nah dyets·keey/vih·soh·keey stool'·cheek*

Where can I change the baby?

Где можно переодеть ребёнка? *gdyeh mozh·nah pee·ree·ah·dyet' ree·byon·kah*

Out & About

Can you recommend something for the kids?	**Можете порекомендовать что-нибудь для детей?** _moh_-zhih-tee pah-ree-kah-meen-dah-_vaht'_ shtoh-nee-boot' dlyah dee-_tyey_
Where's...?	**Где...?** _gdyeh_...
the amusement park	**парк с аттракционами** pahrk s aht-rahk-tsih-_oh_-nah-mee
the arcade	**зал аттракционов** zahl aht-rahk-tsih-_oh_-nahf
the kiddie pool	**детский бассейн** _dyets_-keey bah-_seyn_
the park	**парк** pahrk
the playground	**детская площадка** _dyets_-kah-yah plah-_shchaht_-kah
the zoo	**зоопарк** zah-ah-_pahrk_
Are kids allowed?	**Детям можно?** _dyeh_-tyam _mozh_-nah
Is it safe for kids?	**Здесь неопасно для детей?** zdyes' nee-ah-_pahs_-nah dlyah dee-_tyey_
Is it suitable for...year olds?	**Это подходит для...летних?** _eh_-tah paht-_khoh_-deet dlyah..._let_-neekh

For Numbers, see page 157.

Baby Essentials

Do you have...?	**У Вас есть...?** oo vahs yest'...
a baby bottle	**детская бутылочка** _dyets_-kah-yah boo-_tih_-lahch-kah
baby food	**детское питание** _deht_-skoh-ye pee-_tah_- nee-yeh
baby wipes	**гигиенические салфетки** gee-gee-ee-_nee_-chees-kee-yeh sahl-_fyet_-kee
a car seat	**детское сиденье** _dyets_-kah-yeh see-_dyen'_-yeh
a children's menu/portion	**меню/порции для детей** mee-_nyoo_/ _por_-tsih-ee dlyah dee-_tyey_

a child's seat/ highchair	**детский/высокий стульчик** _dyets_•keey/ vih•soh•keey _stool_•cheek
a crib/cot	**колыбель/детская кроватка** kah•lih•_byel_'/ _dyets_•kah•yah krah•_vaht_•kah
diapers [nappies]	**подгузники** pahd•_gooz_•nee•kee
formula	**молочная смесь** mah•_loch_•nah•yah smyes'
a pacifier [dummy]	**соска** _sos_•kah
a playpen	**манеж** mah•_nyesh_
a stroller [pushchair]	**прогулочная коляска** prah•_goo_•lahch•nah•yah kah•_lyas_•kah
Can I breastfeed the baby here?	**Я могу здесь покормить грудью ребёнка?** yah mah•_goo_ zdyes' pah•kahr•_meet_ _grood_'•yoo ree•_byon_•kah
Where can I breastfeed/ change the baby?	**Где можно покормить/переодеть ребёнка?** gdyeh _mozh_•nah pah•kahr•_meet_'/pee•ree•ah•_dyet_' ree•_byon_•kah

For Dining with Children, see page 66.

YOU MAY HEAR...

Какой хорошенький! _m_ **/Какая хорошенькая** _f_**!** kah•_koy_ khah•_roh_•shen'•keey/ kah•_kah_•yah khah•_roh_•shihn'•kah•yah	How cute!
Как его/её зовут? kak yee•_voh_/yee•_yoh_ zah•_voot_	What's his/her name?
Сколько ему/ей лет? _skol_'•kah ee•moo/ yey lyet	How old is he/she?

Babysitting

Can you recommend a babysitter?	**Вы можете порекомендовать няню?** *vih moh·zhih·tee pah·ree·kah·meen·dah·vaht' nyah·nyoo*
What's the charge?	**Сколько стоит?** *skol'·kah stoh·eet*
We'll be back by...	**Мы вернёмся к...** *mih veer·nyom·syah k...*
I can be reached at...	**Со мной можно связаться...** *sah mnoy mozh·nah svee·zah·tsah...*

For Time, see page 159.

Health & Emergency

Can you recommend a pediatrician?	**Можете порекомендовать педиатра?** *moh·zhih·tee pah·ree·kah·meen·dah·vaht' pee·dee·aht·rah*
My child is allergic to...	**У моего ребёнка аллергия на...** *oo mah·ee·voh ree·byon·kah ah·leer·gee·yah nah...*
My child is missing.	**У меня пропал ребёнок.** *oo mee·nyah prah·pahl ree·byoh·nahk*
Have you seen a boy/girl?	**Вы видели мальчика/девочку?** *vih vee·dee·lee mahl'·chee·kah/dyeh·vahch·koo*

For Meals & Cooking, see page 68.

For Health, see page 145.

For Police, see page 143.

Disabled Travelers

ESSENTIAL

Is there...?	**Есть...?** *yest'...*
access for the disabled	**условия для инвалидов** *oos·loh·vee·yah dlyah een·vah·lee·dahf*

a wheelchair ramp	**пандус для инвалидного кресла** _pahn·doos dlyah een·vah·leed·nah·vah kryes·lah_
a disabled-accessible toilet	**туалет с условиями для инвалидов** _too·ah·lyet s oos·loh·vee·yah·mee dlyaheen·vah·lee·dahf_
I need assistance.	**Мне нужна помощь.** _mnyeh noozh·nah poh·mahshch_
I need an elevator [lift].	**Мне нужен лифт.** _mnyeh noo·zhehn left_
I need a ground-floor room.	**Мне нужен номер на первом этаже.** _mnyeh noo·zhehn noh·meer nah pyer·vahm eh·tah·zheh_

Asking for Assistance

I'm disabled.	**Я инвалид.** _yah een·vah·leet_
I'm deaf.	**Я глухой m /глухая f.** _yah gloo·khoy/ gloo·khah·yah_
I'm visually/hearing impaired.	**У меня плохое зрение/слух.** _oo mee·nyah plah·khoh·yeh zryeh·nee·yeh/slookh_
I'm unable to walk far/use the stairs.	**Я не могу ходить далеко/пользоваться лестницей.** _yah nee mah·goo khah·deet' dah·lee·koh/pol'·zah·vah·tsah lyes·nee·tsey_
Can I bring my wheelchair?	**Я могу привезти своё инвалидное кресло?** _yah mah·goo pree·vees·tee svah·yoh een·vah·leed·nah·yeh kres·lah_
Are guide dogs permitted?	**Сюда допускаются собаки-поводыри?** _syoo·dah dah·poos·kah·yoo·tsah sah·bah·kee pah·vah·dih·ree_
Help me, please.	**Помогите мне, пожалуйста.** _pah·mah·gee·tee mnyeh pah·zhahl·stah_
Please open/hold the door.	**Пожалуйста, откройте/придержите дверь.** _pah·zhahl·stah aht·kroy·tee/pree·deer·zhih·tee dvyer'_

In an Emergency

Emergencies

ESSENTIAL

Help!	**Помогите!** *pah·mah·<u>gee</u>·tee*
Go away!	**Идите отсюда!** *ee·<u>dee</u>·tee aht·<u>syoo</u>·dah*
Stop, thief!	**Держите вора!** *deer·<u>zhih</u>·tee <u>voh</u>·rah*
Get a doctor!	**Вызовите врача!** *<u>vih</u>·zah·vee·tee vrah·<u>chah</u>*
Fire!	**Пожар!** *pah·<u>zhahr</u>*
I'm lost.	**Я заблудился** *m* **/заблудилась** *f.* *yah zah·bloo·<u>deel</u>·syah/zah·bloo·<u>dee</u>·lahs'*
Help me, please.	**Помогите мне, пожалуйста.** *pah·mah·<u>gee</u>·tee mnyeh pah·<u>zhahl</u>·stah*

In an emergency, dial: **02** for the police
01 for the fire brigade
03 for the ambulance

YOU MAY HEAR...

Заполните бланк. *zah·<u>pol</u>·nee·tyeh blahnk*
Please fill out this form.

Ваши документы, пожалуйста. *<u>vah</u>·shih dah·koo·<u>myen</u>·tih pah·<u>zhahl</u>·stah*
Your identification, please.

Где/Когда это произошло? *gdyeh/kahg·<u>dah</u> eh·tah prah·ee·zah·<u>shloh</u>*
When/Where did it happen?

Как он/она выглядит? *kahk on/ah·<u>nah</u> vih·glyah·deet*
What does he/she look like?

Police

ESSENTIAL

Call the police!	**Вызовите милицию!** *vih-zah-vee-tee mee-lee-tsih-yoo*
Where's the police station?	**Где отделение милиции?** *gdyeh aht-dee-lyeh-nee-yeh mee-lee-tsih-ee*
There has been an accident.	**Произошла авария.** *prah-ee-zah-shlah ah-vah-ree-yah*
My child is missing.	**У меня пропал ребёнок.** *oo mee-nyah prah-pahl ree-byoh-nahk*
I need an interpreter.	**Мне нужен переводчик.** *mnyeh noo-zhehn pee-ree-vot-cheek*
I need to contact my lawyer.	**Мне нужно связаться с моим адвокатом.** *mnyeh noozh-nah svyah-zah-tsah s mah-eem ahd-vah-kah-tahm*
I need to make a phone call.	**Мне нужно позвонить.** *mnyeh noozh-nah pah-zvah-neet'*
I'm innocent.	**Я невиновен.** *yah nee-vee-noh-veen*

Crime & Lost Property

I want to report...	**Я хочу заявить о...** *yah khah-chyoo zah-ee-veet' ah...*
a mugging	**ограблении** *ah-grahb-lyeh-nee-ee*
a rape	**изнасиловании** *eez-nah-see-lah-vah-nee-ee*
a theft	**краже** *krah-zheh*
I've been mugged.	**Меня ограбили.** *Meh-nya oh-grah-bee-lee*
I've been robbed.	**Меня ограбили.** *mee-nyah ah-grah-bee-lee*

I've lost my…	**Я потерял *m* /потеряла *f*…** *yah pah•tee•ryahl/pah•tee•ryah•lah…*
My…has been stolen.	**У меня украли…** *oo mee•nyah oo•krah•lee…*
backpack	**рюкзак** *ryoog•zahk*
bicycle	**велосипед** *vee•lah•see•pyet*
camera	**фотоаппарат** *fah•tah•ah•pah•raht*
car	**машину** *mah•shih•noo*
computer	**компьютер** *kahm•pyoo•ter*
credit card	**кредитную карточку** *kree•deet•noo•yoo kahr•tahch•koo*
jewelry	**драгоценности** *drah•gah•tseh•nahs•tee*
money	**деньги** *dyen'•gee*
passport	**паспорт** *pahs•pahrt*
purse [handbag]	**сумочку** *soo•mach•koo*
traveler's cheques	**дорожные чеки** *dah•rozh•nih•ee cheh•kee*
wallet	**бумажник** *boo•mahzh•neek*
I need a police report.	**Мне нужно обратиться в полицию.** *mneh nuzh•noh oh•brah•tee t'•sya v poh•lee•tsih•yoo*
Where is the British/American/Irish embassy?	**Где находится британское/американское/ирландское консульство?** *gdyeh nah•khoh•deet•sya bree•tahn•sko•ye/ah•meh•ree•kahn•sko•ye/eer•lahnd•sko•ye kon•sool'•stvoh*

Health

ESSENTIAL

I'm sick [ill].	**Я заболел** *m* **/заболела** *f.* yah zah•bah•*lyel*/ zah•bah•*lyeh*•lah
I need an English-speaking doctor.	**Мне нужен англоговорящий врач.** mnyeh *noo*•zhen ahn•glah•gah•vah•*ryah*•shcheey vrahch
It hurts here.	**Мне больно вот здесь.** mnyeh *bohl'*•nah voht zdyehs'
I have a stomachache.	**У меня болит живот.** oo mee•*nyah* bah•*leet* zhih•*voht*

Finding a Doctor

Can you recommend a doctor/dentist?	**Можете порекомендовать врача/дантиста?** moh•*zhih*•tee pah•ree•kah•meen•dah•*vaht'* vrah•*chah*/dahn•*tees*•tah
Could the doctor come to see me here?	**Не мог бы врач прийти осмотреть меня здесь?** nee mog bih vrahch pree•*tee* ah•smah•*tryet'* mee•*nyah* zdyes'
I need an English-speaking doctor.	**Мне нужен англоговорящий врач.** mnyeh *noo*•zhihn ahn•glah•gah•vah•*ryah*•shcheey vrahch
What are the office hours?	**Какие часы работы?** kah•*kee*•yeh chah•*sih* rah•*boh*•tih
Can I make an appointment…?	**Можно записаться к врачу на прием…?** mozh•nah zah•pee•*sah*•tsah k vrah•*choo* nah pree•*yom*…
for today	**на сегодня** nah see•*vod*•nyah
for tomorrow	**на завтра** nah *zahf*•trah

| as soon as possible | **как можно скорее** *kahk mozh•nah skah•ryeh•yeh* |
| It's urgent. | **Это срочно.** *eh•tah sroch•nah* |

Symptoms

I'm...	**У меня...** *oo mee•nyah...*
bleeding	**кровотечение** *krah•vah•tee•cheh•nee•yeh*
constipated	**запор** *zah•por*
dizzy	**кружится голова** *kroo•zhih•tsah gah•lah•vah*
I'm nauseous/ vomiting.	**Меня подташнивает/тошнит.** *mee•nyah paht•tahsh•nee•vah•eet/tahsh•neet*
It hurts here.	**Мне больно вот здесь.** *mnyeh bohl'•nah vaht zdyes'*
I have...	**У меня...** *oo mee•nyah...*
an allergic reaction	**аллергическая реакция** *ah•leer•gee•chees•kah•yah ree•ahk•tsih•yah*
a chest pain	**боли в груди** *boh•lee v groo•dee*
cramps	**спазмы** *spah•zmih*
diarrhea	**понос** *pah•nohs*
an earache	**болит ухо** *bah•leet oo•khah*
a fever	**жар** *zhahr*
pain	**боли** *boh•lee*
a rash	**сыпь** *sihp'*
a sprain	**растяжение** *rahs•tee•zheh•nee•yeh*
some swelling	**опухоль** *oh•poo•khahl'*
a sore throat	**болит горло** *boh•leet gohr•loh*
a stomachache	**болит живот** *bah•leet zhih•voht*
sunstroke	**солнечный удар** *sol•neech•niy oo•dahr*
I've been sick [ill] for...days.	**Я болею...дней.** *yah bah•lyeh•yoo...dnyey*

For Numbers, see page 157.

Conditions

I'm...	**У меня...** *oo mee·nyah...*
anemic	**анемия** *ah·nee·mee·yah*
asthmatic	**астма** *ahst·mah*
diabetic	**диабет** *dee·ah·byet*
epileptic	**эпилепсия** *ehpee·lehp·see·ya*

I'm allergic to antibiotics/ penicillin.
У меня аллергия на антибиотики/ пенициллин. *oo mee·nyah ah·leer·gee·yah nah ahn·tee·bee·oh·tee·kee/pee·nee·tsih·leen*

I have arthritis/ high/low blood pressure.
У меня артрит/высокое/низкое давление. *oo mee·nyah ahrt·reet/ vih·soh·kah·ye/nees·kah·yeh dahv·lyeh·nee·yeh*

I have a heart condition.
У меня больное сердце. *oo mee·nyah bahl'·noh·yeh ser·tseh*

I'm on...
Я принимаю... *yah pree·nee·mah·yoo...*

For Meals & Cooking, see page 68.

YOU MAY HEAR...

Что случилось? *shtoh sloo·chee·lahs'*	What's wrong?
Где болит? *gdyeh bah·leet*	Where does it hurt?
Вы принимаете другое лекарство? *vih pree·nee·mah·ee·tee droo·goh·yeh lee·kahr·stvah*	Are you taking any other medication?
Аллергия на что-нибудь? *ah·leer·gee·yah nah shtoh·nee·boot'*	Are you allergic to anything?
Откройте рот. *aht·kroy·tee rot*	Open your mouth.
Дышите глубоко. *dih·shih·tee gloo·bah·koh*	Breathe deeply.
Покашляйте. *poh·kahsch·lyai·tye*	Cough, please.
Обратитесь в больницу. *obh·rah·tee·tehs' v bohl'·nee·tsoo*	Go to the hospital.

Treatment

Do I need a prescription/medicine?	**У меня нет рецепта/лекарства?** *oo meh·nya neht reh·tsehp·tah/leh·kahr·stvah*
Can you prescribe a generic drug [unbranded medication]?	**Вы можете прописать непатентованный препарат [без марочного названия]?** *vih moh·zheh·teh proh·pee·saht' neh·pah·tehn·toh·vah·niy preh·pah·raht [bez naz vah neeya]*
Where can I get it?	**Где можно его приобрести?** *gdyeh mozh·noh ye·voh pree·ohb·rehs·tee*

For Pharmacy, see page 150.

Hospital

Please notify my family.	**Пожалуйста, сообщите моей семье.** *pah·zhahl·stah sah·ahb·shchee·tee mah·yey seem'·yeh*
I'm in pain.	**У меня боли.** *oo mee·nyah boh·lee*
I need a doctor/ nurse.	**Мне нужен врач/нужна медсестра.** *mnyeh noo·zhihn vrahch/noozh·nah myet·sees·trah*
When are visiting hours?	**Когда часы посещений?** *kahg·dah chah·sih pah·see·shcheh·neey*
I'm visiting…	**Я навещаю…** *yah nah·vee·shchah·yoo…*

Dentist

I've broken a tooth/ lost a filling.	**У меня сломался зуб/выпала пломба.** *oo mee·nyah slah·mahl·syah zoop/vih·pah·lah plom·bah*
I have a toothache.	**У меня болит зуб.** *oo mee·nyah bah·leet zoop*
Can you fix this denture?	**Вы можете починить этот протез?** *vih moh·zhih·tee pah·chee·neet' eh·taht prah·tes*

Gynecologist

I have menstrual cramps/a vaginal infection.	**У меня менструальные колики/ вагинальная инфекция.** *oo mee-nyah meen-stroo-ahl'-nih-ee koh-lee-kee/ vah-gee-nahl'-nah-yah een-fyek-tsih-yah*
I missed my period.	**У меня не было менструации.** *oo mee-nyah nyeh-bih-lah meen-stroo-ah-tsih-ee*
I'm on the Pill.	**Я принимаю противозачаточные таблетки.** *yah pree-nee-mah-yoo prah-tee-vah-zah-chah-tahch-nih-ee tahb-lyet-kee*
I'm (...months) pregnant.	**Я беременна (на...месяце).** *ya beh-reh-meh-nah (nah ... meh-sya-tse)*
I'm (not) pregnant.	**Я (не) беременна.** *yah (nee) bee-ryeh-mee-nah*
I haven't had my period for...months.	**У меня нет менструации уже...месяца.** *oo mee-nyah nyet meen-stroo-ah-tsih-ee oo-zheh...myeh-see-tsah*

For Numbers, see page 157.

Optician

I've lost...	**Я потерял m /потеряла f...** *yah pah-tee-ryahl/pah-tee-ryah-lah...*
a contact lens	**контактную линзу** *kahn-tahkt-noo-yoo leen-zoo*
my glasses	**мои очки** *mah-ee ahch-kee*
a lens	**линзу** *leen-zoo*

Payment & Insurance

How much?	**Сколько?** *skol'-kah*
Can I pay by credit card?	**Можно платить кредитной карточкой?** *mozh-nah plah-teet' kree-deet-nie kahr-tahch-kie*
I have insurance.	**У меня есть страховка.** *oo mee-nyah yest' strah-khof-kah*

Can I have a receipt for my insurance? **Можете дать мне квитанцию для моей страховки?** *moh·zhih·tee daht' mnyeh kvee·tahn·tsih·yoo dlyah mah·yey strah·khof·kee*

Pharmacy

ESSENTIAL

Where's the nearest pharmacy? **Где ближайшая аптека?** *gdyeh blee·zhie·shah·yah ahp·tyeh·kah*

What time does it open/close? **Во сколько аптека открывается/ закрывается?** *vah skol'·kah ahp·tyeh·kah aht·krih·vah·ee·tsah/zah·krih·vah·ee·tsah*

What would you recommend for…? **Что порекомендуете от…?** *shtoh pah·ree·kah·meen·doo·ee·tee aht…*

How much should I take? **Сколько нужно принимать?** *skol'·kah noozh·nah pree·nee·maht'*

Can you fill [make up] this prescription for me? **Вы можете приготовить это лекарство?** *vih moh·zhih·tee pree·gah·toh·veet' eh·tah lee·kahr·stvah*

I'm allergic to… **У меня аллергия на…** *oo mee·nyah ah·leer·gee·yah nah…*

In Russia, a wide range of medication is available without a prescription. **Аптека** ahp·*tyeh*·kah (a pharmacy) in Russia's larger cities is likely to carry many brand-name medications. Drugs are also available from kiosks, but it is best to obtain them from a pharmacy or private clinics and hospitals, such as the American Clinic in Moscow or the American Medical Center in St. Petersburg. As a foreigner, you will have to pay for treatment in state-run hospitals. Russian doctors in these facilities are not well paid, and it is customary to give them something to express your gratitude for their care, a box of chocolates or a bottle of wine, for example. Before leaving home, be sure that your insurance coverage is valid for treatment in Russia.

What to Take

How much do I take?	**Какая дозировка?** kah·*kah*·ya doh·zee·*rohv*·kah
How often?	**Как часто?** kahk *chahs*·tah
Is it suitable for children?	**Это можно детям?** *eh*·tah *mozh*·nah *dyeh*·tyahm
I'm taking...	**Я принимаю...** yah pree·nee·*mah*·yoo...
Are there side effects?	**Есть побочные эффекты?** yest' pah·*boch*·nih·ee ee·*fyek*·tih
I'd like some medicine for...	**Мне нужно лекарство от...** mnyeh *noozh*·nah lee·*kahrs*·tvah aht...
a cold	**простуды** prah·*stoo*·dih
a cough	**кашля** *kahsh*·lyah
diarrhea	**поноса** pah·*noh*·sah
a headache	**головной боли** goh·lohv·*noi boh*·lee
insect bites	**укусов насекомых** oo·*koo*·sahf nah·see·*koh*·mihkh
motion [travel] sickness	**морской болезни** mahr·*skoy* bah·*lyez*·nee

a sore throat	**воспаления горла** vahs•pah•_lyeh_•nee•yah _gor_•lah	
sunburn	**солнечного ожёга** _sol_•neech•nah•vah ah•_zhoh_•gah	
a toothache	**зубной боли** zoob•_noi_ _boh_•lee	
an upset stomach	**расстройства желудка** rahs•_troy_•stvah zhih•_loot_•kah	

YOU MAY SEE...

ОДИН/ТРИ РАЗА В ДЕНЬ ah•_deen_/tree _rah_•zah v dyen'	once/three times a day
ТАБЛЕТКИ tahb•_lyet_•kee	tablets
КАПЛИ _kahp_•lee	drops
ДО/ПОСЛЕ/ВО ВРЕМЯ ЕДЫ doh/_pos_•lee/ vah _vryeh_•myah yeh•_dih_	before/after/with meals
НА ПУСТОЙ ЖЕЛУДОК (НАТОЩАК) nah poos•_toy_ zhih•_loo_•dahk (nah•tah•_shchahk_)	on an empty stomach
ТОЛЬКО ДЛЯ НАРУЖНОГО ПРИМЕНЕНИЯ _tol'_•kah dlyah nah•_roozh_•nah•vah pree•mee•_nyeh_•nee•yah	for external use only

Basic Supplies

I'd like...	**Я хотел** m **/хотела** f **бы...** yah khah•_tyel_/ khah•_tyeh_•lah bih...	
acetaminophen [paracetamol]	**парацетамол** pah•rah•tsih•tah•_mol_	
antiseptic cream	**антисептическую мазь** ahn•tee•sep•_tee_•chees•koo•yoo mahz'	
aspirin	**аспирин** ahs•pee•_reen_	
bandages [plasters]	**пластырь** _plahs_•tihr'	
a comb	**расчёску** rah•_shchos_•koo	

I'd like…	**Я хотел *m* /хотела *f* бы…** *yah khah-tyel/ khah-tyeh-lah bih…*
condoms	**презервативы** *pree-zeer-vah-tee-vih*
contact lens	**раствор для контактных линз** *rahst-vor*
solution	*dlyah kahn-tahkt-nihkh leens*
deodorant	**дезодорант** *dee-zah-dah-rahnt*
a hairbrush	**щётку для волос** *shchot-koo dlyah vah-los*
hair spray	**лак для волос** *lahk dlyah vah-los*
ibuprofen	**ибупрофен** *ee-boo-prah-fyen*
insect repellent	**репеллент** *ree-pee-lyent*
lotion	**лосьон** *lohs' yohn*
a nail file	**пилочку для ногтей** *pee-lahch-koo dlyah nahk-tyey*
a (disposable) razor	**(одноразовую) бритву** *(ahd-nah-rah-zah-voo-yoo) breet-voo*
razor blades	**лезвия** *lyez-vee-yah*
sanitary napkins [towels]	**гигиенические салфетки** *gee-gee-ee-nee-chees-kee-yeh sahl-fyet-kee*
shampoo/ conditioner	**шампунь/кондиционер** *shahm-poon'/ kahn-dee-tsih-ah-nyer*
soap	**мыло** *mih-lah*
sunscreen	**крем для загара** *kryem dlyah zah-gah-rah*
tampons	**тампоны** *tahm-poh-nih*
tissues	**бумажные салфетки** *boo-mahzh-nih-ee sahl-fet-kee*
toilet paper	**туалетную бумагу** *too-ah-lyet-noo-yoo boo-mah-goo*
a toothbrush	**зубную щетку** *zoob-noo-yoo shchot-koo*
toothpaste	**зубную пасту** *zoob-noo-yoo pahs-too*

For Baby Essentials, see page 137.

The Basics

Grammar

Verbs

The infinitive of most verbs ends in **–ть**. Russian verbs follow two conjugation patterns in the present and future tenses; following are the patterns for the verbs **жить** *zhiht'* (to live) and **говорить** *gah·vah·reet'* (to speak):

ЖИТЬ (to live)		Present	Future
I	я	живу	буду жить
you (sing.)	ты	живёшь	будешь жить
he/she/it	он/она/оно	живёт	будет жить
we	мы	живём	будем жить
you (pl.)	вы	живёте	будете жить
they	они	живут	будут жить

ГОВОРИТЬ (to speak)		Present	Future
I	я	говорю	буду говорить
you (sing.)	ты	говоришь	будешь говорить
he/she/it	он/она/оно	говорит	будет говорить
we	мы	говорим	будем говорить
you (pl.)	вы	говорите	будете говорить
they	они	говорят	будут говорить

Some verbs have a mixed conjugation, combining the first and second patterns.

The past tense is formed by removing the **–ть** of the infinitive and adding:

–л *(l)*   masculine ending
–ла *(lah)*   feminine ending
–ло *(loh)*   neuter ending
–ли *(lee)*   plural ending

It is the gender and number of the subject that control the ending, for example:

ГОВОРИТЬ (to speak)		Past
I	я	говорил
you (sing.)	ты	говорил
he	он	говорил
she	она	говорила
it	оно	говорило
we	мы	говорили
you (pl.)	вы	говорили
they	они	говорили

There are no irregular verbs in the Russian language.

Word Order

In the Russian language, word order is rather flexible. Though the Russian sentence is generally arranged subject-verb-object, grammar rules allow virtually any combination of subject, verb and object within the sentence. You can form a simple question in Russian by adding an interrogatory intonation (letting the voice rise at the end of the sentence).

Счёт включает обслуживание. *shchot fklyoo•chah•eet ahp•sloo•zhih•vah•nee•yeh*
Service is included.

Счёт включает обслуживание? *shchot fklyoo•chah•eet ahp•sloo•zhih•vah•nee•yeh*
Is service included?

Negation

To form a negative sentence, add **не** *nee* (not) before the verb.
Example:

Мы курим. *mih <u>koo</u>•reem*	We smoke.
Мы не курим. *mih nee <u>koo</u>•reem*	We don't smoke.

Imperatives

Imperative sentences, or sentences that are commands, are formed by adding
the appropriate ending to the stem of the verb (i.e. the verb in the infinitive
without the **–ть**, **–сь**, **–ся** ending). Example: Speak!

you (sing.)	**Говори!** *gah-vah-<u>ree</u>*
you (pl.)	**Говорите!** *gah-vah-<u>ree</u>-tee*

Nouns

There are three genders in Russian: masculine, feminine and neuter. The
endings of nouns vary according to their role in the sentence. There are six
different cases (roles) in both the singular and plural. Adjectives agree in
number and gender with the noun they modify.
There are no articles in Russian.

Adjectives

Adjectives agree in number and gender with the noun they modify.

masculine ending	**–ый, –ой, –ий**
feminine ending	**–ая**
neuter ending	**–ое**

Example:

красный *m* <u>krahs</u>•niy	red
красная *f* krahs•nah•yah	red
красное *n* <u>krahs</u>•nah•yeh	red

Comparatives & Superlatives

The comparative may be formed by adding **более** _boh·lee·yeh_ (more) or
менее _myeh·nee·yeh_ (less) before the adjective or adverb. However, more
often these are formed with the help of the endings **–e** and **–ee** which are
added to the stem.
The superlative is formed by adding **самый** _sah·miy_ (the most) and
наименее _nah·ee·myeh·nee·yeh_ (the least) before the adjective.

большой _bahl'·shoy_	big
больше _bol'·sheh_	bigger
самый большой _sah·miy bahl'·shoy_	biggest
дорогой _dah·rah·goy_	expensive
менее дорогой _myeh·nee·yeh dah·rah·goy_	more expensive
наименее дорогой _nah·ee·myeh·nee·yeh dah·rah·goy_	most expensive

Adverbs & Adverbial Expressions

Many adverbs are formed by adding **–o** to the stem of an adjective:
хороший _khah·roh·shiy_ good   **хорошо** _khah·rah·shoh_ well
красивый _krah·see·viy_ beautiful   **красиво** _krah·see·vah_ beautifully

Numbers

ESSENTIAL

0	**ноль**	_nol'_
1	**один**	_ah·deen_
2	**два**	_dvah_
3	**три**	_tree_
4	**четыре**	_chee·tih·ree_
5	**пять**	_pyaht'_
6	**шесть**	_shest'_
7	**семь**	_syem'_

8	**восемь**	_voh_·seem′
9	**девять**	_dyeh_·veet′
10	**десять**	_dyeh_·seet′
11	**одиннадцать**	ah·dee·_nah_·tsaht′
12	**двенадцать**	dvee·_nah_·tsaht′
13	**тринадцать**	tree·_nah_·tsaht′
14	**четырнадцать**	chee·_tihr_·nah·tsaht′
15	**пятнадцать**	peet·_nah_·tsaht′
16	**шестнадцать**	shihs·_nah_·tsaht′
17	**семнадцать**	seem·_nah_·tsaht′
18	**восемнадцать**	vah·seem·_nah_·tsaht′
19	**девятнадцать**	dee·veet·_nah_·tsaht′
20	**двадцать**	_dvah_·tsaht′
21	**двадцать один**	_dvah_·tsaht′ ah·_deen_
22	**двадцать два**	_dvah_·tsaht′ dvah
30	**тридцать**	_tree_·tsaht′
31	**тридцать один**	_tree_·tsaht′ ah·_deen_
40	**сорок**	_soh_·rahk
50	**пятьдесят**	peet′·dee·_syaht_
60	**шестьдесят**	sheez′·dee·_syaht_
70	**семьдесят**	_syem_′·dee·seet
80	**восемьдесят**	_voh_·seem′·dee·seet
90	**девяносто**	dee·vee·_nos_·tah
100	**сто**	stoh
101	**сто один**	stoh ah·_deen_
200	**двести**	_dvyes_·tee
500	**пятьсот**	peet·_sot_
1,000	**тысяча**	_tih_·see·chah
10,000	**десять тысяч**	_dyeh_·seet′ _tih_·seech
1,000,000	**миллион**	mee·lee·_on_

Ordinal Numbers

first	**первый**	_pyer_·viy
second	**второй**	ftah·_roy_
third	**третий**	_tryeh_·teey
fourth	**четвёртый**	cheet·_vyor_·tiy
fifth	**пятый**	_pyah_·tiy
once	**один раз**	ah·_deen_ rahs
twice	**два раза**	dvah _rah_·zah
three times	**три раза**	tree _rah_·zah

Один ah·_deen_ (one) has three gender forms: **один** m ah·_deen_, **одна** f ahd·_nah_ and **одно** n ahd·_noh_.
Два dvah (two) has two forms: **два** dvah for both masculine and neuter and **две** dveh for feminine.
Ordinal numbers follow the pattern of adjectives.

Time

ESSENTIAL

What time is it?	**Который час?**	kah·_toh_·riy chahs
It's noon [midday].	**Сейчас полдень.**	see·_chahs_ pol·deen'
At midnight.	**В полночь.**	f _pol_·nahch
From nine o'clock	**С девяти до пяти часов.**	s dee·vyah·_tee_ dah
to five o'clock.		pyah·_tee_ chah·_sof_
Twenty after [past]	**Двадцать минут пятого.**	_dvah_·tsaht'
four.		mee·_noot_ _pyah_·tah·vah
A quarter to nine.	**Без четверти девять.**	byes _chet_·veer·tee _dyeh_·veet'
5:30 a.m./p.m.	**Пять тридцать утра/вечера.**	pyaht'
		tree·tsaht' oot·_rah_/_vyeh_·chee·rah

Russians have a different way of thinking about and expressing time. For them, the hour between 12 and 1 is the 'first hour,' the hour between 1 and 2 is the 'second hour,' etc. Up until half past the hour, time is expressed by stating how many minutes into the given hour it is.

Example: **десять минут третьего** _dyeh•seet' mee•noot tryey•tee•vah_ (ten after two) would be 'ten minutes of (into) the third (hour)'.

After half past the hour, time is expressed by using **без** _byez_ (without) and the number of minutes remaining until the next hour.

Example: **без двадцати восемь** _byez dvah•tsah•tee voh•seem'_ (twenty to eight) would be 'eight without twenty'.

Days

ESSENTIAL

Monday	**понедельник**	_pah•nee•dyel'•neek_
Tuesday	**вторник**	_ftohr•neek_
Wednesday	**среда**	_sree•dah_
Thursday	**четверг**	_cheet•vyerk_
Friday	**пятница**	_pyaht•nee•tsah_
Saturday	**суббота**	_soo•boh•tah_
Sunday	**воскресенье**	_vahs•kree•syen'•yeh_

Dates

yesterday	**вчера** *fchee•rah*
today	**сегодня** *see•vod•nyah*
tomorrow	**завтра** *zahf•trah*
day	**день** *dyen'*
week	**неделя** *nee•dyeh•lyah*
month	**месяц** *myeh•seets*
year	**год** *got*

It is standard practice to write dates with the day of the month first followed by the month and then the year. Periods [full stops] are often used to separate the numbers (forward slashes are less common and hyphens are never used). So June 7, 2008 would be expressed as 07.06.08 or 07/06/08.

Months

January	**январь** *yeen•vahr'*
February	**февраль** *feev•rahl'*
March	**март** *mahrt*
April	**апрель** *ahp•ryel'*
May	**май** *mie*
June	**июнь** *ee•yoon'*
July	**июль** *ee•yool'*
August	**август** *ahf•goost*
September	**сентябрь** *seen•tyahbr'*
October	**октябрь** *ahk•tyahbr'*
November	**ноябрь** *nah•yahbr'*
December	**декабрь** *dee•kahbr'*

Seasons

spring	**весна** vees·_nah_
summer	**лето** _lyeh_·tah
fall [autumn]	**осень** _oh_·seen'
winter	**зима** zee·_mah_

Holidays

January 1, New Year's Day	**Новый Год** _noh_·viy got
January 7, Christmas Day	**Рождество** razh·dyes·_tvoh_
March 8, International Women's Day	**Международный Женский День** myezh·doo·nah·_rohd_·nihy _zhen_·skeey dyen'
May 1, May Day/ Labor Day	**1-е мая** _pyer_·vah·yeh _mah_·yah
May 9, Victory in Europe Day	**День Победы** dyen' pah·_byeh_·dih
June 12, Independence Day	**День Независимости России** dyen' nyeh·zah·_vee_·see·mahs·tee rahs·_see_·ee
November 4, Day of National Unity	**День Национального Единства** dyen' nah·tsih·ah·_nahl'_·nah·vah yeh·_deen_·stvah
December 12, Constitution Day	**День Конституции** dyen' kahn·stee·_too_·tsee·ee

| Movable Dates: Easter | **Пасха** _pahs_·khah |

Conversion Tables

When you know	Multiply by	To find
ounces	28.3	grams
pounds	0.45	kilograms
inches	2.54	centimeters
feet	0.3	meters
miles	1.61	kilometers
square inches	6.45	sq. centimeters
square feet	0.09	sq. meters
square miles	2.59	sq. kilometers
pints (U.S./Brit)	0.47/0.56	liters
gallons (U.S./Brit)	3.8/4.5	liters
Fahrenheit	5/9, after 32	Centigrade
Centigrade	9/5, then +32	Fahrenheit

Kilometers to Miles Conversions

1 km	0.62 miles	**20 km**	12.4 miles
5 km	3.10 miles	**50 km**	31.0 miles
10 km	6.20 miles	**100 km**	61.0 miles

Measurement

1 gram	**грамм** *grahm*	= 0.035 oz.
1 kilogram (kg)	**килограмм** *kee·lah·grahm*	= 2.2 lb
1 liter (l)	**литр** *leetr*	= 1.06 U.S./ 0.88 Brit. quarts
1 centimeter (cm)	**сантиметр** *sahn·tee·myetr*	= 0.4 inch
1 meter (m)	**метр** *myetr*	= 3.28 feet
1 kilometer (km)	**километр** *kee·lah·myetr*	= 0.62 mile

Temperature

-40°C – -40°F	**-1°C** – 30°F	**20°C** – 68°F
-30°C – -22°F	**0°C** – 32°F	**25°C** – 77°F
-20°C – -4°F	**5°C** – 41°F	**30°C** – 86°F
-10°C – 14°F	**10°C** – 50°F	**35°C** – 95°F
-5°C – 23°F	**15°C** – 59°F	

Oven Temperature

100°C – 212°F	**177°C** – 350°F
121°C – 250°F	**204°C** – 400°F
149°C – 300°F	**260°C** – 500°F

A

a few несколько _nyeh·skahl'·kah_

a little немного _nee·mnoh·gah_

a lot много _mnoh·gah_

a.m. до полудня _dah pah·lood·nyah_

about (approximately) около
  oh·kah·lah

abroad заграницей _zah·grah·nee·tsey_

accept v принимать _pree·nee·maht'_

access n допуск _doh·poosk_

accessories принадлежности
  pree·nahd·lyezh·nah·stee

accident несчастный случай
  nee·shchas·niy sloo·chie; **(road)**
  авария _ah·vah·ree·yah_

accompany провожать
  prah·vah·zhaht'

accountant бухгалтер _boo·gahl·teer_

acetaminophen парацетамол
  pah·rah·tsih·tah·mol

acne прыщ _prihshch_

across через _cheh·rees_

adapter адаптер _ah·dahp·ter_

address адрес _ah·drees_

adhesive bandage пластырь

plahs·tihr'

admission charge входная плата
  fkhahd·nah·yah plah·tah

adult взрослый _vzros·liy_

after после _pos·lee_

aftershave лосьон после бритья
  las'·yon pos·lee breet'·yah

age n возраст _voz·rahst_

agree соглашаться _sah·glah·shah·tsa_

air воздух _voz·dookh_

air conditioning кондиционер
  kahn·dee·tsih·ah·nyer

air mail авиапочта
  ah·vee·ah·poch·tah

air pump воздушный насос
  vahz·doosh·niy nah·sos

air sickness bag гигиенический
  пакет _gee·gee·ee·nee·chees·keey_
  pah·kyet

airport аэропорт _ah·eh·rah·port_

aisle seat место у прохода _myes·tah_
  oo prah·khoh·dah

alarm clock будильник _boo·deel'·neek_

allergy аллергия _ah·leer·gee·yah_

almost почти _pahch·tee_

adj adjective	**BE** British English	**prep** preposition
adv adverb	**n** noun	**v** verb

alone один _ah·deen_

already уже _oo·zheh_

also также _tahg·zheh_

alter переделывать
pee·ree·dyeh·lih·vaht'

aluminum foil фольга _fahl'·gah_

always всегда _fseeg·dah_

amazing поразительный
pah·rah·zee·teel'·niy

ambassador посол _pah·sol_

ambulance скорая помощь
skoh·rah·yah poh·mahshch

American _adj_ американский
ah·mee·ree·kahn·skeey

amount сумма _soo·mah_

anesthetic обезболивающее _ah·beez·boh·lee·vah·yoo·shchee·yeh_

animal животное _zhih·vot·nah·yeh_

another другой _droo·goy_

antibiotic _n_ антибиотик
ahn·tee·bee·oh·teek

antique антикварный
ahn·tee·kvahr·niy

antiques store антикварный
магазин _ahn·tee·kvahr·niy_
mah·gah·zeen

antiseptic _n_ антисептик
ahn·tee·sep·teek

any какой-либо _kah·koy·lee·bah_

anyone кто-нибудь _ktoh·nee·boot'_

anything что-нибудь _shtoh·nee·boot'_

apartment квартира _kvahr·tee·rah_

apologize просить прощения
prah·seet' prah·shcheh·nee·yah

appendix аппендикс _ah·pyen·deeks_

appointment приём _pree·yom_

approximately приблизительно
pree·blee·zee·teel'·nah

area code код _kot_

arm рука _roo·kah_

around (place) по _pah;_ **(time)** около
oh·kah·lah

arrive прибывать _pree·bih·vaht'_

art gallery картинная галерея
kahr·teen·nah·yah gah·lee·ryeh·yah

ashtray пепельница
pyeh·peel'·nee·tsah

ask просить _prah·seet'_

aspirin аспирин _ah·spee·reen_

asthmatic _n_ астматик _ahst·mah·teek_

at в _v_

ATM банкомат _bahn·kah·maht_

attack _n_ нападение
nah·pah·dyeh·nee·yeh

attractive привлекательный
pree·vlee·kah·teel'·niy

authentic настоящий
nah·stah·yah·shcheey

authenticity подлинность
pod·leen·nahst'

available (unoccupied) свободный
svah·bod·niy

B

baby ребёнок *ree-byoh-nahk*

babysitter няня *nyah-nyah*

back спина *spee-nah*

backache боль в спине *bol' f spee-nyeh*

backpack рюкзак *ryoog-zahk*

bad плохой *plah-khoy*

baggage [BE] багаж *bah-gahzh*

baggage check багажная квитанция *bah-gahzh-nah-yah kvee-tahn-tsih-yah*

bakery булочная *boo-lahch-nah-yah*

balcony балкон *bahl-kon*

ball мяч *myahch*

ballet балет *bah-lyet*

band (musical group) группа *groo-pah*

bank банк *bahnk*

bar бар *bahr*

barber парикмахер *pah-reekh-mah-kheer*

basement подвал *pahd-vahl*

basket корзина *kahr-zee-nah*

basketball баскетбол *bahs-keet-bol*

battery (car) аккумулятор *ah-kah-moo-lyah-tahr;* **(camera, etc.)** батарея *bah-tah-ryeh-yah*

be быть *biht'*

beach пляж *plyahsh*

beautiful красивый *krah-see-viy*

because потому что *pah-tah-moo-shtah*

bed кровать *krah-vaht'*

bedding постельное бельё *pahs-tel'-nah-yeh beel'-yoh*

bedroom спальня *spahl'-nyah*

before (time) до *dah*

begin начинать *nah-chee-naht'*

belong принадлежать *pree-nahd-lee-zhaht'*

belt ремень *ree-myen'*

bicycle велосипед *vee-lah-see-pyet*

big большой *bahl'-shoy*

bikini бикини *bee-kee-nee*

bill счёт *shchot*

binoculars бинокль *bee-noh-kahl'*

bird птица *ptee-tsah*

birthday день рождения *dyen' rahzh-dyeh-nee-yah*

bite *n* укус *oo-koos; v* кусать *koo-saht'*

bizarre причудливый *pree-chood-lee-viy*

bladder мочевой пузырь *mah-chee-voy poo-zihr'*

blanket одеяло *ah-dee-yah-lah*

bleach отбеливатель *aht-byeh-lee-vah-teel'*

bleeding *n* кровотечение *krah-vah-tee-cheh-nee-yeh*

blister волдырь *vahl-dihr'*

blood кровь *krof'*

blood pressure кровяное давление
krah•vee•noh•yeh dahv•lyeh•nee•yeh

blouse блузка *bloos•kah*

blow-dry фен *fyen*

boarding card посадочный талон
pah•sah•dahch•niy tah•lon

boat лодка *lot•kah*

boat trip водная экскурсия
vod•nah•yah ehks•koor•see•yah

bone кость *kost'*

book *n* книга *knee•gah;* *v* заказывать
zah•kah•zih•vaht'

bookstore книжный магазин
kneezh•niy mah•gah•zeen

boots сапоги *sa•pah•gee*

borrow одолжить *ah•dahl•zhit'*

botanical garden ботанический сад
bah•tah•nee•chees•keey saht

bottle opener открывалка
aht•krih•vahl•kah

boy мальчик *mahl'•cheek*

boyfriend друг *drook*

bra бюстгальтер *byoost•gahl•tyer*

bracelet браслет *brahs•lyet*

break *v* сломать *slah•maht'*

break down *v* сломаться
slah•mah•tsah

break-in *n* взлом *vzlom*

breast грудь *groot'*

breathe дышать *dih•shaht'*

breathtaking захватывающий
zah•khvah•tih•vah•yoo•shcheey

bridge мост *most*

British *adj* британский
bree•tahn•skeey

brochure брошюра *brah•shoo•rah*

brooch брошь *brosh*

browse *v* просматривать
prah•smah•tree•vaht'

bruise *n* синяк *see•nyahk*

bucket ведро *veed•roh*

build строить *stroh•eet'*

building здание *zdah•nee•yeh*

burn *n* ожог *ah•zhok*

bus автобус *ahf•toh•boos*

bus route автобусный маршрут
ahf•toh•boos•niy mahrsh•root

bus station автобусная станция
ahf•toh•boos•nah•yah stahn•tsih•yah

bus stop автобусная остановка
ahf•toh•boos•nah•yah ahs•tah•nof•kah

business бизнес *beez•nees*

business trip командировка
kah•mahn•dee•rof•kah

busy *adj* (occupied) занятый
zah•nyah•tiy

but но *noh*

butane gas газовый баллон
gah•zah•viy bah•lon

button кнопка *knop•kah*

buy покупать *pah•koo•paht'*

by (time) к *k*

C

cabin каюта *kah·yoo·tah*

calendar календарь *kah·leen·dahr'*

call *v* звать *zvaht'*; **(for someone)** заходить за *zah·khah·deet' zah*; **(phone)** звонить *zvah·neet'*

camera фотоаппарат *foh·tah·ah·pah·raht*

camera case футляр *foot·lyahr*

campbed раскладушка *rahs·klah·doosh·kah*

camping кемпинг *kyem·peenk*

camping equipment снаряжение *snah·ree·zheh·nee·yeh*

campsite палаточный лагерь *pah·lah·tahch·niy lah·geer'*

can *n* банка *bahn·kahn*; *v* мочь *moch*

can opener консервный нож *kahn·syerv·niy nosh*

cancel отменять *aht·mee·nyaht'*

candle свеча *svee·chah*

cap (dental) коронка *kah·ron·kah*

car машина *mah·shih·nah*; **(train compartment)** вагон *vahh·gon*

car hire [BE] прокат автомобилей *prah·kaht ahf·tah·mah·bee·leey*

car park [BE] автостоянка *ahf·tah·stah·yahn·kah*

carafe графин *grah·feen*

careful осторожный *ahs·tah·rozh·niy*

carpet (rug) ковер *kah·vyor*

cart тележка *tee·lyesh·kah*

carton пакет *pah·kyet*

cash наличные *nah·leech·nih·yeh*

cash desk касса *kah·sah*

cashier кассир *kah·seer*

casino казино *kah·zee·noh*

castle замок *zah·mahk*

cathedral собор *sah·bor*

cave пещера *pee·shcheh·rah*

CD компакт-диск *kahm·pahkt deesk*

CD player лазерный проигрыватель *lah·zeer·niy prah·eeg·rih·vah·teel'*

cell phone мобильный телефон *mah·beel'·niy tee·lee·fon*

center центр *tsentr*

ceramics керамика *kee·rah·mee·kah*

certificate свидетельство *svee·dyeh·teel'·stvah*

chain цепочка *tsih·poch·kah*

change *n* сдача *zdah·chah*; *v* **(alter)** поменять *pah·mee·nyaht'*; **(buses, etc.)** делать пересадку *dyeh·laht' pee·ree·saht·koo* **(baby)** перепеленать *pee·ree·pee·lee·naht'*; **(money)** обменять *ahb·mee·nyaht'*

charge *n* плата *plah·tah*

charter flight чартерный рейс *chahr·ter·niy reys*

cheap дешёвый *dee·shoh·viy*

check *n* чек *chek*; *v* проверять *prah·veh·ryaht'*

check in v регистрироваться
ree·gees·*tree*·rah·vah·tsah

check-in desk регистрационная
стойка ree·gee·strah·tsih·*on*·nah·yah
stoy·kah

check out v **(hotel)** выезжать
vih·eezh·*zhaht'*

chemist [BE] аптека ahp·*tyeh*·kah

cheque [BE] чек chek

chess шахматы *shahkh*·mah·tih

chest (body part) грудная клетка
grood·*nah*·yah *klyet*·kah

child adj детский *dyets*·keey; n
ребёнок ree·*byoh*·nahk

child seat (in car) детское сиденье
dyets·kah·yeh see·*dyen'*·yeh

children дети *dyeh*·teeh

church церковь *tser*·kahf'

cigarette сигарета see·gah·*ryeh*·tah

cigar сигара see·*gah*·rah

cinema [BE] кинотеатр
kee·nah·tee·*ahtr*

class (type of seat, etc.) класс klahs

clean adj чистый *chees*·tiy; v чистить
chees·teet'

cliff скала skah·*lah*

cling film [BE] продуктовая плёнка
prah·dook·*toh*·vah·yah *plyon*·kah

clock часы chah·*sih*

close v **(store, etc.)** закрываться
zah·krih·*vah*·tsah

clothes одежда ah·*dyezh*·dah

cloudy облачный *ob*·lahch·niy

clubs (golf) клюшки *klyoosh*·kee

coach (long-distance bus)
междугородний автобус
meezh·doo·gah·*rod*·niy ahf·*toh*·boos

coast побережье pah·bee·*ryezh*·yeh

coat пальто pahl'·*toh*

coatcheck гардероб gahr·dee·*rop*

code (area, dialing) код kot

coin монета mah·*nyeh*·tah

cold adj холодный khah·*lod*·niy; n
(flu) простуда prah·*stoo*·dah

colleague коллега kah·*lyeh*·gah

collect v забирать zah·bee·*raht'*

color цвет tsvyet

comb расчёска rah·*shchos*·kah

come приходить pree·khah·*deet'*

commission комиссионный сбор
kah·mee·see·*oh*·niy zbor

compact компактный
kahm·*pahk*·tniy

company (business) предприятие
preet·pree·*yah*·tee·yeh;
(companionship) компания
kahm·*pah*·nee·yah

compartment (train) купе koo·*peh*

complaint жалоба *zhah*·lah·bah

concert концерт kahn·*tsert*

concert hall концертный зал
kahn·*tsert*·niy zahl

concussion сотрясение мозга
sah·tree·syeh·nee·yeh moz·gah

conditioner кондиционер
kahn·dee·tsih·ah·nyer

condom презерватив
pree·zeer·vah·teev

conductor дирижёр *dee·ree·zhor*

confirm (reservation) подтвердить
paht·tveer·deet'

consulate консульство
kon·sool'·stvah

consult v консультироваться
kahn·sool'·tee·rah·vah·tsah

contact v связаться *svyah·zah·tsah*

contagious инфекционный
een·feek·tsih·oh·niy

contain v содержать *sah·deer·zhaht'*

cook n повар *poh·vahr;* v готовить
gah·toh·veet'

cooker [BE] плита *plee·tah*

copper медь *myet'*

copy n копия *koh·pee·yah*

corkscrew штопор *shtoh·pahr*

corner угол *oo·gahl*

correct adv правильно *prah·veel'·nah*

cosmetics косметика
kahs·myeh·tee·kah

cottage дача *dah·chah*

cotton вата *vah·tah*

cough n кашель *kah·shihl';* v кашлять
kahsh·lyaht'

country (nation) страна *strah·nah*

cramps судороги *soo·dah·rah·gee*

credit card кредитная карточка
kree·deet·nah·yah kahr·tahch·kah

crib детская кроватка *dets·kah·yah
krah·vaht·kah*

crossroad перекрёсток
pee·ree·kryos·tahk

cruise n круиз *kroo·eez*

crutches костыли *kahs·tih·lee*

crystal хрусталь *khroos·tal'*

cup чашка *chahsh·kah*

cupboard шкаф *shkahf*

currency валюта *vah·lyoo·tah*

currency exchange office обмен
валюты *ahb·myen vah·lyoo·tih*

curtains занавеси *zah·nah·vee·see*

customs таможня *tah·mozh·nyah*

customs declaration таможенная
декларация *tah·moh·zhih·nah·yah
deek·lah·rah·tsih·yah*

cut порез *pah·ryes*

cycle route велосипедный маршрут
vee·lah·see·pyed·niy mahrsh·root

cycling велоспорт *vyeh·lah·sport*

D

daily ежедневно *ee·zhee·dnyev·nah*

damage v повредить *pah·vree·deet'*

damp adv сыро *sih·rah;* n сырость
sih·rahst'

dance *n* танец _tah_•neets

dangerous *adj* опасный ah•_pahs_•niy

dark тёмный _tyom_•niy

dawn рассвет rahs•_vyet_

day день dyen'

deaf глухой gloo•_khoy_

deck chair шезлонг shez•_lonk_

declare предъявлять
  preed•yahv•_lyaht'_

deep глубокий gloo•_boh_•keey

degree (temperature) градус
  grah•doos

delay задержка zah•_dyersh_•kah

deliver доставлять dah•stahv•_lyat'_

denim джинсовый dzhihn•_soh_•viy

dentist зубной врач zoob•_noy_ vrahch

dentures протез prah•_tes_

deodorant дезодорант
  dee•zah•dah•_rahnt_

depart (train, bus) отправляться
  aht•prahv•_lyah_•tsah

department отдел aht•_dyel_

departure lounge зал вылета zahl
  vih•lee•tah

deposit аванс ah•_vahns_

describe описывать ah•_pee_•sih•vaht'

destination место назначения
  myes•tah nahz•nah•_cheh_•nee•yah

details подробности
  pahd•_rob_•nahs•tee

detergent моющее средство
  moh•yoo•shchee•yeh _sryet_•stvah

diabetes диабет dee•ah•_byet_

diabetic *n* диабетик dee•ah•_byeh_•teek

diagnosis диагноз dee•_ahg_•nahs

diamond брильянт breel'•_yahnt_

diaper пелёнка pee•_lyon_•kah

diarrhea понос pah•_nos_

dice кости _kos_•tee

dictionary словарь slah•_vahr'_

diesel дизельное топливо
  dee•zeel'•nah•yeh _top_•lee•vah

diet *n* диета dee•_yeh_•tah

difficult трудный _trood_•niy

dining car вагон-ресторан vah•_gon_
  rees•tah•_rahn_

dining room столовая
  stah•_loh_•vah•yah

dinner ужин _oo_•zhihn

direct *adj* (train) прямой pryah•_moy;_
  v направлять nah•prahv•_lyaht'_

direction направление
  nah•prahv•_lyeh_•nee•yeh

director директор dee•_ryek_•tahr

directory (telephone) телефонный
  справочник tee•lee•_foh_•niy
  sprah•vahch•neek

dirty грязный _gryahz_•niy

disabled инвалид een•vah•_leet_

discount скидка _skeet_•kah

dish (meal) блюдо _blyoo_•dah

dishcloth тряпка _tryahp_•kah

dishwasher посудомоечная машина
*pah·soo·dah·moh·eech·nah·yah
mah·shih·nah*

dishwashing liquid средство для
мытья посуды *sryet·stvah dlyah
miht'·yah pah·soo·dih*

disturb беспокоить *bees·pah·koh·eet'*

dive нырять *nih·ryaht'*

diving equipment снаряжение для
дайвинга *snah·ree·zheh·nee·yeh
dlyah die·veen·gah*

divorce развод *rahz·vod*

doctor врач *vrahch*

doll кукла *kook·lah*

door дверь *dvyer'*

double bed двуспальная кровать
dvoo·spahl'·nah·yah krah·vaht'

double room двухместный номер
dvookh·myes·niy noh·meer

downtown area центр города *tsentr
goh·rah·dah*

dozen дюжина *dyoo·zhih·nah*

dress платье *plaht'·yeh*

drink *v* пить *peet'*

drive *v* ехать *yeh·khaht'*

driver водитель *vah·dee·teel'*

driver's licence водительские права
vah·dee·teel'·skee·ye prah·vah

drugstore аптека *ahp·tyeh·kah*

drunk *adj* пьяный *pyah·niy*

dry clean *v* отдавать в химчистку

aht·dah·vaht' f kheem·cheest·koo

dry cleaner химчистка
kheem·cheest·kah

during во время *vah vrye·myah*

dustbin [BE] мусорный бак
moo·sahr·niy bahk

duty пошлина *posh·lee·nah*

E

ear ухо *oo·khah*

earache боль в ухе *bol' v oo·khee*

early ранний *rahn·neey*

earrings серьги *syer'·gee*

easy лёгкий *lyokh·keey*

eat есть *yest'*

economy class пассажирский класс
pah·sah·zhihr·skeey klahs

electric outlet розетка *rah·zyet·kah*

electric shaver электробритва
eh·lyek·trah·breet·vah

electricity электричество
eh·leek·tree·cheest·vah

elevator лифт *leeft*

else еще *ee·shchoh*

e-mail электронная почта
ee·leek·troh·nah·yah poch·tah

e-mail address адрес электронной
почты *ah·drees ee·leek·tron·nie
poch·tih*

e-ticket электронный билет
ee·leek·tron·niy bee·lyet

embassy посольство *pah·sol'·stvah*

emerald изумруд *ee·zoom·root*

emergency крайний случай *krie·neey sloo·chie*

emergency exit аварийный выход *ah·vah·reey·niy vih·khaht*

empty *adj* пустой *poos·toy*

enamel эмаль *ee·mahl'*

end *v* кончаться *kahn·chah·tsah*

England Англия *ahn·glee·yah*

English *adj* английский *ahn·gleey·skeey*

enjoy нравиться *nrah·vee·tsah*

enough достаточно *dah·stah·tahch·nah*

entrance fee входная плата *fkhahd·nah·yah plah·tah*

entry visa въездная виза *vyezd·nah·yah vee·zah*

envelope конверт *kahn·vyert*

epileptic *n* эпилептик *ee·pee·lyep·teek*

equipment оборудование *ah·bah·roo·dah·vah·nee·yeh;* **(sports)** снаряжение *snah·ryah·zheh·nee·yeh*

error ошибка *ah·shihp·kah*

escalator эскалатор *ees·kah·lah·tahr*

essential основной *ahs·nahv·noy*

European Union (EU) Европейский союз *yev·rah·pey·skeey sah·yoos*

event событие *sah·bih·tee·yeh*

every каждый *kahzh·diy*

example пример *pree·myer*

except кроме *kroh·mee*

excess luggage перевес багажа *pee·ree·vyes bah·gah·zhah*

exchange *v* обменивать *ahb·myeh·nee·vaht'*

exchange rate курс обмена *koors ahb·myeh·nah*

excursion экскурсия *eks·koor·see·yah*

exit *n* выход *vih·khaht*

expensive дорогой *dah·rah·goy*

express экспресс *eks·pres*

extension добавочный номер *dah·bah·vahch·niy noh·meer*

extra *adv* ещё *ee·shchoh*

extract *v* удалять *oo·dah·lyaht'*

eye глаз *glahs*

F

fabric (material) ткань *tkahn'*

face лицо *lee·tsoh*

facial чистка лица *cheest·kah lee·tsah*

facilities удобства *oo·dops·tvah*

family семья *seem'·yah*

fan (air) вентилятор *veen·tee·lyah·tahr*

far далеко *dah·lee·koh*

far-sighted дальнозоркий *dahl'·nah·zor·keey'*

fare плата *plah·tah*

farm ферма _fyer_•mah

fast adv быстро _bihst_•rah

faucet кран krahn

favorite любимый lyoo•_bee_•miy

fax факс faks

feed кормить kar•_meet'_

ferry паром pah•_rom_

fever жар zhahr

few мало _mah_•lah

filling (dental) пломба _plom_•bah

film [BE] **(movie)** фильм feel'm;
  (camera) плёнка _plyon_•kah

filter фильтр feel'•tr

finger палец _pah_•leets

fire n пожар pah•_zhahr_

fire alarm пожарная тревога
  pah•_zhahr_•nah•yah tree•_voh_•gah

fire escape пожарная лестница
  pah•_zhahr_•nah•yah _lyes_•nee•tsah

fire extinguisher огнетушитель
  ahg•nee•too•_shih_•teel'

firewood дрова drah•_vah_

first class первый класс _pyer_•viy klahs

fit v **(clothes)** подходить
  paht•khah•_deet'_

fitting room примерочная
  pree•_myeh_•rahch•nah•yah

fix v чинить chee•_neet'_

flashlight фонарь fah•_nahr'_

flight рейс reys

floor этаж eh•_tahsh_

florist цветочный магазин
  tsvyeh•toch•_niy_ mah•gah•_zeen_

flower цветок tsvee•_tok_

flu грипп greep

fog туман too•_mahn_

folk народный nah•_rod_•niy

follow v **(pursue)** преследовать
  pree•_slyeh_•dah•vaht'

food n еда yee•_dah_

foot (body) нога nah•_gah_

football [BE] футбол food•_bol_

footpath тропинка trah•_peen_•kah

for на nah

foreign currency иностранная
  валюта ee•nah•_strah_•nah•yah
  vah•_lyoo_•tah

forest лес lyes

forget забывать zah•bih•_vaht'_

fork вилка veel•kah

form n бланк blahnk

fountain фонтан fahn•_tahn_

foyer (hotel, theater) фойе fie•yeh

fracture (a bone) перелом
  pee•ree•_lom_

frame n **(glasses)** оправа ah•_prah_•va

free adj **(not busy/available)**
  свободный svah•_bod_•niy

freezer морозильная камера
  mah•rah•_zeel'_•nah•yah _kah_•mee•rah

frequently часто _chahs_•tah

fresh свежий _syeh_•zhiy

friend друг *drook*

friendly *adj* дружеский
droo·zhees·keey

from (place) из *eez*; **(time)** с *s*

frost мороз *mah·roz*

frying pan сковорода
skah·vah·rah·dah

full *adj* полный *pol·niy*

fun веселье *vee·syel'·yeh*

furniture мебель *myeh·beel'*

G

game игра *eeg·rah*

garage гараж *gah·rash*

garbage bag мусорный мешок
moo·sahr·niy mee·shok

garden сад *saht*

gas (fuel) бензин *been·zeen*

gas station заправочная
станция *zah·prah·vahch·nah·yah*
stahn·tsih·yah

gate (airport) выход *vih·khaht*

gauze бинт *beent*

genuine настоящий
nah·stah·yah·shcheey

get (receive) получать
pah·loo·chaht'; **(to destination)**
добираться до *dah·bee·rah·tsah doh*

gift подарок *pah·dah·rahk*

gift store магазин подарков
mah·gah·zeen pah·dahr·kahf

girl девочка *dyeh·vahch·kah*

girlfriend подруга *pah·droo·gah*

give давать *dah·vaht'*

glass стакан *stah·kahn*

glasses (optical) очки *ahch·kee*

glove перчатка *peer·chaht·kah*

go ходить *khah·deet'*

go away уходить *oo·khah·deet'*

gold золото *zoh·lah·tah*

golf гольф *gol'f*

golf course поле для гольфа *poh·lyeh*
dlyah gol'·fah

good хороший *khah·roh·shiy*

gram грамм *grahm*

grass трава *trah·vah*

gray серый *syeh·riy*

Great Britain Великобритания
vee·lee·kah·bree·tah·nee·yah

group группа *groo·pah*

guarantee гарантия
gah·rahn·tee·yah

guide (tour) гид *geet*

guidebook путеводитель
poo·tee·vah·dee·teel'

guided tour экскурсия
eks·koor·see·yah

guitar гитара *gee·tah·rah*

gum десна *dees·nah*

gym спортзал *sport·zahl*

gynecologist гинеколог
gee·nee·koh·lahk

H

hair волосы _voh·lah·sih_

hairbrush щётка для волос
shchot·kah dlyah vah·los

haircut стрижка _streesh·kah_

hairdresser парикмахер
pah·reek·mah·kheer

hairspray лак для волос _lahk dlyah_
vah·los

half половина _pah·lah·vee·nah_

hand рука _roo·kah_

hand luggage ручная кладь
rooch·nah·yah klahd'

handbag [BE] сумка _soom·kah_

handicapped инвалид _een·vah·leet_

handicraft ремесло _ree·mees·loh_

handkerchief платок _plah·tok_

hanger вешалка _vyeh·shahl·kah_

hangover похмелье _pahkh·myel'·yeh_

harbor гавань _gah·vahn'_

hat шапка _shahp·kah_

hay fever сенная лихорадка
see·nah·yah lee·khah·raht·kah

head голова _gah·lah·vah_

headache головная боль
gah·lahv·nah·yah bol'

health insurance медицинское
страхование _mee·dee·tsihn·skah·yah_
strah·khof·kah

hear слышать _slih·shaht'_

hearing aid слуховой аппарат

sloo·khah·voy ah·pah·raht

heart сердце _syer·tseh_

heart attack сердечный приступ
seer·dyech·niy prees·toop

heart condition заболевание сердца
zah·bah·lee·vah·nee·yeh syer·tsah

heater обогреватель
ah·bah·gree·vah·teel'

heating _n_ отопление
ah·tahp·lyeh·nee·yeh

heavy тяжёлый _tee·zhoh·liy_

height рост _rost_

helmet шлем _shlyem_

help _v_ помогать _pah·mah·gaht'_

here здесь _zdyes'_

high высокий _vih·soh·keey_

high blood pressure высокое
давление _vih·soh·kha·yeh_
dahv·lyeh·nee·yeh

highlight _v_ **(hair)** мелировать
mee·lee·rah·vaht'

highway шоссе _shah·seh_

hiking _n_ поход _pah·khot_

hill холм _kholm_

hire [BE] _v_ взять напрокат _vzyaht'_
nah·prah·kaht

hobby хобби _khoh·bee_

hold on _v_ подождать _pah·dah·zhdah_

hole (in clothes) дырка _dihr·kah_

holiday [BE] отпуск _ot·poosk_

home дом _dom_

honeymoon медовый месяц
mee•doh•viy myeh•syahts

horse лошадь *loh•shahd'*

horseracing бега *bee•gah*

hospital больница *bahl'•nee•tsah*

hot *adj* горячий *gah•ryah•cheey*

hotel гостиница *gahs•tee•nee•tsah*

hotel room номер *noh•meer*

hour час *chahs*

house дом *dom*

hungry голодный *gah•lod•niy*

hurt *v* болеть *bah•lyet'*

husband муж *moosh*

I

icy гололёд *gah•lah•lyot*

identification документ
dah•koo•myent

ill [BE] больной *bahl'•noy*

illegal незаконный *nee•zah•koh•niy*

immediately немедленно
nee•myeh•dlee•nah

in (place) в *v;* **(time)** через *cheh•rees*

incredible невероятный
nee•vee•rah•yaht•niy

indigestion изжога *eezh•zhoh•gah*

indoor закрытый *zah•krih•tiy*

inexpensive недорогой
nee•dah•rah•goy

infect заразить *zah•rah•zeet'*

infection инфекция *een•fyek•tsih•yah*

inflammation воспаление
vahs•pah•lyeh•nee•yeh

information информация
een•fahr•mah•tsih•yah

injection укол *oo•kol*

injury травма *trahv•mah*

innocent невиновен
nee•vee•noh•veen

insect насекомое
nah•see•koh•mah•yeh

insert *v* вставлять *fstahv•lyat'*

inside внутри *vnoo•tree*

insist настаивать *nah•stah•ee•vaht'*

insomnia бессоница
bees•soh•nee•tsah

instructions инструкция
een•strook•tsih•yah

insulin инсулин *een•soo•leen*

insurance страховка *strah•khof•kahh*

insurance claim страховой иск
strah•khah•voy eesk

insurance company страховая
компания *strah•khah•vah•yah
kahm•pah•nee•yah*

interesting интересный
een•tee•ryes•niy

internet интернет *een•ter•net*

internet cafe интернет-кафе
een•ter•net kah•feh

interpreter переводчик
pee•ree•vot•cheek

intersection перекресток
pee•ree•kryos•tahk

invitation приглашение
pree•glah•sheh•nee•yeh

invite приглашать *pree•glah•shaht'*

iron утюг *oo•tyook*

itemized bill детальный счёт
dee•tahl'•niy shchot

J

jacket куртка *koort•kah*

jar банка *bahn•kah*

jaw челюсть *cheh•lyoost'*

jazz джаз *dzhahs*

jeans джинсы *dzhihn•sih*

jeweler ювелирный магазин
yoo•vee•leer•niy mah•gah•zeen

job работа *rah•boh•tah*

joke шутка *shoot•kah*

journalist журналист *zhoor•nah•leest*

journey поездка *pah•yest•kah*

K

kettle чайник *chie•neek*

key ключ *klyooch*

key card электронный ключ
eh•leek•tron•niy klyooch

key ring брелок *bree•lok*

kiddie pool детский бассейн
dyets•keey bah•seyn

kidney почка *poch•kah*

kind (pleasant) любезный
lyoo•byez•niy

kiss *v* целовать *tsih•lah•vaht'*

kitchen кухня *kookh•nyah*

knee колено *kah•lyeh•nah*

knife нож *nosh*

kosher кошерный *kah•sher•niy*

L

label *n* ярлык *yahr•lihk*

lace кружево *kroo•zhih•vah*

ladder стремянка *stree•myahn•kah*

lake озеро *oh•zee•rah*

lamp лампа *lahm•pah*

land *v* приземляться
pree•zeem•lyah•tsah

language course языковые курсы
yah•zih•kah•vih•yeh koor•sih

large большой *bahl'•shoy*

last *adj* последний *pahs•lyed•neey*

late *adj* поздний *poz•neey*

laugh *v* смеяться *smee•yah•tsah*

launderette [BE] прачечная
prah•cheech•nah•yah

laundromat прачечная
prah•cheech•nah•yah

lawyer адвокат *ahd•vah•kaht*

leader (of group) руководитель
roo•kah•vah•dee•teel'

leaflet брошюра *brah•shoo•rah*

leak *v* **(roof, pipe)** течь *tyech*

learn (language) изучать
ee·zoo·chaht'

leather кожа *koh·zhah*

leave *v* уезжать *oo·eezh·zhaht'*

left *adj* левый *leh·viy*

left-luggage office [BE]
камера хранения *kah·mee·rah khrah·nyeh·nee·yah*

leg нога *nah·gah*

legal законный *zah·koh·niy*

lend дать взаймы *daht' vzie·mih*

length длина *dlee·nah*

less меньше *myen'·sheh*

lesson урок *oo·rok*

letter письмо *pees'·moh*

library библиотека
bee·blee·ah·tyeh·kah

lifeboat спасательная лодка
spah·sah·teel'·nah·yah lot·kah

lifeguard спасатель *spah·sah·teel'*

lifejacket спасательный жилет
spah·sah·teel'·niy zhih·lyet

lift [BE] *n* лифт *leeft*

lift pass пропуск на подъёмник
proh·poosk nah pahd·yom·neek

light *adj* **(weight)** лёгкий *lyokh·keey;*
(color) светлый *svyet·liy;* **(electric)**
свет *svyet*

light bulb лампочка *lahm·pahch·kah*

lighter (cigarette) зажигалка
zah·zhih·gahl·kah

like *v* нравиться *nrah·vee·tsah*

line (subway) линия *lee·nee·yah*

linen лён *lyon*

lip губа *goo·bah*

lipstick губная памада *goob·nah·yah pah·mah·dah*

liquor store винный магазин *vee·niy mah·gah·zeen*

little (small) маленький
mah·leen'·keey

liver печень *pyeh·cheen'*

living room гостиная
gahs·tee·nah·yah

lobby (theater, hotel) фойе *fah·yeh*

local местный *mes·niy*

lock *n* замок *zah·mok*

login вход в систему *fhot f sees·tyeh·moo*

long длинный *dlee·niy*

long-distance bus междугородний
автобус *myezh·doo·gah·rod·niy ahf·toh·boos*

long-sighted [BE] дальнозоркий
dahl'·nah·zor·keey

loose (clothing) свободный
svah·bod·niy

lose потерять *pah·tee·ryaht'*

lost-and-found бюро находок
byoo·roh nah·khoh·dahk

loud громкий *grom·keey*

love *v* любить *lyoo·beet'*

luggage багаж *bah·gahsh*
lunch обед *ah·byet*
lung лёгкое *lyokh·kah·yeh*

M

magazine журнал *zhoor·nahl*
magnificent великолепный *vee·lee·kah·lyep·niy*
mail *n* почта *poch·tah;* *v* отправлять *aht·prahv·lyaht'*
mailbox почтовый ящик *pahch·toh·viy yah·shcheek*
main главный *glahv·niy*
main course второе *ftah·roh·yeh*
make-up макияж *mah·kee·yahsh*
male мужской *moosh·skoy*
mall (shopping) торговый центр *tahr·goh·viy tsentr*
man (male) мужчина *moo·shchee·nah*
manicure маникюр *mah·nee·kyoor*
manual *n* **(for smth)** руководство *roo·kah·vod·stvah*
many много *mnoh·gah*
map карта *kahr·tah*
market рынок *rih·nahk*
married (man) женат *zhih·naht;* **(woman)** замужем *zah·moo·zhem*
mascara тушь *toosh*
mask (diving) маска *mahs·kah*
massage массаж *mah·sahsh*

match (sport) матч *mahch*
matches спички *speech·kee*
mattress матрас *maht·rahs*
meal блюдо *blyoo·dah*
mean *v* значить *znah·cheet'*
measure *v* измерить *eez·myeh·reet'*
measurement измерение *eez·mee·ryeh·nee·yeh*
medication лекарство *lee·kahr·stvah*
meet *v* встречаться *fstree·chah·tsah*
message сообщение *sah·ahp·shcheh·nee·yeh*
metal металл *mee·tahl*
microwave микроволновая печь *meek·rah·vahl·noh·vah·yah pyech*
migraine мигрень *meeg·ryen'*
mileage километраж *kee·lah·mee·trahsh*
mine мой *moy*
minute минута *mee·noo·tah*
mirror зеркало *zyer·kah·lah*
miss *v* **(pass)** пропустить *prah·poos·teet';* **(get lost)** пропасть *prah·pahst'*
mistake ошибка *ah·shihp·kah*
misunderstanding недоразумение *nee·dah·rah·zoo·myeh·nee·yeh*
mobile phone [BE] мобильный телефон *mah·beel'·niy tee·lee·fon*
modern современный *sah·vree·myen·niy*

money деньги <u>dyen</u>'-gee

month месяц <u>myeh</u>-syahts

mop швабра <u>shvahb</u>-rah

more больше <u>bol</u>'-sheh

mosque мечеть mee-<u>chet</u>'

mosquito bite комариный укус
kah-mah-<u>ree</u>-niy oo-<u>koos</u>

motion sickness морская болезнь
mahr-<u>skah</u>-yah bah-<u>lyezn</u>'

motorboat моторка mah-<u>tor</u>-kah

motorway [BE] шоссе shah-<u>seh</u>

mountain гора gah-<u>rah</u>

mouth рот rot

movie фильм feel'm

movie theater кинотеатр
kee-nah-tee-<u>ahtr</u>

Mr. господин gahs-pah-<u>deen</u>

Mrs. госпожа gahs-pah-<u>zhah</u>

much много <u>mnoh</u>-gah

mug n кружка <u>kroosh</u>-kah; v ограбить
ah-<u>grah</u>-beet'

mugging n ограбление
ah-grahb-<u>lyeh</u>-nee-yeh

museum музей moo-<u>zyey</u>

music музыка <u>moo</u>-zih-kah

my мой moy

myself сам <u>sahm</u>

N

name (first name) имя <u>ee</u>-myah;
  (family name) фамилия

fah-<u>mee</u>-lee-yah

napkin салфетка sahl-<u>fyet</u>-kah

nappy [BE] пелёнка pee-<u>lyon</u>-kah

narrow узкий <u>oos</u>-keey

national национальный
nah-tsih-ah-<u>nahl</u>'-niy

nationality национальность
nah-tsih-ah-<u>nahl</u>'-nahst'

nature reserve заповедник
zah-pah-<u>vyed</u>-neek

near около <u>oh</u>-kah-lah

nearby рядом <u>ryah</u>-dahm

near-sighted близорукий
blee-za-<u>roo</u>-keey

neck шея <u>sheh</u>-yah

necklace ожерелье ah-zhih-<u>ryel</u>'-yeh

nerve нерв nyerf

nesting doll матрёшка
maht-<u>ryosh</u>-kah

never никогда nee-kahg-<u>dah</u>

new новый <u>noh</u>-viy

newspaper газета gah-<u>zyeh</u>-tah

newsstand газетный киоск
gah-<u>zyet</u>-niy kee-<u>osk</u>

next следующий
<u>slyeh</u>-doo-yoo-shcheey

nice хороший khah-<u>roh</u>-shiy

niece племянница
plee-<u>myah</u>-nee-tsah

no нет nyet

no one никто nee-<u>ktoh</u>

noisy шумный *shoom·niy*
non-alcoholic безалкогольный
  beez·ahl·kah·gol'·niy
non-smoking некурящий
  nee·koo·ryah·shcheey
nonsense ерунда *ee·roon·dah*
normal нормальный *nahr·mahl'·niy*
nose нос *nos*
nothing ничего *nee·chee·voh*
notify сообщать *sah·aph·shchaht'*
number (phone) номер *noh·meer*
nurse сестра *sees·trah*

O

occupied занятый *zah·nee·tiy*
odds (betting) шансы *shahn·sih*
off-license [BE] винный магазин
  vee·niy mah·gah·zeen
office офис *oh·fees*
often часто *chahs·tah*
old старый *sta·riy*
on (day, date) в *v;* **(place)** на *nah*
once один раз *ah·deen rahs*
one-way ticket билет в один конец
  bee·lyet v ah·deen kah·nyets
open *adj* открытый *aht·krih·tiy;* *v*
  открывать *aht·krih·vaht'*
opening hours часы работы *chah·sih*
  rah·boh·tih
opera опера *oh·pee·rah*
operation операция

  ah·pee·rah·tsih·yah
opposite напротив *nah·proh·teef*
optician оптика *op·tee·kah*
or или *ee·lee*
orchestra оркестр *ahr·kyestr*
order *v* заказывать *zah·ka·zih·vaht'*
ordering заказ *zah·kahs*
Orthodox православный
  prah·vah·slahv·niy
other другой *droo·goy*
outdoor на открытом воздухе *nah*
  aht·krih·tahm voz·doo·khee
outside на улице *nah oo·lee·tseh*
oven духовка *doo·khof·kah*
overheat перегреться
  pee·ree·gryeh·tsah
overlook *n* смотровая площадка
  smah·trah·vah·yah plah·shchaht·kah
owner владелец *vlah·dyeh·leets*

P

pacifier соска *sos·kah*
pack *v* упаковывать
  oo·pah·koh·vih·vaht'
package посылка *pah·sihl·kah*
packet пакет *pah·kyet*
paddling pool [BE] детский бассейн
  dyets·keey bah·seyn
pain боль *bol'*
painkiller болеутоляющее *boh·lee·oo*
  ·tah·lyah·yoo·shchee·yeh

painting картина *kahr·tee·nah*

pair пара *pah·rah*

palace дворец *dvah·ryets*

panorama панорама
pah·nah·rah·mah

pants брюки *bryoo·kee*

paper бумага *boo·mah·gah*

paracetamol [BE] парацетамол
pah·rah·tsih·tah·mol

parents родители *rah·dee·tee·lee*

park парк *pahrk*

parking lot автостоянка
ahf·tah·stah·yahn·kah

party (social) вечеринка
vee·chee·reen·kah

pass v проезжать *prah·eezh·zhaht'*

passport паспорт *pahs·pahrt*

pastry store кондитерская
kahn·dee·teer·skah·yah

patch v заштопать *zah·shtoh·paht'*

path тропинка *trah·peen·kah*

patient n пациент *pah·tsih·yent*

pay v платить *plah·teet'*

pay phone телефон-автомат
tee·lee·fon ahf·tah·maht

payment оплата *ah·plah·tah*

peak пик *peek*

pearl жемчуг *zhem·chook*

pedestrian crossing переход
pee·ree·khot

pedestrian zone пешеходная зона

pee·shih·khod·nah·yah zoh·nah

pedicure педикюр *pee·dee·kyoor*

pen ручка *rooch·kah*

pencil карандаш *kah·rahn·dahsh*

people люди *lyoo·dee*

perhaps может быть *moh·zhiht biht'*

period n **(historical)** период
pee·ree·aht; **(menstrual)**
менструация *meen·stroo·ah·tsih·yah*

petrol [BE] бензин *been·zeen*

pharmacy аптека *ahp·tyeh·kah*

phone v звонить *zvah·neet'*

phone card телефонная карточка
tee·lee·foh·nah·yah kahr·tahch·kah

phone call звонок *zvah·nok*

photo фотография
fah·tah·grah·fee·yah

photocopier ксерокс *ksyeh·rahks*

photography фотография
fah·tah·grah·fee·yah

phrase фраза *frah·zah*

phrase book разговорник
rahz·gah·vor·neek

pick up v **(get)** взять *vzyaht'*; **(collect)**
забирать *zah·bee·raht'*

picnic пикник *peek·neek*

piece n кусочек *koo·soh·cheek*

pill таблетка *tahb·lyet·kah*

pillow подушка *pah·doosh·kah*

pipe (smoking) трубка *troop·kah*

piste [BE] трасса *trah·sah*

pizzeria пиццерия *pee·tsih·ree·yah*

place (space) место *myes·tah*

plane самолёт *sah·mah·lyot*

plan план *plahn*

plant n растение *rahs·tyeh·nee·yeh*

plastic bag пакет *pah·kyet*

plastic wrap продуктовая плёнка *prah·dook·toh·vah·yah plyon·kah*

plate тарелка *tah·rel·kah*

platform [BE] платформа *plaht·for·mah*

platinum платина *plah·tee·nah*

play n игра *eeg·rah*; v **(games, etc.)** играть *eeg·raht'*; **(perform)** исполнять *ees·pahl·nyat'*

playground детская площадка *dyets·kah·yah plah·shchaht·kah*

playpen манеж *mah·nyesh*

pleasant приятный *pree·yaht·niy*

please пожалуйста *pah·zhahl·stah*

plug штепсель *shtep·seel'*

plunger вантуз *vahn·toos*

point v **(at)** показывать (на) *pah·kah·zih·vaht' (nah)*

poison n яд *yaht*

poles палки *pahl·kee*

police милиция *mee·lee·tsih·yah*

police station отделение милиции *aht·dee·lyeh·nee·yeh mee·lee·tsih·ee*

popular популярный *pah·poo·lyahr·niy*

port (harbor) порт *port*

porter носильщик *nah·seel·'shcheek*

portion порция *por·tsih·yah*

possible возможно *vahz·mozh·nah*

post n почта *poch·tah*; v отправлять *aht·prahv·lyaht'*

postbox [BE] почтовый ящик *pahch·toh·viy yah·shcheek*

postcard открытка *aht·kriht·kah*

pottery керамика *kee·rah·mee·kah*

pound (sterling) фунт *foont*

pregnant беременная *bee·reh·mee·nah·yah*

prescribe выписывать *vih·pee·sih·vaht'*

prescription рецепт *ree·tsept*

present n **(gift)** подарок *pah·dah·rahk*

press v гладить *glah·deet'*

pretty красивый *krah·see·viy*

print v печатать *pee·chah·taht'*

program n программа *prah·grah·mah*

pronounce v произносить *prah·eez·nah·seet'*

pump насос *nah·sos*

puncture прокол *prah·kol*

puppet show кукольный театр *koo·kahl'·niy tee·ahtr*

pure (material) чистый *chees·tiy*

purpose цель *tsel'*

purse сумка _soom_·kah

pushchair [BE] прогулочная коляска
prah·_goo_·lahch·nah·yah kah·_lyas_·kah

put v поставить pah·_stah_·veet'

Q

quality качество _kah_·chees·tvah

queue [BE] v стоять в очереди
stah·_yaht'_ v oh·chee·ree·dee

quick быстрый _bihs_·triy

quiet тихий _tee_·kheey

R

racetrack ипподром ee·pah·_drom_

racket (tennis) ракетка rah·_kyet_·kah

railroad железная дорога
zhee·_lyez_·nah·yah dah·_roh_·gah

railway [BE] железная дорога
zhee·_lyez_·nah·yah dah·_roh_·gah

rain v идёт дождь ee·_dyot_ doshch

raincoat плащ plahshch

rape n изнасилование
eez·nah·_see_·lah·vah·nee·yeh

rapids пороги pah·_roh_·gee

rash сыпь sihp'

razor бритва _breet_·vah

read v читать chee·_taht'_

ready готовый gah·_toh_·viy

real (genuine) настоящий
nah·stah·_yah_·shcheey

receipt квитанция kvee·_tahn_·tsih·yah

reception (desk) регистрация
ree·gee·_strah_·tsih·yah

receptionist портье pahrt'·_yeh_

recommend рекомендовать
ree·kah·meen·dah·_vaht'_

reduction (in price) скидка _skeet_·kah

refrigerator холодильник
khah·lah·_deel'_·neek

refund вернуть деньги veer·_noot'_
dyen'·gee

region район rah·_yon_

regular adj **(size)** средний _sryed_·neey

religion религия ree·_lee_·gee·yah

remember помнить _pom_·neet'

rent v взять напрокат vzyat'
nah·prah·_kaht_

repair v чинить chee·_neet'_

repeat v повторять pahf·tah·_ryaht'_

report v заявить zah·yah·_veet'_

reservation заказ zah·_kahs_

reserve v заказать zah·kah·_zaht'_

rest v отдыхать aht·dih·_khaht'_

restaurant ресторан rees·tah·_rahn_

restroom туалет too·ah·_lyet_

retail торговля tahr·_gov_·lyah

retired на пенсии nah _pyen_·see·ee

return v **(surrender)** возвратить
vahz·vrah·_teet'_

return ticket [BE] билет туда
и обратно bee·_lyet_ too·_dah_ ee
ahb·_raht_·nah

revolting отвратительный
aht·vrah·tee·teel·niy

rib ребро *reeb·roh*

right adj (correct) правильный
prah·veel·niy

ring кольцо *kahl'·tsoh*

river река *ree·kah*

road дорога *dah·roh·gah*

road map карта дорог *kahr·tah
dah·rok*

robbery грабеж *grah·byosh*

romantic романтичный
rah·mahn·teech·niy

roof (house, car) крыша *krih·shah*

room комната *kom·nah·tah*

room service
обслуживание номеров
*ahp·sloo·zhih·vah·nee·yeh
nah·mee·rof*

rope веревка *vee·ryof·kah*

round adj круглый *kroog·liy;* n **(of
game)** раунд *rah·oond*

round-trip ticket билет туда
и обратно *bee·lyet too·dah ee
ahb·raht·nah*

rubbish [BE] мусор *moo·sahr*

ruble [rouble] рубль *roobl'*

Russia Россия *rahs·see·yah*

Russian adj русский *roos·keey*

Russian language русский язык
roos·kee yah·zihk

S

safe adj безопасный *bee·zah·pahs·niy*
n сейф *seyf*

safety безопасность
bee·zah·pahs·nahst'

safety pin булавка *boo·lahf·kah*

sailboat яхта *yahkh·tah*

sales tax НДС *en deh es*

same тот же самый *tot zheh sah·miy*

sand песок *pee·sok*

sandals сандалии *sahn·dah·lee*

sandy beach песчаный пляж
pee·shchah·niy plyahsh

sanitary napkins
гигиенические салфетки
*gee·gee·ee·nee·chees·kee·yeh
sahl·fyet·kee*

saucepan кастрюля *kahs·tryoo·lyah*

sauna сауна *sah·oo·nah*

say v говорить *gah·vah·reet'*

scarf шарф *shahrf*

scenic route живописный маршрут
zhi·vah·pees·niy mahrsh·root

schedule n расписание
rahs·pee·sah·nee·yeh

scissors ножницы *nozh·nee·tsih*

screwdriver отвёртка *aht·vyort·kah*

sea море *moh·ryeh*

seat место *myes·tah*

second class (train) купейный вагон
koo·pey·niy vah·gon

second-hand подержанный
pah·dyer·zhah·niy

secretary секретарь *seek·ree·tahr'*

sedative успокаивающее *oos·pah·ka h·ee·vah·yoo·shchee·yeh*

see видеть *vee·deet'*

self-service самообслуживание *sah· mah·ahp·sloo·zhih·vah·nee·yeh*

sell продавать *prah·dah·vaht'*

send посылать *pah·sih·laht'*

senior citizen пенсионер
pyen·see·ah·nyer

separately отдельно *ahd·del'·nah*

serious серьёзный *see·ryoz·niy*

service (religious)
служба *sloozh·bah;* **(in restaurant)** обслуживание
ahp·sloo·zhih·vah·nee·yeh

shade тень *tyen'*

shallow мелкий *myel·keey*

shampoo шампунь *shahm·poon'*

shape *n* форма *for·mah*

share *v* **(a room)** делить *dee·leet'*

sheet (bedding) простыня
prahs·tih·nyah

ship корабль *kah·rahbl'*

shirt рубашка *roo·bahsh·kah*

shoe repair ремонт обуви *ree·mont oh·boo·vee*

shoe store обувной магазин
ah·boov·noy mah·gah·zeen

shoes туфли *toof·lee*

shop магазин *mah·gah·zeen*

shop assistant продавец
prah·dah·vyets

shopping basket корзинка
kahr·zeen·kah

shopping centre [BE] торговый
центр *tahr·goh·viy tsentr*

short *adj* **(height)** низкий *nees·keey*

short-sighted [BE] близорукий
blee·zah·roo·keey

shorts шорты *shor·tih*

shoulder плечо *plee·choh*

shovel совок *sah·vok*

show *v* показывать *pah·kah·zih·vaht'*

shower душ *doosh*

shut *adj* закрытый *zah·krih·tiy; v*
закрываться *zah·krih·vah·tsah*

sick больной *bahl'·noy;*

side *n* **(of road)** сторона *stah·rah·nah*

sightseeing tour обзорная
экскурсия *ahb·zor·nah·yah eeks·koor·see·yah*

sign (road) знак *znahk*

silk шёлк *sholk*

silver серебро *see·ree·broh*

single (unmarried) холостой
khah·lash·toy

single room одноместный номер
ahd·nah·myes·niy noh·meer

single ticket [BE] билет в один конец

bee•lyet *v* ah•deen kah•*nyets*

sink раковина *rah*•kah•vee•nah

sit *v* сесть syest'

size размер rahz•*myer*

skates коньки kahn'•*kee*

ski boots лыжные ботинки
lihzh•nih•yeh bah•*teen*•kee

skin кожа *koh*•zhah

skirt юбка *yoop*•kah

skis лыжи *lih*•zhih

sleep *v* спать spaht'

sleeping bag спальный мешок
spahl'•niy mee•*shok*

sleeping pill снотворное
snaht•*vor*•nah•yeh

sleeve рукав roo•*kahf*

slippers тапочки *tah*•pach•kee

slow *adj* медленный *myed*•lee•niy

small (in size) маленький
mah•leen'•keey

smell *n* запах *zah*•pahkh

smoke *v* курить koo•*reet'*

smoking *adj* курящий
koo•*ryah*•shcheey

snack bar буфет boo•*fyet*

sneakers теннисные туфли
teh•nees•nih•ee *toof*•lee

snorkel *n* трубка *troop*•kah

snow снег snyek

soap мыло *mih*•lah

soccer футбол food•*bol*

socket розетка rah•*zyet*•kah

socks носки nahs•*kee*

sole (shoes) подошва pah•*dosh*•vah

some какой-то kah•*koy* tah

someone кто-то *ktoh*•tah

something что-то *shtoh*•tah

sometimes иногда ee•nahg•*dah*

soon скоро *skoh*•rah

soother [BE] соска sos•kah

sore throat ангина ahn•*gee*•nah

souvenir сувенир soo•vee•*neer*

souvenir store магазин сувениров
mah•gah•*zeen* soo•vee•*nee*•rahf

spa спа spah

space место *myes*•tah

spare (extra) лишний *leesh*•neey

speak *v* говорить gah•vah•*reet'*

specialist специалист
spee•tsih•ah•*leest*

spell *v* называть по буквам
nah•zih•*vaht'* pah *book*•vahm

spend *v* тратить *trah*•teet'

spine позвоночник
pahz•vah•*noch*•neek

spoon ложка *losh*•kah

sport спорт sport

sports club спортклуб sport•*kloop*

sporting goods store спорттовары
spor•tah•*vah*•rih

sprain *n* растяжение
rahs•tee•zheh•nee•yeh

square *adj* квадратный
kvahd-raht-niy; *n* площадь
ploh-shchaht'

stadium стадион *stah-dee-on*

staff персонал *peer-sah-nahl*

stainless steel нержавеющая сталь
nee-rzhah-vye-yoo-shchah-yah stahl'

stamp марка *mahr-kah*

stand *v* стоять *stah-yaht'*

start *v* **(commence)** начинать
nah-chee-naht'; **(car)** заводить
zah-vah-deet'

station вокзал *vahg-zahl*

stationery канцелярские товары
kahn-tsih-lyahr-skee-yeh tah-vah-rih

statue статуя *stah-too-yah*

stay *v* остаться *ah-stah-tsah*

sting укус *oo-koos*

stockings чулки *chool-kee*

stomach живот *zhih-vot*

stomachache болит живот *bah-leet zhih-vot*

stop *n* **(bus, etc.)** остановка
ah-stah-nof-kah; *v* останавливаться
ah-stah-nahv-lee-vah-tsah

store магазин *mah-gah-zeen*

store guide перечень отделов
pyeh-ree-cheen' ahd-dyeh-lahf

storm буря *boo-ryah*

stove плита *plee-tah*

strange странный *strah-niy*

stream ручей *roo-chey*

stroller прогулочная коляска
*prah-goo-lahch-nah-yah
kah-lyas-kah*

strong (potent) сильный *seel'-niy*

student студент *stoo-dyent*

study *v* учиться *oo-chee-tsah*

stunning ошеломляющий
ah-shih-lahm-lyah-yoo-shcheey

style стиль *steel'*

subtitled с субтитрами *s
soop-teet-rah-mee*

subway метро *meet-roh*

subway station станция метро
stahn-tsih-yah meet-roh

suggest предлагать *preed-lah-gaht'*

suit костюм *kahs-tyoom*

sunbathe *v* загорать *zah-gah-raht'*

sunburn солнечный ожёг
sol-neech-niy ah-zhok

sunglasses солнечные очки
sol-neech-nih-ee ahch-kee

sunny солнечно *sol-nyech-nah*

sunstroke солнечный удар
sol-neech-niy oo-dahr

superb превосходный
pree-vahs-khod-niy

supermarket универсам
oo-nee-veer-sahm

supervision присмотр *pree-smotr*

supplement доплата *dah-plah-tah*

surfboard доска для серфинга
dahs•kah dlyah ser•feen•gah

surname фамилия *fah•mee•lee•yah*

suspicious подозрительный
pah•dah•zree•teel'•niy

sweater пуловер *poo•loh•veer*

sweatshirt байка *bie•kah*

swelling опухоль *oh•poo•khahl'*

swim *v* плавать *plah•vaht'*

swimming плавание
plah•vah•nee•yeh

swimming pool бассейн *bah•seyn*

swimming trunks плавки *plahf•kee*

swimsuit купальник *koo•pahl'•neek*

symptoms симптомы *seemp•toh•mih*

synagogue синагога *see•nah•goh•gah*

synthetic синтетический
seen•teh•tee•chees•keey

T

T-shirt майка *mie•kah*

table столик *stoh•leek*

take (carry) нести *nyes•tee;*
(medication) принимать
pree•nee•maht'; **(time)** занимать
zah•nee•maht'

talk *v* разговаривать
rahz•gah•vah•ree•vaht'

tall высокий *vih•soh•keey*

tampon тампон *tahm•pon*

tan загар *zah•gahr*

taxi такси *tahk•see*

taxi rank [BE] стоянка такси
stah•yahn•kah tahk•see

taxi stand стоянка такси
stah•yahn•kah tahk•see

team команда *kah•mahn•dah*

teaspoon чайная ложка *chie•nah•yah
losh•kah*

teddy bear мишка *meesh•kah*

telephone *n* телефон *tee•lee•fon*

telephone bill счёт за телефон
shchot zah tee•lee•fon

telephone booth телефон-автомат
tee•lee•fon•ahf•tah•maht

telephone call телефонный звонок
tee•lee•foh•niy zvah•nok

telephone directory телефонный
справочник *tee•lee•foh•niy
sprah•vahch•neek*

telephone number номер телефона
noh•meer tee•lee•foh•nah

tell *v* рассказывать
rahs•kah•zih•vaht'

temperature (body) температура
teem•pee•rah•too•rah

tennis теннис *teh•nees*

tennis court теннисный корт
teh•nees•niy kort

tent палатка *pah•laht•kah*

tent pegs колышки *koh•lihsh•kee*

tent pole шест *shest*

terminal (bus) (авто) вокзал *(ahf·tah)* vahg·*zahl*

terrible ужасный ooh·*zhahs*·niy

theater театр tee·*ahtr*

theft кража *krah*·zhah

then (time) затем zah·*tyem*

there там tahm

thermometer термометр teer·*moh*·meetr

thermos термос *ter*·mahs

thick толстый *tols*·tiy

thief вор vor

thigh бедро beed·*roh*

thin тонкий *ton*·keey

think думать *doo*·maht'

throat горло *gor*·lah

through через *chyeh*·rees

thumb большой палец bahl'·*shoy* *pah*·leets

ticket билет bee·*lyet*

ticket office билетные кассы bee·*lyet*·nih·yeh *kah*·sih

tie галстук *gahls*·took

tight (loose) тесно *tyehs*·niy

tights колготки kahl·*got*·kee

time время *vryeh*·myah

timetable [BE] расписание rahs·pee·*sah*·nee·yeh

tin [BE] банка *bahn*·kah

tin opener [BE] консервный нож kahn·*serv*·niy nosh

tire n шина *shih*·nah

tired усталый oos·*tah*·liy

tissue бумажная салфетка boo·*mahzh*·nah·yah salh·*fyet*·kah

to (place) в v

tobacco табак tah·*bahk*

toe палец ноги *pah*·leets nah·*gee*

together вместе *vmyes*·tee

toilet [BE] туалет too·ah·*lyet*

toilet paper туалетная бумага too·ah·*lyet*·nah·yah boo·*mah*·gah

tongue язык yah·*zihk*

too слишком *sleesh*·kahm

tooth зуб zoop

toothache зубная боль zoob·*nah*·yah bol'

toothbrush зубная щётка zoob·*nah*·yah *shchot*·kah

toothpaste зубная паста zoob·*nah*·yah *pahs*·tah

top крышка *krihsh*·kah

tour экскурсия eeks·*koor*·see·yah

tour guide экскурсовод eeks·koor·sah·*vot*

tourist турист too·*reest*

tourist office туристическое бюро too·rees·*tee*·chees·kah·yeh byoo·*roh*

tow truck буксир book·*seer*

tow v отбуксировать aht·book·*see*·rah·vaht'

towel полотенце pah·lah·*tyen*·tseh

tower башня _bahsh_•nyah

town город _goh_•raht

town hall горсовет _gor_•sah•_vyet_

toy игрушка _eeg_•_roosh_•kah

track платформа _plaht_•_for_•mah

traditional традиционный
trah•dee•tsih•_oh_•niy

traffic дорожное движение
dah•_rozh_•nah•yeh dvee•_zheh_•nee•yeh

traffic jam пробка _prop_•kah

traffic lights светофор _svee_•tah•_for_

trail трасса _trah_•sah

trailer трейлер _trey_•leer

train поезд _poh_•eest

train station вокзал _vahg_•_zahl_

tram трамвай _trahm_•_vie_

transit n проездом _prah_•_yez_•dahm

translate v переводить
pee•ree•vah•_deet'_

translation перевод _pee_•ree•_vot_

translator переводчик
pee•ree•_vot_•cheek

trash мусор _moo_•sahr

trash can мусорный бак _moo_•sahr•niy
bahk

travel agency бюро путешествий
byoo•_roh_ poo•tee•_shest_•veey

travel sickness [BE] морская болезнь
mahr•_skah_•yah bah•_lyezn'_

traveler's check дорожный чек
dah•_rozh_•niy chehk

tray поднос _pahd_•_nos_

tree дерево _dyeh_•ree•vah

trim (hair) постричь _pah_•_streech_

trip (journey) поездка _pah_•_yest_•kah

trolley [BE] тележка _tee_•_lyesh_•kah

trousers [BE] брюки _bryoo_•kee

true правда _prahv_•dah

tunnel тунель _too_•_nel'_

turn down (volume, heat)
уменьшать _oo_•meen'•_shaht'_

turn off выключать _vih_•klyoo•_chaht'_

turn on включать _fklyoo_•_chaht'_

turn up (volume, heat) увеличивать
_oo_•vee•lee•chee•vaht'

turning поворот _pah_•vah•_rot_

TV телевизор _teh_•leh•_vee_•zahr

typical типичный _tee_•_peech_•niy

U

ugly некрасивый _nee_•krah•_see_•viy

ulcer язва _yahz_•vah

umbrella зонт _zont_

uncle дядя _dyah_•dyah

unconscious без сознания _byes_
sahz•_nah_•nee•yah

under под _paht_

underground [BE] метро _meet_•_roh_

underground station [BE] станция
метро _stahn_•tsih•yah meet•_roh_

understand понимать
pah•nee•_maht'_

uneven (ground) неровный
nee·_rov_·niy

unfortunately к сожалению k
sah·zhih·_lyeh_·nee·yoo

uniform форма _for_·mah

unit (for phonecard, etc.) единица
ee·dee·_nee_·tsah

unleaded (gas) без свинца bees
sveen·_tsah_

unlock отпирать aht·pee·_raht'_

unpleasant неприятный
nee·pree·_yaht_·niy

upper (berth) верхний _vyerkh_·neey

urgent срочно _sroch_·nah

urine моча mah·_chah_

use v пользоваться _pol'_·zah·vah·tsah

V

vacant свободный svah·_bod_·niy

vacation отпуск _oht_·poosk

vacuum cleaner пылесос pih·lee·_sos_

vaginal infection вагинальная
инфекция vah·gee·_nahl'_·nah·yah
een·_fyek_·tsih·yah

valid действителен deey·_stvee_·tee·len

valley долина dah·_lee_·nah

valuable ценный _tseh_·niy

value стоимость _stoh_·ee·mahst'

VAT [ВЕ] НДС en deh es

vegetarian вегетарианец
vee·gee·tah·ree·_ah_·neets

vein вена _vyeh_·nah

very очень _oh_·cheen'

village деревня dee·_ryev_·nyah

visa виза _vee_·zah

visit n визит vee·_zeet_; v посещать
pah·see·_shchaht'_

visiting hours часы посещений
chee·sih pah·see·_shcheh_·neey

vitamins витамины
vee·tah·_mee_·nih

volleyball волейбол vah·leey·_bol_

voltage напряжение
nah·pree·_zheh_·nee·yeh

vomit тошнить tahsh·_neet'_

W

wait ждать zhdaht'

waiter официант ah·fee·tsih·_ahnt_

waiting room зал ожидания zahl
ah·zhih·_dah_·nee·yah

wake (someone) разбудить
rahz·boo·_deet'_

walk v идти eet·_tee_

walking route пешеходный
маршрут pee·shih·_khod_·niy
mahrsh·_root_

wallet кошелёк kah·shih·_lyohk_

want хотеть khah·_tet'_

war memorial мемориал
mee·mah·ree·_ahl_

ward (hospital) палата pah·_lah_·tah

warm тёплый _tyop_•liy

washing machine стиральная машина stee•_rahl'_•nah•yah mah•_shih_•nah

watch часы chah•_sih_

water вода vah•_dah_

water skis водные лыжи _vod_•nih•yeh _lih_•zhee

waterfall водопад vah•dah•_paht_

waterproof водонепроницаемый voh•dah•nee•prah•nee•_tsah_•ee•miy

wave волна vahl•_nah_

wear v одевать ah•dee•_vaht'_

weather погода pah•_goh_•dah

weather forecast прогноз погоды prahg•_nos_ pah•_goh_•dih

wedding свадьба _svahd'_•bah

week неделя nee•_deh_•lyah

weekend выходные vih•khahd•_nih_•yeh

weigh вес vyes

wheelchair инвалидное кресло een•vah•_leed_•nah•yeh _kryes_•lah

wide широкий shih•_roh_•keey

wife жена zhih•_nah_

windbreaker ветровка veet•_rof_•kah

window окно ahk•_noh_

window seat место у окна _myes_•tah oo ahk•_nah_

windscreen ветровое стекло vee•trah•_voh_•yeh steek•_loh_

windsurfer виндсерфер veend•_syer_•fyer

windy ветер _vyeh_•teer

wireless internet беспроводной интернет bees•prah•vahd•_noy_ een•ter•_net_

with с s

withdraw снимать snee•_maht'_

without без bes

wood лес lyes

wool шерсть sherst'

work v работать rah•_boh_•taht'

wound n рана _rah_•nah

wrong неправильный nee•_prah_•veel'•niy

X

X-ray рентген reen•_gyen_

Y

yacht яхта _yahkh_•tah

yellow жёлтый _zhol_•tiy

young молодой mah•lah•_doy_

youth hostel общежитие ahp•shchee•_zhih_•tee•yeh

Z

zebra crossing переход pee•ree•_khot_

zipper молния _mol_•nee•yah

zoo зоопарк zah•ah•_pahrk_

A

аванс *ah-vahns* deposit

аварийный выход *ah-vah-reey-niy vih-khaht* emergency exit

автобус *ahf-toh-boos* bus

автобусная остановка *ahf-toh-boos-nah-yah ahs-tah-nof-kah* bus stop

автобусная станция *ahf-toh-boos-nah-yah stahn-tsih-yah* bus station

автовокзал *ahf-tah vahg-zahl* terminal (bus)

автостоянка *ahf-tah-stah-yahn-kah* parking lot [car park BE]

адаптер *ah-dahp-ter* adapter

адвокат *ahd-vah-kaht* lawyer

адрес *ah-drees* address

адрес электронной почты *ah-drees ee-leek-tron-nie poch-tih* e-mail address

аккумулятор *ah-kah-moo-lyah-tahr* battery

аллергия *ah-leer-gee-yah* allergy

американский *ah-mee-ree-kahn-skeey adj* American

ангина *ahn-gee-nah* sore throat

английский *ahn-gleey-skeey* English

антибиотики *ahn-tee-bee-oh-tee-kee* antibiotics

антикварный *ahn-tee-kvahr-niy* antique

антисептик *ahn-tee-sep-teek* antiseptic

аппендикс *ah-pyen-deeks* appendix

аптека *ahp-tyeh-kah* pharmacy [chemist BE]

аспирин *ah-spee-reen* aspirin

астматик *ahst-mah-teek n* asthmatic

аэропорт *ah-eh-rah-port* airport

Б

багаж *bah-gahsh* luggage [baggage BE]

багажная квитанция *bah-gahzh-nah-yah kvee-tahn-tsih-yah* baggage check

багажная тележка *bah-gahzh-nah-yah tee-lyesh-kah* luggage cart [trolley BE]

байка *bie-kah* sweatshirt

балет *bah-lyet* ballet

балкон *bahl-kon* balcony

банк *bahnk* bank

банка *bahn-kah* jar; can [tin BE]

банкомат *bahn-kah-maht* ATM

бар *bahr* bar (hotel, etc.)

баскетбол *bahs-keet-bol* basketball

бассейн bah-*seyn* swimming pool

башня *bahsh*-nyah tower

бега bee-*gah* horse racing

бедро beed-*roh* thigh

без byez without

без сознания byes sah-*znah*-nee-yah unconscious

безопасность bee-zah-*pahs*-nahst' safety

безопасный bee-zah-*pahs*-niy adj safe

бензин been-*zeen* gas [petrol BE]

беременна bee-*ryeh*-mee-nah pregnant

беспокоить bees-pah-*koh*-eet' disturb

беспроводной интернет bees-prah-vahd-*noy* een-ter-*net* wireless internet

бессоница bees-*soh*-nee-tsah insomnia

библиотека bee-blee-ah-*tyeh*-kah library

бизнес *beez*-nees business

бикини bee-*kee*-nee bikini

билет bee-*lyet* ticket

билет в один конец bee-*lyet* v ah-*deen* kah-*nyets* one-way [single BE] ticket

билет туда и обратно bee-*lyet* too-*dah* ee ahb-*raht*-nah round-trip [return BE] ticket

билетная касса bee-*lyet*-nah-yah *kah*-sah ticket office

бинокль bee-*noh*-kahl' binoculars

близорукий blee-zah-*roo*-keey near-sighted [short-sighted BE]

блузка *bloos*-kah blouse

болеть bah-*lyet'* v hurt

болеутоляющее boh-lee-oo-tah-*lya* h-yoo-shchee-yeh painkiller

боль bol' pain

больница bahl'-*nee*-tsah hospital

большой bahl'-*shoy* big

большой палец bahl'-*shoy* *pah*-leets thumb

ботанический сад bah-tah-*nee*-chees-keey saht botanical garden

бояться bah-*yah*-tsah frightened

браслет brahs-*lyet* bracelet

брат braht brother

брильянт breel'-*yahnt* diamond

британский bree-*tahn*-skeey British

бритва *breet*-vah razor

бронхит brahn-*kheet* bronchitis

брошь brosh brooch

брошюра brah-*shoo*-rah brochure

брюки *bryoo*-kee pants [trousers BE]

будильник boo-*deel'*-neek alarm clock

буксир book-*seer* tow truck

буксировать book-*see*-rah-vaht' tow

булавка boo-*lahf*-kah safety pin

булочная *boo*-lahch-nah-yah bakery

бумага boo-*mah*-gah paper

бумажная салфетка boo-*mahzh*-nah-yah sahl-*fyet*-kah tissue

буря *boo*-ryah storm

буфет boo-*fyet* snack bar

бухгалтер boo-*gahl*-teer accountant

быстрый *bihs*-triy quick

быть biht´ be

бюро находок byoo-*roh* nah-*khoh*-dahk lost-and-found [lost property office BE]

бюстгальтер byoost-*gahl*-ter bra

В

вагинальная инфекция vah-gee-*nahl´*-nah-yah een-*fyek*-tsih-yah vaginal infection

вагон vah-*gon* car [coach BE] (train)

вагон-ресторан vah-*gon* rees-tah-*rahn* dining car

валюта vah-*lyoo*-tah currency

вантуз *vahn*-toos plunger

вата *vah*-tah cotton

вегетарианец vee-gee-tah-ree-*ah*-neets vegetarian

ведро veed-*roh* bucket

Великобритания vee-lee-kah-bree-*tah*-nee-yah Great Britain

великолепный vee-lee-kah-*lyep*-niy magnificent

велосипед vee-lah-see-*pyet* bicycle

велосипедный маршрут vee-lah-see-*pyed*-niy mahrsh-*root* cycle route

велоспорт vyeh-lah-*sport* cycling

вена vyeh-nah vein

вентилятор veen-tee-lyah-tahr fan (air)

веревка vee-*ryof*-kah rope

верхний *vyerkh*-neey upper

вес vyes weight

веселье vee-*syel´*-yeh fun

ветер *vyeh*-teer wind

ветровка veet-*rof*-kah windbreaker

ветровое стекло vee-trah-*voh*-yeh steek-*loh* windscreen

вечеринка vee-chee-*reen*-kah party (social)

вешалка *vye*-shahl-kah peg

взлом vzlom break-in

взрослый *vzros*-liy adult

взять напрокат vzyat´ nah-prah-*kaht* v rent [hire BE]

видеть *vee*-deet´ see

виза *vee*-zah visa

визит vee-*zeet* n visit

вилка *veel*-kah fork

виндсерфер veend-*syer*-fyer windsurfer

винный магазин *vee·niy mah·gah·zeen* liquor store [off-license BE]

витамины *vee·tah·mee·nih* vitamins

витрина *vee·tree·nah* window (in store)

владелец *vlah·dyeh·leets* owner

вместе *vmyes·tee* together

внутри *vnoo·tree* inside

вовремя *voh·vryeh·myah* on time

вода *vah·dah* n water

водитель *vah·dee·teel'* driver

водительские права *vah·dee·teel'·skee·yeh prah·vah* driver's license

водная экскурсия *vod·nah·yah eks·koor·see·yah* boat trip

водные лыжи *vod·nih·yeh lih·zhih* water skis

водонепроницаемый *voh·dah·nee·prah·nee·tsah·ee·miy* waterproof

водопад *vah·dah·paht* water fall

воздух *voz·dookh* air

возраст *voz·rahst* n age

вокзал *vahg·zahl* train [railway BE] station

волдырь *vahl·dihr'* blister

волейбол *vah·leey·bol* volleyball

волна *vahl·nah* n wave

волосы *voh·lah·sih* hair

вор *vor* thief

воспаление *vahs·pah·lyeh·nee·yeh* inflammation

врач *vrahch* doctor

время *vryeh·myah* time

все *fsyoh* all

все еще *vsyoh ee·shchoh* still

всегда *fseeg·dah* always

вставлять *fstahv·lyat'* v insert

встречаться *fstree·chah·tsah* meet

второй *ftah·roy* second

вход в систему *fkhot f sees·tyeh·moo* n login

входная плата *fkhahd·nah·yah plah·tah* entrance fee

въездная виза *vyezd·nah·yah vee·zah* entry visa

вывихнуть *vih·veekh·noot'* v twist

выезжать *vih·eezh·zhaht'* check-out (hotel)

вызывать *vih·zih·vaht'* v call (the police)

выписывать *vih·pee·sih·vaht'* prescribe

высокий *vih·soh·keey* high

высокий *vih·soh·keey* tall

высокое давление *vih·soh·kah·yeh dahv·lyeh·nee·yeh* high blood pressure

выход *vih·khaht* n exit

выходные *vih·khahd·nih·yeh* weekend

г

гавань *gah-vahn'* harbor

газета *gah-zyeh-tah* newspaper

газетный киоск *gah-zyet-niy kee-osk* newsstand

галлон *gah-lon* gallon

галстук *gahls-took* tie

гандикап *gahn-dee-kahp* handicap (golf)

гараж *gah-rahsh* garage

гарантия *gah-rahn-tee-yah* guarantee

гардероб *gahr-dee-rop* coatcheck

гигиенические салфетки *gee-gee-ee-nee-chees-kee-yeh sahl-fyet-kee* sanitary napkins [pads BE]

гид *geet* guide (tour)

гинеколог *gee-nee-koh-lahk* gynecologist

гитара *gee-tah-rah* guitar

главный *glahv-niy* main

глаз *glahs* eye

глубокий *gloo-boh-keey* deep

глухой *gloo-khoy* deaf

говорить *gah-vah-reet'* speak

голова *gah-lah-vah* head

головная боль *gah-lahv-nah-yah bol'* headache

голодный *gah-lod-niy* hungry

гололёд *gah-lah-lyot* icy

гольф *gol'f* golf

гора *gah-rah* mountain

горло *gor-lah* throat

город *goh-raht* town

горсовет *gor-sah-vyet* town hall

горячий *gah-rya-cheey* hot

гостиная *gahs-tee-nah-yah* living room

гостиница *gahs-tee-nee-tsah* hotel

готовить *gah-toh-veet'* prepare

готовый *gah-toh-viy* ready

грабеж *grah-byosh* robbery

градус *grah-doos* degree (temperature)

грамм *grahm* gram

графин *grah-feen* carafe

грипп *greep* flu

громче *grom-chee* louder

грудная клетка *grood-nah-yah klyet-kah* chest (body)

грудь *groot'* breast

группа *groo-pah* group

группа крови *groo-pah kroh-vee* blood group

грязный *gryahz-niy* dirty

губа *goo-bah* lip

губная памада *goob-nah-yah pah-mah-dah* lipstick

д

давать *dah-vaht'* give

далеко *dah-lee-koh* far

дальнозоркий dahl'·nah·<u>zor</u>·keey far-sighted [long-sighted BE]

дать взаймы daht' vzie·<u>mih</u> lend

дача <u>dah</u>·chah summer cottage

дверь dvyer' door

движение dah·<u>rozh</u>·nah·yeh dvee·<u>zheh</u>·nee·yeh traffic

дворец dvah·<u>ryets</u> palace

двухместный dvookh·<u>myes</u>·niy double

девочка <u>dyeh</u>·vahch·kah girl

дезодорант dee·zah·dah·<u>rahnt</u> deodorant

действителен deey·<u>stvee</u>·tee·lyen valid

делать ставку <u>dyeh</u>·laht' stahf·koo place a bet

день dyen' day

день рождения dyen' rahzh·<u>dyeh</u>·nee·yah birthday

деньги <u>dyen</u>'·gee money

деревня dee·<u>ryev</u>·nyah village

дерево <u>dyeh</u>·ree·vah tree

десна dees·<u>nah</u> gum

детальный счёт dee·<u>tahl</u>'·niy shchot itemized bill

дети <u>dyeh</u>·tee children

детская площадка <u>dyets</u>·kah·yah plah·<u>shchaht</u>·kah playground

детское сиденье <u>dyets</u>·kah·yeh see·<u>dyen</u>'·yeh child seat (in car)

дешевле dee·<u>shev</u>·lee cheaper

дешёвый dee·<u>shoh</u>·viy cheap

джаз dzhahs jazz

джинсовый dzhihn·<u>soh</u>·viy adj denim

джинсы <u>dzhihn</u>·sih jeans

диабет dee·ah·<u>byet</u> diabetes

диабетик dee·ah·<u>byeh</u>·teek diabetic (person)

диагноз dee·<u>ahg</u>·nahs diagnosis

диета dee·<u>yeh</u>·tah n diet

дизельное топливо dee·zeel'·nah·yeh <u>top</u>·lee·vah diesel

директор dee·<u>ryek</u>·tahr director (of company)

дирижёр dee·ree·<u>zhor</u> conductor (orchestra)

длина dlee·<u>nah</u> length

длинный <u>dlee</u>·niy long

дневное представление dneev·<u>noh</u>·yeh preet·stahv·<u>lyeh</u>·nee·yeh matinée

до dah until

добавочный номер dah·<u>bah</u>·vahch·niy <u>noh</u>·meer extension

добираться dah·bee·<u>rah</u>·tsah get (to destination)

дождь doshch n rain

долина dah·<u>lee</u>·nah valley

дом dom house

допуск <u>doh</u>·poosk n access

дорога dah·*roh*·gah road

дорогой dah·rah·*goy* expensive

дорожная пробка dah·*rozh*·nah·yah *prop*·kah traffic jam

дорожный чек dah·*rozh*·niy chehk traveler's check [cheques BE]

доска для серфинга dahs·kah dlyah *ser*·feen·gah surfboard

доставлять dah·stahv·*lyat'* deliver

достаточно dah·*stah*·tahch·nah enough

дрова drah·*vah* firewood

друг drook friend

другие droo·*gee*·yeh others

другой droo·*goy* other

дружеский *droo*·zhees·keey friendly

дублирован doob·lee·rah·vahn dubbed

думать *doo*·maht' think

духовка doo·*khof*·kah oven

душ doosh shower

дырка *dihr*·kah hole (in clothes)

дышать dih·*shaht'* breathe

дюжина *dyoo*·zhih·nah dozen

дядя *dyah*·dyah uncle

E

Европейский союз yev·rah·*pey*·skeey sah·*yoos* European Union (EU)

ежедневно ee·zhee·*dnyev*·nah daily

ерунда *zhah*·lah·bah nonsense

есть yest' eat

ехать *yeh*·khaht' drive

ещё ee·*shchoh* extra (additional)

Ж

жалоба *zhah*·lah·bah complaint

жар zhahr fever

ждать zhdaht' wait

жёлтый *zhol*·tiy yellow

жемчуг *zhem*·chook pearl

жена zhih·nah wife

женат zhih·naht married (man)

живописный маршрут zhih·vah·pees·niy mahrsh·root scenic route

живот zhih·vot stomach

животное zhi·*vot*·nah·yeh animal

журнал zhoor·nahl magazine

З

забирать zah·bee·*raht'* collect

заблокирован zah·blah·*kee*·rah·vahn blocked

заболевание сердца zah·bah·lee·*vah*·nee·yeh *syer*·tsah heart condition

заболеть zah·bah·*lyet'* get sick [ill BE]

забывать zah·bih·*vaht'* forget

загар zah·*gahr* tan

загорать zah·gah·*raht'* sunbathe

заграницей *zah-grah-nee-tsey* abroad

задержка *zah-dyersh-kah* n delay

зажигалка *zah-zhih-gahl-kah* lighter (cigarette)

заказывать *zah-kah-zih-vaht'* v order

законный *zah-kon-niy* legal

закрываться *zah-krih-vah-tsah* v close (store, etc.)

закрытый *zah-krih-tiy* adj shut

закрытый бассейн *zah-krih-tiy bah-seyn* indoor pool

зал вылета *zahl vih-lee-tah* departure lounge

зал ожидания *zahl ah-zhih-dah-nee-yah* waiting room

замок *zah-mahk* castle

замок *zah-mok* n lock

замужем *zah-moo-zhihm* married (woman)

занят *zah-nyaht* busy

занятый *zah-nee-tiy* occupied

запах *zah-pahkh* smell

заповедник *zah-pah-vyed-neek* nature reserve

заправочная станция *zah-prah-vahch-nah-yah stahn-tsih-yah* gas station

затем *zah-tyem* then (time)

захватывающий *zah-khvah-tih-vah-yoo-shcheey* breathtaking

заштопать *zah-shtoh-paht'* patch

звонить *zvah-neet'* v call (phone)

здание *zdah-nee-yeh* building

здесь *zdyes'* here

зелёный *zee-lyoh-niy* green

зеркало *zyer-kah-lah* mirror

знак *znahk* sign (road)

значить *znah-cheet'* v mean

золото *zoh-lah-tah* gold

зонт *zont* umbrella

зоопарк *zah-ah-pahrk* n zoo

зуб *zoop* tooth

зубная боль *zoob-nah-yah bol'* tooth-ache

зубная паста *zoob-nah-yah pahs-tah* toothpaste

зубная щётка *zoob-nah-yah shchot-kah* toothbrush

зубной врач *zoob-noy vrahch* dentist

И

игра *eeg-rah* game

играть *eeg-raht'* v play (games, etc.)

игрушка *eeg-roosh-kah* n toy

идти за покупками *eet-tee zah pah-koop-kah-mee* go shopping

идти пешком *eet-tee peesh-kom* v walk

из-за *eez-zah* because of

измерение *eez·mee·<u>ryeh</u>·nee·yeh* measurement

измерить *eez·<u>myeh</u>·reet'* v measure

изнасилование *eez·nah·<u>see</u>·lah·vah·nee·yeh* n rape

изумруд *ee·zoom·<u>root</u>* emerald

изучать *ee·zoo·<u>chaht</u>'* learn (language)

имя <u>*ee*</u>·*myah* name (first name)

инвалид *een·vah·<u>leet</u>'* n handicapped [disabled BE]

инвалидное кресло *een·vah·<u>leed</u>·nah·yeh kryes·lah* wheelchair

иногда *ee·nahg·<u>dah</u>* sometimes

иностранная валюта *ee·nah·<u>strah</u>·nah·yah vah·<u>lyoo</u>·tah* foreign currency

инструкция *een·<u>strook</u>·tsih·yah* instructions

инсулин *een·soo·<u>leen</u>* insulin

интересный *een·tee·<u>ryes</u>·niy* interesting

интернет *een·ter·<u>net</u>* internet

интернет-кафе *een·ter·<u>net</u> kah·<u>feh</u>* internet cafe

инфекция *een·<u>fyek</u>·tsih·yah* infection

информация *een·fahr·<u>mah</u>·tsih·yah* information

ипподром *ee·pah·<u>drom</u>* racetrack

исполнять *ees·pahl·<u>nyaht</u>'* perform

К

к сожалению *k sah·zhih·<u>lyeh</u>·nee·yoo* unfortunately

к счастью *k shchahst'·yoo* fortunately

каждый *<u>kahzh</u>·diy* every

казино *kah·zee·<u>noh</u>* casino

какой-либо *kah·<u>koy</u>·lee·bah* any
какой-то kah·<u>koy</u> tah some

календарь *kah·leen·<u>dahr</u>'* calendar

камера хранения <u>*kah*</u>·*mee·rah khrah·<u>nyeh</u>·nee·yah* luggage locker

канцелярские товары *kahn·tsih·<u>lyahr</u>·skee·yeh tah·<u>vah</u>·rih* stationery

карандаш *kah·rahn·<u>dahsh</u>* pencil

карта <u>*kahr*</u>·*tah* map

карта дорог <u>*kahr*</u>·*tah dah·<u>rok</u>* road map

картина *kahr·<u>tee</u>·nah* painting

картинная галерея *kahr·<u>teen</u>·nah·yah gah·lee·<u>ryeh</u>·yah* art gallery

карты <u>*kahr*</u>·*tih* cards

кассета *kah·<u>syeh</u>·tah* cassette

кассир *kah·<u>seer</u>* cashier

кастрюля *kahs·<u>tryoo</u>·lyah* saucepan

качество <u>*kah*</u>·*chees·tvah* quality

кашель <u>*kah*</u>·*shihl'* n cough

кашлять <u>*kahsh*</u>·*lyaht'* v cough

каюта *kah·<u>yoo</u>·tah* cabin

квадратный *kvahd-raht-niy adj*
square

квартира *kvahr-tee-rah* apartment
[flat BE]

кемпинг *kyem-peenk* camping

керамика *kee-rah-mee-kah* pottery

километраж *kee-lah-mee-trahsh*
mileage

кинотеатр *kee-nah-tee-ahtr* movie
theater [cinema BE]

кишечник *kee-shech-neek* bowel

класс *klahs* class (type of seat, etc.)

ключ *klyooch* key

клюшка *klyoosh-kah* club (golf)

книга *knee-gah* book

книжный магазин *kneezh-niy
mah-gah-zeen* bookstore

кнопка *knop-kah* button

ковер *kah-vyor* carpet (rug)

код *kot* area code

кожа *koh-zhah* leather (material); skin
(body)

колготки *kahl-got-kee* tights

колено *kah-lyeh-nah* knee

кольцо *kahl-tsoh n* ring

команда *kah-mahn-dah* team

командировка
kah-mahn-dee-rof-kah business
trip

комариный укус *kah-mah-ree-niy
oo-koos* mosquito bite

комиссионный сбор
kah-mee-see-oh-niy zbor n
commission

комната *kom-nah-tah* room (house)

компакт-диск kahm-pahkt deesk CD

компания *kahm-pah-nee-yah*
company (companionship)

конверт *kahn-vyert* envelope

кондитерская
kahn-dee-teer-skah-yah pastry store

кондиционер *kahn-dee-tsih-ah-nyer*
conditioner

консервный нож *kahn-syerv-niy
nosh* can [tin BE] opener

консульство *kon-sool'-stvah*
consulate

консультироваться
kahn-sool-tee-rah-vah-tsah consult

контактные линзы
kahn-tahkt-nih-yeh leen-zih contact
lenses

концерт *kahn-tsert* concert

концертный зал *kahn-tsert-niy zahl*
concert hall

кончаться *kahn-chah-tsah v* end

коньки *kahn'-kee* skates

копия *koh-pee-yah* copy

корабль *kah-rahbl'* ship

корзина *kahr-zee-nah* basket

кормить *kahr-meet'* feed

коронка *kah-ron-kah* cap (dental)

косметика kahs-_myeh_-tee-kah cosmetics

костыли kahs-tih-_lee_ crutches

кость kost' bone

костюм kahs-_tyoom_ n suit

кошелёк kah-shih-_lyok_ wallet

кошерный kah-_sher_-niy kosher

кража _krah_-zhah theft

крайний случай _krie_-neey _sloo_-chie emergency

кран krahn faucet [tap BE]

красивый krah-_see_-viy beautiful

кредитная карточка kree-_deet_-nah-yah _kahr_-tahch-kah credit card

крем для загара kryem dlyah zah-_gah_-rah sun-tan cream

кровать krah-_vaht'_ bed

кровотечение krah-vah-tee-_cheh_-nee-yeh bleeding

кровь krof' blood

кровяное давление krah-vee-_noh_-yeh dahv-_lyeh_-nee-yeh blood pressure

кроме _kroh_-mee except

круглый _kroog_-liy round

кружево _kroo_-zhih-vah lace

кружка _kroosh_-kah n mug

круиз kroo-_ees_ cruise

крыша _krih_-shah roof (house, car)

ксерокс _ksyeh_-rahks photocopier

кто-нибудь _ktoh_-nee-boot' anyone

кто-то _ktoh_-tah someone

кукла _kook_-lah doll

кукольный meamp _koo_-kahl'-niy tee-_ahtr_ puppet show

купальник koo-_pahl'_-neek swimsuit

купе koo-_peh_ compartment (train)

курить koo-_reet'_ v smoke

курс обмена koors ahb-_myeh_-nah exchange rate

курящий koo-_ryah_-shcheey adj smoking

кусочек koo-_soh_-cheek piece

Л

лавина lah-_vee_-nah avalanche

лазерный проигрыватель _lah_-zeer-niy prah-_eeg_-rih-vah-teel' CD-player

лак для волос lahk dlyah vah-_los_ hair spray

лампа _lahm_-pah lamp

лампочка _lahm_-pahch-kah light bulb

лёгкий _lyokh_-keey light (opp. heavy); easy

лёгкое _lyokh_-kah-yeh lung

лезвие _lyez_-vee-yeh razor blade

лекарство lee-_kahr_-stvah medication

лес lyes forest

линия _lee_-nee-yah line (metro)

лифт leeft elevator [lift BE]

лицо _lee•tsoh_ face

лишний _leesh•neey_ spare (extra)

лодка _lot•kah_ boat

ложка _losh•kah_ spoon

лосьон после бритья _lahs'•yon pos•lee breet'•yah_ after-shave

лошадь _loh•shahd'_ horse

лучше _looch•sheh_ better

лыжи _lih•zhih_ skis

лыжные ботинки _lizh•nih•yeh bah•teen•kee_ ski boots

любезный _lyoo•byez•niy_ kind (pleasant)

любимый _lyoo•bee•miy_ favorite

любить _lyoo•beet'_ v love

люди _lyoo•dee_ people

М

магазин _mah•gah•zeen_ store

майка _mie•kah_ T-shirt

макияж _mah•kee•yash_ n make-up

маленький _mah•leen'•keey_ little (small)

мало _mah•lah_ few; little

мальчик _mahl'•cheek_ boy

манеж _mah•nyesh_ playpen

маникюр _mah•nee•kyoor_ manicure

марка _mahr•kah_ stamp

маска _mahs•kah_ mask (diving)

массаж _mah•sahsh_ n massage

матрас _maht•rahs_ mattress

матрёшка _maht•ryosh•kah_ nesting doll

матч _mahch_ match (sport)

машина _mah•shih•nah_ car

мебель _myeh•beel'_ furniture

медленный _myed•lee•niy_ slow

медовый месяц _mee•doh•viy myeh•syats_ honeymoon

медсестра _myet•sees•trah_ nurse

медь _myet'_ copper

междугородний автобус _meezh•doo•gah•rod•niy ahf•toh•boos_ coach (long-distance bus)

мелировать _mee•lee•rah•vaht'_ v highlight (hair)

мелкий _mel•keey_ shallow

мемориал _mee•mah•ree•ahl_ war memorial

менять _mee•nyaht'_ v change

местный _myes•niy_ local

местный наркоз _myes•niy nahr•kos_ local anesthetic

место _myes•tah_ place (space)

место багажа _myes•tah bah•gah•zhah_ piece of luggage

место назначения _myes•tah nahz•nah•cheh•nee•yah_ destination

место у окна _myes•tah oo ahk•nah_ window seat

место у прохода _myes•tah oo prah•khoh•dah_ aisle seat

месяц *myeh•syahts* month

металл *mee•tahl* metal

метро *meet•roh* subway [underground BE]

мечеть *mee•chet'* mosque

мигрень *meeg•ryen'* migraine

микроволновая печь *meek•rah•vahl•noh•vah•yah pyech* microwave

милиция *mee•lee•tsih•yah* police

минута *mee•noo•tah* minute

мобильный телефон *mah•beel'•niy tee•lee•fon* cell [mobile BE] phone

мой *moy* my

молния *mol•nee•yah* zipper

молодой *mah•lah•doy* young

монета *mah•nyeh•tah* coin

море *moh•ryeh* sea

мороз *mah•ros* frost

морозильная камера *mah•rah•zeel'•nah•yah kah•mee•rah* freezer

морская болезнь *mahr•skah•yah bah•lyezn'* motion [travel BE] sickness

мост *most* bridge

моторка *mah•tor•kah* motorboat

мотоцикл *mah•tah•tsihkl* motorbike

моча *mah•chah* urine

мочевой пузырь *mah•chee•voy poo•zihr'* bladder

моющее средство *moh•yoo•shchee•yeh sryet•stvah* detergent

муж *moosh* husband

мужчина *moo•shchee•nah* man (male)

музей *moo•zyey* museum

музыка *moo•zih•kah* music

мусор *moo•sahr* trash [rubbish BE]

мусорный бак *moo•sahr•niy bahk* trash can [dustbin BE]

мы *mih* we

мыло *mih•lah* soap

мышца *mihsh•tsah* muscle

мяч *myahch* ball

Н

на открытом воздухе *nah aht•krih•tahm voz•doo•khee* outdoor

на пенсии *nah pyen•see•ee* retired

на улице *nah oo•lee•tseh* outside

называть по буквам *nah•zih•vaht' pah book•vahm* v spell

наконец *nah•kah•nyets* at last

наличные *nah•leech•nih•yeh* n cash

нападение *nah•pah•dyeh•nee•yeh* n attack

направление *nah•prahv•lyeh•nee•yeh* direction

направлять *nah•prahv•lyaht'* v direct

например *nah•pree•myer* for example

напротив nah·*proh*·teef opposite

напряжение nah·pree·*zheh*·nee·yeh voltage

народная музыка nah·*rod*·nah·yah *moo*·zih·kah folk music

народное искусство nah·*rod*·nah·yeh ees·*koos*·tvah folk art

насекомое nah·see·*koh*·mah·yeh insect

насос nah·*sos* n pump

настаивать nah·*stah*·ee·vaht' insist

настоящий nah·stah·*yah*·shcheey real (genuine)

национальность nah·tsih·ah·*nahl'*·nahst' nationality

национальный nah·tsih·ah·*nahl'*·niy national

начинать nah·chee·*naht'* begin

начинаться nah·chee·*nah*·tsah v start

НДС en deh es sales tax [VAT BE]

невероятный nee·vee·rah·*yaht*·niy incredible

невиновен nee·vee·*noh*·veen innocent

неделя nee·*deh*·lyah week

недоразумение nee·dah·rah·zoo·*myeh*·nee·yeh misunderstanding

недорогой nee·dah·rah·*goy* inexpensive

незаконный nee·zah·*kon*·niy illegal

некрасивый nee·krah·*see*·viy ugly

некурящий nee·koo·*ryah*·shcheey a non-smoking

немедленно nee·*myeh*·dlee·nah immediately

неплохо nee·*ploh*·khah not bad

неправильный nee·*prah*·veel'·niy wrong

неприятный nee·pree·*yaht*·niy unpleasant

нерв *nyerf* nerve

нержавеющая сталь nee·rzhah·*vyeh*·yoo·shchah·yah stah stainless steel

неровный nee·*rov*·niy uneven (ground)

несложный nyeh·*slozh*·niy easy

несчастный случай nee·*shchahs*·n *sloo*·chie accident

низкий *nees*·keey short (height)

никогда nee·kahg·*dah* never

никто nee·*ktoh* no one

ничего nee·chee·*voh* nothing

новый *noh*·viy new

нога nah·*gah* foot; leg

нож *nosh* knife

ножницы *nozh*·nee·tsih scissors

номер *noh*·meer number (telephone)

нормальный nahr·*mahl'*·niy norma

нос *nos* nose

носильщик *nah-<u>seel</u>'-shcheek* porter

носки *nahs-<u>kee</u>* socks

ночной *nahch-<u>noy</u>* all-night

ночью <u>noh</u>-chyoo at night

нравиться <u>nrah</u>-vee-tsah *v* enjoy

нырять *nih-<u>ryat</u>' v* dive

О

обед *ah-<u>byet</u>* lunch

обезболивающее *ah-beez-<u>boh</u>-lee-v ah-yoo-shchee-yeh* anaesthetic

обзорная экскурсия *ahb-<u>zor</u>-nah-yah eeks-<u>koor</u>-see-yah* sightseeing tour

облачно <u>ob</u>-lahch-nah cloudy

обмен валюты *ahb-<u>myen</u> vah-<u>lyoo</u>-tih* currency exchange office

обменивать *ahb-<u>myeh</u>-nee-vaht'* exchange

обогреватель *ah-bah-gree-<u>vah</u>-teel'* heater

обслуживание номеров *ahp-<u>sloo</u>-zhih-vah-nee-yeh nah-mee-<u>rof</u>* room service

обувной магазин *ah-boov-<u>noy</u> mah-gah-<u>zeen</u>* shoe store

общежитие *ahp-shchee-<u>zhih</u>-tee-yeh* youth hostel

обязательный *ah-bee-<u>zah</u>-teel'-niy* necessary

огнетушитель *ahg-nee-too-<u>shih</u>-teel'* fire extinguisher

ограбление *ah-grahb-<u>lyeh</u>-nee-yeh* mugging; robbery

одевать *ah-dee-<u>vat</u>'* put on; wear

одежда *ah-<u>dyezh</u>-dah* clothes

одеяло *ah-dee-<u>yah</u>-lah* blanket

один <u>ah</u>-deen alone

один раз <u>ah</u>-deen rahs once

одноместный номер *ahd-nah-<u>myes</u>-niy <u>noh</u>-meer* single room

одолжить *ah-dahl-<u>zhit</u>'* borrow

ожерелье *ah-zhih-<u>ryel</u>'-yeh* necklace

ожог *ah-<u>zhok</u> n* burn

озеро <u>oh</u>-zee-rah lake

окно *ahk-<u>noh</u>* window

около <u>oh</u>-kah-lah about (approximately); near

опаздывать *ah-<u>pahz</u>-dih-vaht'* be delayed

опасный *ah-<u>pahs</u>-niy* dangerous

опера <u>oh</u>-pee-rah opera

операция *ah-pee-<u>rah</u>-tsih-yah* operation

описывать *ah-<u>pee</u>-sih-vaht'* describe

оплата *ah-<u>plah</u>-tah* payment

оправа *ah-<u>prah</u>-vah n* frame (glasses)

оптика <u>op</u>-tee-kah optician

оркестр *ahr-<u>kyestr</u>* orchestra

осмотр *ahs·motr* examination (medical)

основной *ahs·nahv·noy* essential

останавливаться *as·stah·nahv·lee·vah·tsah* v stop

остановка *ah·stah·nof·kah* n stop (bus, etc.)

остаться *ah·stah·tsah* v stay

осторожный *ahs·tah·rozh·niy* careful

отбеливатель *aht·byeh·lee·vah·teel'* bleach

отвёртка *aht·vyort·kah* screwdriver

отвратительный *aht·vrah·tee·teel'·niy* revolting

отдавать в химчистку *aht·dah·vaht' f kheem·cheest·koo* v dry clean

отдел *aht·dyel* department (in store)

отделение милиции *aht·dee·lyeh·nee·yeh mee·lee·tsih·ee* police station

отдельно *ahd·del'·nah* separately

отдыхать *aht·dih·khat'* v rest

открывать *aht·krih·vaht'* v open

открытка *aht·kriht·kah* postcard

открытый *aht·krih·tiy adj* open

отменять *aht·mee·nyat'* cancel (reservation)

отопление *ah·tahp·lyeh·nee·yeh* heating

отпирать *aht·pee·raht'* v unlock

отправляться *aht·prahv·lyah·tsah* depart (train, bus)

отпуск *ot·poosk* vacation [holiday BE]

официант *ah·fee·tsih·ahnt* waiter

очень *oh·cheen'* very

очередь *oh·chee·reet' n* queue

очки *ahch·kee* glasses (optical)

ошеломляющий *ah·shih·lahm·lyah·yoo·shcheey* stunning

ошибка *ah·shihp·kah n* mistake

П

пакет *pah·kyet* carton; packet

палата *pah·lah·tah* ward (hospital)

палатка *pah·laht·kah* tent

палаточный лагерь *pah·lah·tahch·niy lah·geer'* campsite

палец *pah·leets* finger

палец ноги *pah·leets nah·gee* toe

пальто *pahl'·toh* coat

панорама *pah·nah·rah·mah* panorama

пара *pah·rah* pair

парацетамол *pah·rah·tsih·tah·mol* acetaminophen [paracetamol BE]

парикмахер *pah·reek·mah·kheer* hairdresser

парк *pahrk* park

паром *pah·rom* ferry

паспорт *pahs·pahrt* passport

пассажирский класс *pah·sah·zhihr·skeey klahs* economy class

пациент *pah·tsih·yent* n patient

пачка сигарет *pahch·kah see·gah·ryet* packet of cigarettes

педикюр *pee·dee·kyoor* pedicure

пелёнка *pee·lyon·kah* diaper [nappy BE]

пепельница *pyeh·peel'·nee·tsah* ashtray

перевес багажа *pee·ree·vyes bah·gah·zhah* excess luggage

перевод *pee·ree·vot* translation

переводить *pee·ree·vah·deet'* translate

переводчик *pee·ree·vot·cheek* translator (text); interpreter (speech)

перегреться *pee·ree·gryeh·tsah* overheat

перед *pyeh·reet* before

переделывать *pee·ree·dyeh·lih·vaht'* alter

перекрёсток *pee·ree·kryos·tahk* crossroad

перелом *pee·ree·lom* fracture (of a bone)

переход *pee·ree·khot* pedestrian crossing

период *pee·ree·aht* period (historical)

персонал *peer·sah·nahl* n staff

перчатка *peer·chaht·kah* glove

песок *pee·sok* sand

песчаный пляж *pee·shchah·niy plyahsh* sandy beach

печатать *pee·chah·taht'* v print

печень *pyeh·cheen'* liver

пешеходная зона *pee·shih·khod·nah·yah zoh·nah* pedestrian zone [precinct BE]

пешеходный маршрут *pee·shih·khod·niy mahrsh·root* walking route

пешком *peesh·kom* on foot

пещера *pee·shcheh·rah* cave

пикник *peek·neek* picnic

письмо *pees'·moh* letter

пить *peet'* v drink

пиццерия *pee·tsih·ree·yah* pizzeria

плавание *plah·vah·neeh·yeh* swimming

плавать *plah·vaht'* swim

плавки *plahf·kee* swimming trunks

план *plahn* n plan

пластырь *plahs·tihr'* adhesive bandage

плата *plah·tah* n charge

платина *plah·tee·nah* platinum

платить *plah·teet'* v pay

платок *plah·tok* handkerchief

платформа *plaht·for·mah* n track [platform BE]

платье _plaht'_•yeh dress

плащ _plahshch_ raincoat

плёнка _plyon_•kah n film (camera)

плечо _plee_•choh shoulder

плита _plee_•tah stove [cooker BE]

пломба _plom_•bah filling (dental)

плохой _plah_•khoy bad

пляж _plyahsh_ beach

по делу _pah dyeh_•loo on business

по крайней мере _pah kray_•neey _myeh_•ryeh at least

по почте _pah poch_•tyeh by mail

побережье _pah_•bee•_ryezh_•yeh coast

повар _poh_•vahr n cook

поворот _pah_•vah•_rot_ n turning

повредить _pah_•vree•_deet'_ v damage

повторять _pahf_•tah•_ryaht'_ v repeat

погода _pah_•goh•dah weather

под _pahd_ under

подарок _pah_•dah•rahk n present (gift)

подвал _pahd_•vahl basement

подвозить _pahd_•vah•zeet' give a lift

подержанный _pah_•dyer•zhah•niy second-hand

поднос _pahd_•nos tray

пододеяльник _pah_•dah•dee•_yahl'_•neek duvet

подозрительный _pah_•dah•_zree_•teel'•niy suspicious

подошва _pah_•dosh•vah sole (shoes)

подробности _pahd_•rob•nahs•tee details

подруга _pahd_•roo•gah girlfriend

подтвердить _paht_•tveer•_deet'_ confirm (reservation)

подушка _pah_•doosh•kah pillow

поезд _poh_•eest train

поездка _pah_•yest•kah trip (journey)

пожар _pah_•zhahr fire

пожарная лестница _pah_•zhahr•nah•yah _lyes_•nee•tsah fire escape

позвоночник _pahz_•vah•_noch_•neek spine

поздний _poz_•neey adj late

пойти по магазинам _pie_•tee pah mah•gah•_zee_•nahm go shopping

пойти потанцевать _pie_•tee pah•tahn•tsih•_vaht'_ go dancing

показывать _pah_•kah•zih•vaht' v show

покупать _pah_•koo•_paht'_ buy

полный _pol_•niy full

половина _pah_•lah•_vee_•nah half

полотенце _pah_•lah•_tyen_•tseh towel

получать _pah_•loo•_chaht'_ get (receive)

пользоваться _pol'_•zah•vah•tsah v use

помедленнее _pah_•_myed_•lee•nee•yeh slow down

поменьше _pah_•_myen'_•sheh smaller

помнить _pom·neet'_ remember

помогать _pah·mah·gaht'_ v help

понимать _pah·nee·maht'_ understand

популярный _pah·poo·lyahr·niy_ popular

поразительный _pah·rah·zee·teel'·niy_ amazing

порез _pah·ryes_ n cut (finger)

пороги _pah·roh·gee_ rapids

порт _port_ port (harbor)

портье _pahrt'·yeh_ receptionist

посадочный талон _pah·sah·dahch·niy tah·lon_ boarding card

посещать _pah·see·shchaht'_ v visit

после _pos·lee_ after (time/place)

последний _pahs·lyed·neey_ last

посол _pah·sol_ ambassador

посольство _pah·sol'·stvah_ embassy

постельное бельё _pahs·tel'·nah·yeh beel'·yoh_ n bedding

постричь _pah·streech_ v trim (hair)

построенный _pah·stroh·yeh·niy_ built

посуда _pah·soo·dah_ crockery

посудомоечная машина _pah·soo·dah·moh·eech·nah·yah mah·shih·nah_ dishwasher

посылать _pah·sih·laht'_ send

посылка _pah·sihl·kah_ package (mail)

потерять _pah·tee·ryaht'_ v lose

потерять сознание _pah·tee·ryaht' sah·znah·nee·yeh_ v collapse

потише _pah·tee·sheh_ quieter

потому что _pah·tah·moo·shtah_ because

похмелье _pahkh·myel'·yeh_ n hangover

починить _pah·chee·neet'_ v repair

почка _poch·kah_ kidney

почта _poch·tah_ post office

почта _poch·tah_ mail (letters)

почти _pahch·tee_ almost

почтовый ящик _pahch·toh·viy yah·shcheek_ mailbox [postbox BE]

пошлина _posh·lee·nah_ duty

правда _prahv·dah_ true

правильный _prah·veel'·niy_ right (correct)

православный _prah·vah·slahv·niy_ Orthodox

прачечная _prah·cheech·nah·yah_ laundromat (launderette BE]

превосходный _pree·vahs·khod·niy_ superb

предлагать _preed·lah·gaht'_ suggest

предприятие _preet·pree·yah·tee·yeh_ company (business)

предъявлять _preed·yahv·lyaht'_ declare

презерватив _pree·zeer·vah·teef_ condom

преследовать pree·*slyeh*·dah·vaht' follow (pursue)

приблизительно
pree·blee·*zee*·teel'·nah approximately

прибывать pree·bih·*vaht'* arrive

привлекательный
pree·vlee·*kah*·teel'·niy attractive

приглашать pree·glah·*shaht'* invite

приглашение
pree·glah·*sheh*·nee·yeh invitation

приземляться pree·zeem·*lyah*·tsah v land

примерочная
pree·*myeh*·rahch·nah·yah fitting room

принадлежать pree·nahd·lee·*zhaht'* belong

принадлежности
pree·nahd·*lyezh*·nah·stee accessories

принимать лекарство
pree·nee·*maht'* lee·*kahr*·stvah take medication

присмотр pree·*smotr* supervision

приходить pree·khah·*deet'* come

причудливый pree·*chood*·lee·viy bizarre

приятный pree·*yaht*·niy pleasant

пробор prah·*bor* parting (hair)

проверить prah·*vyeh*·reet' v check [cheque BE]

провожать prah·vah·*zhaht'* accompany

прогноз погоды prahg·*nos* pah·*goh*·dih weather forecast

программа prah·*grah*·mah program

продавать prah·dah·*vaht'* sell

продавец prah·dah·*vyets* shop assistant

проездом prah·*yez*·dahm in transit

проезжать prah·eezh·*zhaht'* v pass

произносить prah·eez·nah·*seet'* pronounce

прокол prah·*kol* puncture

просить prah·*seet'* ask for

просматривать
prah·*smah*·tree·vaht' v browse

простуда prah·*stoo*·dah cold; flu

простыня prahs·tih·*nyah* sheet (bedding)

протез prah·*tes* denture

противозачаточное средство pr oh·tee·vah·zah·*chah*·tahch·nah·yeh *sryet*·stvah n contraceptive

профессия prah·*fyeh*·see·yah line (profession)

прыщ prihshch acne

прямой pryah·*moy* adj direct (train)

птица ptee·tsah bird

пустой poos·*toy* adj empty

путеводитель poo·tee·vah·*dee*·teel' guide book

пылесос *pih·lee·sos* vacuum cleaner

пьяный *pyah·niy adj* drunk

Р

работа *rah·boh·tah* job

работать *rah·boh·taht' v* work

разбудить *rahz·boo·deet'* wake someone

разговаривать *rahz·gah·vah·ree·vaht' v* talk

разговорник *rahz·gah·vor·neek* phrasebook

размер *rahz·myer* size

район *rah·yon* region

ракетка *rah·kyet·kah* racket (tennis)

раковина *rah·kah·vee·nah* sink

рана *rah·nah n* wound

ранний *rahn·neey* early

раскладушка *rahs·klah·doosh·kah* camp bed

расписание *rahs·pee·sah·nee·yeh n* schedule [timetable BE]

рассвет *rahs·vyet* dawn

рассказывать *rahs·kah·zih·vaht'* tell

растение *rahs·tyeh·nee·yeh n* plant

растяжение *rahs·tee·zheh·nee·yeh n* sprain

расчёска *rah·shchos·kah n* comb

раунд *rah·oond* round (of golf)

ребёнок *ree·byoh·nahk* baby; child

ребро *reeb·roh* rib

регистрационная стойка *ree·gee·strah·tsih·on·nah·yah stoy·kah* check-in desk

регистрация *ree·gee·strah·tsih·yah* reception (desk)

регистрироваться *ree·gees·tree·rah·vah·tsah v* check-in

рейс *reys* flight

река *ree·kah* river

рекомендовать *ree·kah·meen·dah·vaht'* recommend

религия *ree·lee·gee·yah* religion

ремень *ree·myen'* belt

ремесла *ree·myos·lah* handicrafts

ремонт обуви *ree·mont oh·boo·vee* shoe repair

рентген *reen·gyen* X-ray

ресторан *rees·tah·rahn* restaurant

рецепт *ree·tsept* prescription

родители *rah·dee·tee·lee* parents

розетка *rah·zyet·kah* electric outlet

романтичный *rah·mahn·teech·niy* romantic

Россия *rah·see·yah* Russia

рост *rost* height

рот *rot* mouth

рубашка *roo·bahsh·kah* shirt

рубль *roobl'* ruble [rouble]

рука *roo·kah* arm; hand

рукав *roo·kahf* sleeve

руководитель *roo•kah•vah•dee•teel'* leader (of group)

руководство *roo•kah•vod•stvah* manual (car)

русский *roos•keey adj* Russian

русский язык *roos•keey yah•zihk* Russian language

ручей *roo•chey n* stream

ручка *rooch•kah* pen

ручная кладь *rooch•nah•yah klaht'* hand luggage

рыба *rih•bah* fish

рынок *rih•nahk* market

рюкзак *ryoog•zahk* rucksack

рядом *ryah•dahm* nearby

рядом с *ryah•dahm s* next to

С

с *s* with

с субтитрами *s soop•teet•rah•mee* subtitled

сад *saht* garden

салфетка *sahl•fyet•kah* napkin

самолёт *sah•mah•lyot* plane

самообслуживание *sah•mah•ahp•s loo•zhih•vah•nee•yeh* self-service

сандалии *sahn•dah•lee* sandals

сапоги *sah•pah•gee* boots

сауна *sah•oo•nah* sauna

сахар *sah•khahr* sugar

свадьба *svahd'•bah* wedding

свежий *svye•zhiy* fresh

свет *svyet n* light (electic)

светлый *svyet•liy adj* light (opp. dark)

светофор *svee•tah•for* traffic lights

свеча *svee•chah* candle

свидетельство *svee•dyeh•teel'•stvah* certificate

свитер *svee•teer* sweater

свободное время *svah•bod•nah•yeh vryeh•myah* free time

свободный *svah•bod•niy* available (unoccupied, free)

связаться *svyah•zah•tsah v* contact

сдача *zdah•chah* change (coins)

сейф *seyf n* safe (lock up)

секретарь *seek•ree•tahr'* secretary

семья *seem'•yah n* family

сенная лихорадка *see•nah•yah lee•khah•raht•kah* hay fever

сердечный приступ *seer•dyech•niy prees•toop* heart attack

сердце *syer•tseh* heart

серебро *see•ree•broh n* silver

серый *syeh•riy* gray

серьги *syer'•gee* earrings

серьёзный *seer'•yoz•niy* serious

сесть *syest'* sit

сигара *see•gah•rah* cigar

сигарета *see•gah•ryeh•tah* cigarette

сильный *seel'•niy* strong (potent)

симптомы *seemp•toh•mih* symptoms

синагога *see·nah·goh·gah* synagogue

синтетический
seen·teh·tee·chees·key synthetic

синяк *see·nyahk* bruise

скала *skah·lah* cliff

скидка *skeet·kah* discount

сковорода *skah·vah·rah·dah* frying pan

скорая помощь *skoh·rah·yah poh·mahshch* ambulance

скоро *skoh·rah* soon

слева *slyeh·vah* on the left

следующий *slyeh·doo·yoo·shcheey* next

словарь *slah·vahr'* dictionary

сломан *sloh·mahn* broken

сломать *slah·maht'* v break

сломаться *slah·mah·tsah* v break down (car)

служба *sloozh·bah* n service (religious)

слуховой аппарат *sloo·khah·voy ah·pah·raht* hearing aid

слышать *slih·shaht'* hear

смеяться *smee·yah·tsah* v laugh

смотровая площадка
smah·trah·vah·yah plah·shchaht·kah overlook

снаряжение *snah·ree·zheh·nee·yeh* equipment (sports)

снаряжение для дайвинга
snah·ree·zheh·nee·yeh dlyah die·veen·gah diving equipment

снег *snyek* n snow

снотворное *snah·tvor·nah·yeh* sleeping pill

собор *sah·bor* cathedral

событие *sah·bih·tee·yeh* event

совок *sah·vok* shovel

современный *sah·vree·myen·niy* modern

современный танец
sah·vree·myen·niy tah·neets contemporary dance

содержать *sah·deer·zhaht'* contain

Соединенные Штаты
sah·ee·dee·nyoh·nih·ee shtah·tih United States

соленый *sah·lyoh·niy* salty

солнечно *sol·neech·nah* sunny

солнечные очки *sol·neech·nih·ee ahch·kee* sunglasses

солнечный ожёг *sol·neech·niy ah·zhok* sunburn

солнечный удар *sol·neech·niy oo·dahr* sunstroke

сообщение *sah·ahp·shcheh·nee·yeh* message

соска *sos·kah* pacifier [soother BE]

сотрясение мозга
sah·tree·syeh·nee·yeh moz·gah concussion

спа *spah* spa

спальный мешок _spahl'·niy mee·shok_ sleeping bag

спальня _spahl'·nyah_ bedroom

спасатель _spah·sah·teel'_ lifeguard

спасательная лодка _spah·sah·teel'·nah·yah lot·kah_ lifeboat

спасательный жилет _spah·sah·teel'·niy zhih·lyet_ lifejacket

спать _spaht'_ v sleep

специалист _spee·tsih·ah·leest_ specialist

спина _spee·nah_ back

спички _speech·kee_ matches

спорт _sport_ sport

спортзал _sport·zahl_ gym

спортклуб _sport·kloop_ sports club

спорттовары _spor·tah·vah·rih_ sporting goods store

справа _sprah·vah_ on the right

срочно _sroch·nah_ urgent

стадион _stah·dee·on_ stadium

стакан _stah·kahn_ glass

станция метро _stahn·tsih·yah meet·roh_ subway [underground BE] station

старый _stah·riy_ old

старый город _stah·riy goh·raht_ old town

статуя _stah·too·yah_ statue

стиль _steel'_ style

стиральная машина _stee·rahl'·nah·yah mah·shih·nah_ washing machine

стоимость _stoh·ee·mahst'_ value

столик _stoh·leek_ table

сторона _stah·rah·nah_ side (of road)

стоянка _stah·yahn·kah_ pitch (for camping)

стоянка такси _stah·yahn·kah tahk·see_ taxi stand [rank BE]

стоять в очереди _stah·yaht' v oh·chee·ree·dee_ stand in line

страна _strah·nah_ country (nation)

странный _strah·niy_ strange

страховка _strah·khof·kah_ insurance

стремянка _stree·myahn·kah_ ladder

стрижка _streesh·kah_ haircut

строить _stroh·eet'_ build

студент _stoo·dyent_ student

сувенир _soo·vee·neer_ souvenir

судороги _soo·dah·rah·gee_ cramps

сумка _soom·kah_ purse [handbag BE]

сумма _soo·mah_ amount

сухая стрижка _soo·khah·yah streesh·kah_ dry cut

счёт _shchot_ n bill

счёт за телефон _shchot zah tee·lee·fon_ telephone bill

США _seh sheh ah_ U.S.A.

сыпь _sihp'_ rash

сыро _sih·rah_ adj damp

T

табак *tah·bahk* tobacco

таблетка *tahb·lyet·kah* pill (tablet)

также *tahk·zheh* also

такси *tahk·see* taxi

там *tahm* there

таможенная декларация
*tah·moh·zhih·nah·yah
deek·lah·rah·tsih·yah* customs
declaration

таможня *tah·mozh·nyah* customs

тампон *tahm·pon* tampon

танец *tah·neets n* dance
(performance)

тапочки *tah·pahch·kee* slippers

тарелка *tah·ryel·kah* plate

театр *tee·ahtr* theater

телевизор *tee·lee·vee·zahr* TV-set

тележка *tee·lyesh·kah* cart [trolley BE]

телефон *tee·lee·fon n* phone

телефон-автомат *tee·lee·fon
ahf·tah·maht* pay phone

телефонный *справочник*
tee·lee·foh·niy sprah·vahch·neek
directory (telephone)

тёмный *tyom·niy* dark

температура *teem·pee·rah·too·rah*
temperature

теннис *teh·nees* tennis

теннисные туфли *teh·nees·nih·ee
toof·lee* sneakers

теннисный корт *teh·nees·niy kort*
tennis court

тень *tyen'* shade

тёплый *tyop·liy* warm

термометр *teer·moh·meetr*
thermometer

термос *ter·mahs* thermos flask

тесно *tyes·nah* crowded

тесный *tyes·niy* tight (loose)

течь *tyech v* leak (roof, pipe)

типичный *tee·peech·niy* typical

тихий *tee·kheey* quiet

ткань *tkahn'* fabric (material)

толстый *tols·tiy* thick

тонкий *ton·keey* thin

тонуть *tah·noot'* drown

торговый центр *tahr·goh·viy tsentr*
mall [shopping centre]

тот же самый *tot zheh sah·miy* same

трава *trah·vah* grass

традиционный *trah·dee·tsih·oh·niy*
traditional

трамвай *trahm·vie* tram

трасса *trah·sah* trail [piste BE]

тратить *trah·teet'* spend

трейлер *trey·leer* caravan

тропинка *trah·peen·kah* path

трубка *troop·kah* pipe (smoking)

трудный *trood·niy* difficult

тряпка *tryahp·kah* dish cloth

туалет *too·ah·lyet* restroom [toilet BE]

туалетная бумага
too•ah•lyet•nah•yah boo•mah•gah
toilet paper

туман *too•mahn* fog

туннель *too•nel'* tunnel

турист *too•reest* tourist

туфли *toof•lee* shoes

тушь *toosh* mascara

ты *tih* you (informal)

тяжёлый *tee•zhoh•liy* heavy

У

угол *oo•gahl* corner

уголь *oo•gahl'* charcoal

удалять *oo•dah•lyaht'* extract (tooth)

удобства *oo•dops•tvah* facilities

удостоверение
oo•dah•stah•vee•ryeh•nee•yeh
identification

уезжать *oo•eezh•zhaht'* v leave

ужасный *oo•zhahs•niy* terrible

уже *oo•zheh* already

ужин *oo•zhih* dinner

узкий *oos•keey* narrow

укол *oo•kol* injection

Украина *oo•krah•ee•nah* Ukraine

укус *oo•koos* sting (wasp); bite (dog)

универсам *oo•nee•veer•sahm* supermarket

упаковочная пленка

oo•pah•koh•vahch•nah•yah plyon•kah
plastic wrap [cling film BE]

упаковывать *oo•pah•koh•vih•vaht'* v pack

урок *oo•rok* lesson

успокаивающее *oos•pah•kah•ee•va h•yoo•shchee•yeh* sedative

усталый *oos•tah•liy* tired

утюг *oo•tyook* n iron

ухо *oo•khah* ear

уходить *oo•khah•deet'* go away

учитель *oo•chee•teel'* teacher

Ф

факс *fahks* n fax

фамилия *fah•mee•lee•yah* surname

фен *fyen* blow-dry

ферма *fyer•mah* farm

фильм *feel'm* movie [film BE]

фильтр *feel'tr* filter

фойе *fei•yeh* foyer (hotel, theater)

фольга *fahl'•gah* aluminium foil

фонтан *fahn•tahn* fountain

форма *for•mah* uniform

фотоаппарат *foh•tah•ah•pah•raht* camera

фотография *fah•tah•grah•fee•yah* photograph

фраза *frah•zah* phrase

фунт *foont* pound (sterling)

футбол *food•bol* soccer [football BE]